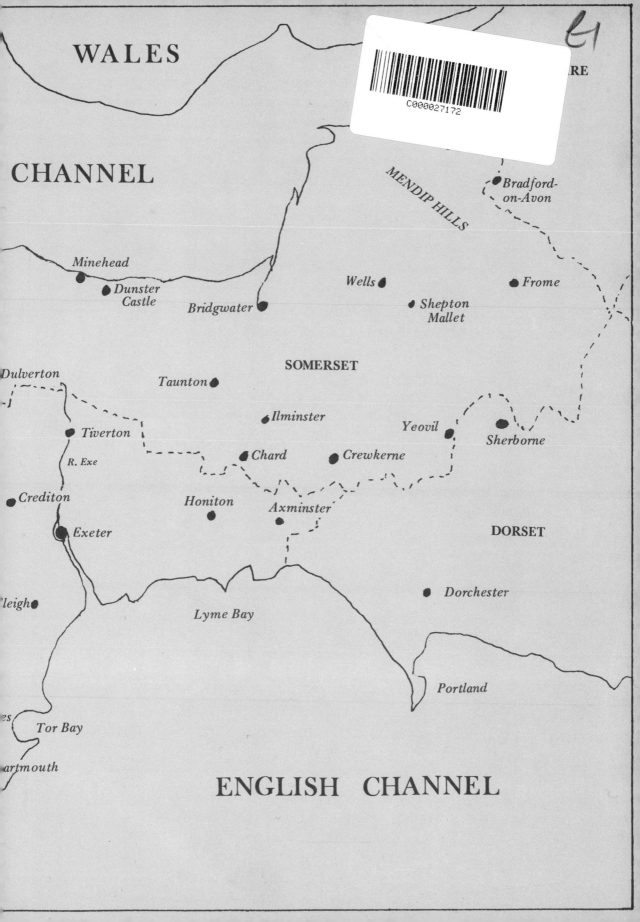

SIR BEVILL GRENVILE
AND HIS TIMES

SIR BEVILL GRENVILE
and his times
1596~1643

John Stucley

Phillimore

1983

Published by
PHILLIMORE & CO. LTD.
Shopwyke Hall, Chichester, Sussex

ISBN 0 85033 512 4

Typeset in the United Kingdom by
Fidelity Processes - Selsey - Sussex

Printed and bound in Great Britain by
THE CAMELOT PRESS LTD
Southampton, England

CONTENTS

FOR NATALIA

*without whose support I would
never have written this book*

LIST OF PLATES

(between pages 50 and 51)

1. Elizabeth Bevill, mother of Sir Bevill Grenvile
2. Bevill Grenvile, 1626
3. Locket containing miniature portrait of Sir Bevill Grenvile
4. The Lodge or New Castle of Sherborne
5. John, 1st Baron Mohun of Okehampton
6. Sir John Eliot
7. Sir Bevill Grenvile, *c.* 1636, painting by Sir Anthony Van Dyke
8. Richard Grenvile, eldest son of Sir Bevill
9. Plaster fireplace from Sir Bevill's house at Bideford
10. Sir Nicholas Slanning
11. View of Falmouth Harbour and Pendennis Castle
12. Colonel John Trevannion
13. Ralph, 1st Baron Hopton of Stratton
14. Sidney Godolphin
15. Radford Manor
16. Launceston Castle
17. Anthony Payne
18. Sir William Waller
19. Cold Ashton Parsonage, now the Old Rectory
20. John Grenvile, Sir Bevill's second son

FOREWORD

One of the oddities of writing about a member of the Grenvile family is that its members have invariably been called 'Grenville' by other writers. It could be argued that the spelling of surnames varied from generation to generation in the 16th and 17th centuries, and this is undoubtedly true of the Grenviles. Admiral Sir Richard signed himself 'Greynvile', his son Sir Barnard, and his grandson Bevill 'Grenvile'. The misspelling of the name may be because of the existence of a totally different family called Grenville (later Dukes of Buckingham) who were not only unrelated to the Grenviles, but according to J. Horace Round, originated from quite different areas of France. To add to the confusion, both families lived in houses called 'Stow' or 'Stowe'.

Bevill's eldest surviving son John Grenvile changed his name to Granville on becoming Earl of Bath, and some of his descendants in the female line have adopted that name. One such descendant, Roger Granville, was fortunate in being able to copy the great hoard of letters — or at least those that were not destroyed by George, Lord Carteret — which were found by Mrs. Hawker, the first wife of the vicar of Morwenstow, when lunching at Stowe Barton. Her hostess used them for making frills on lamb cutlets! Others have since come to light in Los Angeles and at Longleat. Those living authors on whom I have relied are listed under 'Principal Sources'.

Bevill lived out his life at a period which has always fascinated me. It was the twilight of feudalism. Religious fervour submerged the ablest intellects. The new middle class, enriched by the dissolution of the monasteries, felt competent to challenge the King himself. Democracy was nascent. When the Civil War began, archers still had their rôle; both sides wore armour capable of withstanding lead shot fired from smooth-bored weapons, and atrocities were few. Battles before mid-1643 caused few fatalities. Officers were exchanged, and others sent home without their weapons. Our internecine war was still chivalrous in nature, and our island's warriors were only savage towards priests, foreigners, and Catholics, as second class citizens.

No one today, in our modern welfare state, should disregard the comparative novelty of present day political thought. It is little more than ten generations ago since men died in England and Scotland for their religion, and their belief in the divinity of Kings.

Bevill Grenvile exemplified the squirearchy of his day. His portraits show that artists saw him in many different lights; the man-about-town in London, the squire in Cornwall, the soldier pursuing his family's traditions, the fringe courtier of the Carolean Court. His letters, and those of his wife Grace, throw much light on the domestic issues of his day.

London 1983

JOHN STUCLEY

xi

ACKNOWLEDGEMENTS

I am grateful to a large number of people who have helped me publish this book; some are listed at the end of it. But Major Malcolm Munthe proved its inspiration, giving me photo-copies of his Grenvile papers. These proved to have been seen and copied by Roger Granville in his history of his family published in 1895, but Mary Robertson, Curator of Manuscripts at the Huntington Library in California, and Miss Fowles, Curator of the Longleat Library, helped with others not previously printed. Mr. James Derriman, engaged in researching the History of Talland allowed me to use documents he had found in the Northants Record Office and in the Talland/West Looe Legal Records.

Mr. Penhallurick the Cornish Archivist and Mr. Douch of the Royal Institute of Cornwall, Col. Peter Shakerly, the present owner of Tremeer, Mr. Eaves, the Keeper of Armour at the Tower, and many others contributed to the story.

Of those who kindly allowed me to photograph their pictures I must particularly thank Mr. Prideaux-Brune of Padstow, Major Fortescue of Boconnoc, Lord Egremont of Petworth, and Sir Dennis Stucley of Hartland. The North Devon Gas Board were good enough to allow photographs to be taken of their premises, once Bevill's house at Bideford.

I have also had help from the staff of the London Library, British Library, the Victoria and Albert Museum, and the Record Offices of London and Exeter.

Major Charles Chichester of Hall gave me the history of Bevill's canteen of silver and his jewelled locket. The Earl Fortescue and Mr. Tait of the British Museum were kind enough to let me inspect them.

Chapter One

A CORNISH HEIR COMES OF AGE

BEVILL GRENVILE was born on 23 March 1596 at Great Brinn, his mother's old home, near Withiel in Cornwall. He was baptised two days later at Withiel parish church, some five miles south west of Bodmin. Had he been a sickly child his christening would have taken place immediately he was born, lest he die and be denied heaven. His arrival was a happy event for his parents — an heir-at-law for their respective estates. Both parents were of land-owning families: Sir Barnard, his father, inherited Stow and elsewhere on the death of his famous father, Sir Richard, in the *Revenge* in 1591 off the Azores; his mother, Elizabeth Bevill, whom Sir Barnard married in 1592, was the heiresss of the Bevill estates at Killigarth and Brinn.

While both Grenviles and Bevills boasted Norman ancestry, it is important to remember that Bevill regarded himself as first and foremost a Cornishman. His son Jack, who was to become John, Earl of Bath, believed himself to be descended from the 9th-century conquerer of Normandy, Rollo the Viking, and hence by inheritance the 23rd Earl of Corboile, and Lord of Granville and Thorigny. It seems unlikely that Bath thought up the story for himself, and it is a fair assumption that the Grenvile family had at least an oral tradition to that effect. The very learned J. Horace Round poured scorn on the Grenvile ancestry, but was never quite able to explain the coats of arms reported at Corbeil and elsewhere in France, 'gules three lance rests or', which have been the bearings of the Grenviles for some centuries. He suggests that the lance rests are mouth-organs and derive from the county of Glam-organ in Wales. Whether or not he be right, it seems clear that Bevill believed himself the scion of an illustrious line, and that belief may well have inspired not only his heroic charge at Lansdowne, but also his grandfather's heroism at the Azores.

Satisfactory though his ancestry may have been, it is necessary to understand where his family stood in the economic climate of his day. In the days of the first Queen Elizabeth, who still had seven years of her reign to enjoy when Bevill was born, social status was very much a question of parentage, and the social barriers between the nobility, the gentry, trade, artisans, and labourers were not only well defined but equally difficult to surmount.

Professor A. L. Rowse considered the Grenviles second only to the Arundells in terms of wealth, when Bevill's famous grandfather was alive. The Admiral added nothing to the family fortune save honour. Nor did his wife, Mary St

1

Leger, bring any money with her. Mary was the daughter of Sir John St Leger who lived at Annery, up river from Bideford, overlooking the Torridge. The St Legers, too, were as well bred as anyone could wish; they had an undeniable ancestry through the Butlers to the Plantagenets, but were bankrupt and crooked. Sir John had married a great fortune and spent it, and the family pursued a headlong downward course. They were an easy-going, good-for-nothing, hard-drinking lot. A brother was convicted at Middlesex Quarter Sessions of highway robbery on Hounslow Heath. To make ends meet they borrowed from all and sundry. Sir John married his daughters to West Country gentry, Grenviles, Stucleys, Bellews, and Tremaynes, but no son-in-law ever received the promised dowry.

Bevill's father, Sir Barnard, did better in choosing himself a wife. Elizabeth Bevill was sole heiress to her parents and inherited many substantial manors throughout Cornwall. It was she who introduced red hair into the family, which continues among some of her descendants to this day. Sir Barnard was content to live the life of a county magnate, interesting himself in the military affairs of his county. He was appointed High Sheriff of Cornwall the year Bevill was born, and served as a member for Bodmin in the Parliament of 1597: He was very much an establishment figure, and avoided the improvident investments his father had made in attempting to colonise Roanoke Island, in support of his cousin Sir Walter Ralegh, or the Province of Munster in Ireland. Sir Richard had been one of the 'undertakers' in that ill-fated venture, in partnership with his wife's cousin, Warham St Leger, whose father Sir Anthony had been Lord Deputy of Ireland in the reign of Henry VIII. Sir Warham had gone to Ireland in 1579 as provost marshal. The plan approved by Queen Elizabeth was to re-people Munster with Englishmen, a province devastated in the course of putting down the rebellion of the last Earl of Desmond. A campaign of scorched earth and genocide in Munster led Hooker to write:

> The curse of God was so great and the land so barren, both of man and beast, that whosoever did travel from one end to the other of all Munster, even from Waterford to Smerwick, about six score miles, he should not meet man, woman, or child, saving in cities and towns, nor yet see any beast save foxes, wolves, or other ravening beasts.

Sir Richard took 99 settlers from England, St Leger 46; including his son John Grenvile, a nephew, Thomas Stucley, a half-brother John Arundell, Christopher Harris a prospective son-in-law, and a number of farmers and labourers from the West Country.

When Sir Richard was killed in the Battle of the Azores, the crown leases granted him and St Leger passed to John Grenvile, and consisted of about five hundred square miles in southern Ireland. But John sailed with Sir Walter Ralegh on his penultimate voyage to the Caribbean in search of El Dorado, the fabulous city of gold in South America. John was drowned when one of Ralegh's ships foundered on passage, and his holdings passed to Sir Barnard, his elder brother. Barnard went to Ireland with the new Lord Deputy, Arthur Chichester, a younger son of the Chichesters of Hall, and involved himself to some extent in the Munster settlement, but the Irish had crept back into their expropriated lands as squatters, and there was little return for the £8,000 invested in the project. Poor John Grenvile's inheritance was eventually sold to the Lord Treasurer, Lionel Cranfield, recently created Earl of Middlesex and a creature of the Duke of Buckingham, in about 1621. Middlesex never paid Sir Barnard a penny, but nevertheless purported to sell the Munster property to Lord Cork for £4,500. In fine, the Munster investment proved at least as great a drain on the Grenvile fortunes as Roanoke, when every settler was killed by the American Indians, and the only profit arose from the capture of a Spanish treasure ship met by chance on Grenvile's return from America. Lady Grenvile's brother-in-law, John Stucley, having taken his part in settling the colonists on Roanoke, appropriated as his share a pearl necklace taken from the Spaniards. When Grenvile's ship, the *Tiger*, reached Plymouth, Sir Walter Ralegh hurried down to welcome them from London, and insisted on claiming the pearls for the Queen. Stucley, who had sold farms to help finance the voyage, was less than pleased, and his son was to bear a grudge which gave rise to tragic consequences later.

In later years Bevill was to complain of the improvidence of his ancestors, but his father Sir Barnard seems to have lived quietly enough at his wife's house of Killigarth in Talland, overlooking the bay in south-east Cornwall. It was by no means his only house. He owned the manor of Bideford in North Devon, and his house stood on the site of the present town hall. There were other houses belonging to him in the town. Stow, as the old house was then called, between Kilkhampton and the sea in North Cornwall, had also been a home of the Grenvile's since the 14th century, on land which had belonged to them since the 12th. A chapel in the house was licensed by the bishop in 1386, and Grenvile deeds and burials at Kilkhampton suggest the family regarded Stow as their principal seat, yet Barnard Grenvile preferred living in the south to be sheltered, perhaps, from the westerly gales which stunt and distort the trees along the savage north Cornish coastline.

Sir Barnard was able to lay his hands on considerable sums of money when required to do so. His grandfather, Sir John St Leger, owned the island of Lundy, a bleak granite outcrop in the Bristol Channel between Hartland Point and the Welsh coast. Sir John having borrowed £200 from a London mercer and finding himself unable to repay it, Sir Barnard paid the debt in return for the conveyance of Lundy to himself. There was also St Leger House which stood near the Southwark end of London Bridge. That, too, fell to Sir Barnard in similar circumstances.

None of the Cornish gentry were very rich or lived in great mansions, and the Grenviles were no different from their fellows. The only church land which came their way on the dissolution of the monasteries was Buckland, in Devon, and Barnard's father, Sir Richard, had been obliged to sell it. Sir Richard loved Buckland and, when the abbey was put up for sale, he turned down Sir Francis Drake as a prospective purchaser, preferring to sell to a gentleman rather than a parvenue. There may have been some jealousy, too, since Drake had been far more successful in his raids on the Spanish treasure ships than Sir Richard. In the end Drake had his way, buying Buckland under cover of nominee purchasers.

Near neighbours of the Grenviles at Killigarth were the Eliots. The Eliot family originated in Devon, and the Champernownes, another Devon family, had obtained the Priory of St Germans at the Dissolution. The Champernownes, who owned large estates in Devon, were happy to exchange St Germans for the Eliot lands in that country. The Priory was a substantial building, and the Eliot of the day was able to share his son John's tutor with other boys. Killigarth was too small for such a purpose.

It is more than probable that young Bevill received his education at St Germans. The son of the house, John Eliot, was nearly four years older than Bevill; (he was baptised at St Germans, 20 April 1592). Another boy seems to have been William Coryton from nearby West Newton, and a fourth was young Moyle, another neighbour's son.

In the early 17th century sons of gentry sometimes entered service with great noblemen as pages, obtaining their education with the sons of the house. Endymion Porter, a distant relation of Bevill's, was sent as page to the Conde de Olivares in Spain (his family having Spanish interests).

Bevill's education would have been based on the precept that 'Manners maketh man', the motto William of Wykeham chose for both his creations, Winchester College and New College, Oxford. The real work of education in England was done in grammar schools. As their name implies, grammar schools existed to teach Latin grammar, Latin being the universal language of learning throughout western Europe, and 'grammar' being defined as 'the art of speaking and writing correctly, as used by the writers of prose and poetry'. In 1513 Lily's *Latin Grammar* was published, and was made compulsory reading in all grammar schools in 1528, remaining without any serious rival for 350 years. The tutor at St Germans would have made all the boys in his care thumb Lily exhaustively. Without a first-class knowledge of Latin there could be no matriculation into a University or the Inns of Court.

Sir Barnard had been up at Oxford and was a graduate of University College; Bevill was destined to follow his father in due course.

Bevill would have had to learn the martial arts as well as grammar, and great emphasis was placed on boys being taught to write well and to be able to compose formal polished letters. Riding a horse was an attribute of a gentleman as necessary as the breath of life itself. The Grenvile's kept a good stable and bred their animals with care. When the great Queen died in 1603 all the world flocked to London to see their new King, James the Sixth of Scotland and First of England. The Countess of Bath (née Lady Elizabeth Russell) wrote to Sir Barnard from her house of Tawstock near Barnstaple in North Devon:

'I think I may be thus bold with you at this time to entreat your kind favour in this little request; which is to let me exchange with you for your sorrell gelding which I hear you have. For my hap is such as I had thought I had been well fitted for two geldings for my coach. The one I had from Mr. Stucley that will by no means serve, and our time in stay is short to enquire further of . . .'.

The letter was dated 24 April and the new King was due in London on 7 May — the journey from Barnstaple to London taking five or six days.

By 1607, Bevill was eleven or twelve. His mother, Elizabeth Grenvile had married in 1592 and had given birth to at least five children in addition to Bevill, who survived. The rate of infant mortality, and indeed death in child-bed, was appallingly high. A brother Barnard was born in 1597–8, Richard, the rascal of the family in 1600, John who became a barrister in 1601, and Roger, the youngest, was christened at Bideford in 1603. Two infants were buried in 1605 at Kilkhampton and only one daughter, Gartrud, lived long enough to marry. Lady Elizabeth, as Knight's wives were then called, seems to have died in or shortly after 1607, as there is no mention of her after that date. She was a tall attractive looking girl and Sir Barnard never remarried, preferring to live at her house of Killigarth in which he would have had at least a life interest.

Meanwhile Bevill was being schooled at St Germans. Young Eliot was a slim slight sensitive looking youth with a quick temper and open-handed ways. Moyle sneaked to Eliot's father about John's extravagant ways and no doubt earned John a wigging from his parent. John considered himself unfairly treated, and drawing his sword, wounded Moyle in his side. Moyle survived his injury and, after becoming High Sheriff of Cornwall in 1624, was appointed one of the Parliamentary sequestrators of Royalist lands during the Civil War. But even if the wound was not a serious one, he was entitled to an apology. John Eliot wrote him the following letter:

> 'I do acknowledge I have done you a great injury, which I wish I had never done, and so desire you to remit; and I do desire that all unkindness may be forgiven and forgotten betwixt us, and henceforth I shall desire and deserve your love in all friendly offices, as I hope you will mine.'

This letter between teenagers was signed by Eliot and his signature was witnessed by William Coryton and Bevill Grenvile.

Eliot, Coryton, and Bevill Grenvile remained friends all their lives, save for a brief period when Coryton, a pragmatist, reneged on his friends. All became members of a Parliament, in which Latin was frequently used in debate to amplify or clarify a point to be made. His education enabled Bevill to matriculate into Exeter College, Oxford at the age of 15 in June 1611. Bevill's father Sir Barnard had been at University College, and it may have been because John Eliot preceded him there that Bevill went to Exeter instead.

Exeter had always been frequented by young men of West Country families, having been founded as early as 1314 by a bishop of Exeter. It was established in its original buildings just inside the north wall of Oxford close by the Turl Gate, a minor gateway in the city's defences. The College still stands at the corner of Broad Street and the Turl across the road from Balliol, but has been much altered since 1611.

To get from Killigarth to Oxford Bevill had a lengthy ride to face, taking perhaps five days to complete. His route passed through Exeter, the county town of Devon, where at Madford House in Heavitree, just beyond the city's walls, lived Sir George Smith. Sir George was a considerable magnate, and related to Bevill and Stucley cousins by marriage. One of Sir George's daughters had married a Monck of Potheridge, a family of great antiquity and great penury. Their son George Monck had little prospect of achieving a decent education; such money as was available would be spent on his elder brother. Fortunately for George, his grandfather took a great liking to him (he had no sons of his own though twice married) and offered to educate the boy on condition that he spent half his year at Madford with his grandparents.

By his second marriage, Sir George Smith acquired another daughter, Grace, and it is likely that, en route to and from Oxford during his time as an undergraduate, Bevill would have met the infant Monck, later Duke of Albermarle and the man responsible for restoring the monarchy, and his future wife.

Life at Oxford was essentially monastic. The Fellows have only been permitted to marry in recent years. Plumbing and heating was until recently medieval. In 1611 there was no very distinct line between the grammar schools and the universities of England. Boys might come up to a university at the age of thirteen or fourteen, although 17 was the more usual age, and the less advanced students would continue to study Latin there. The study of more advanced subjects, of which theology and law were the most important, was by means of attending lectures given by Masters of Arts, and the candidate for the degree of Bachelor of Arts did not, as he does now, have to pass an examination. All he had to do was produce certificates that he had attended lectures and a recommendation from his teachers that he was worthy of a degree.

In spite of frequent prohibitions, the students often wore swords and daggers, and had no hesitation in using them. A university education may have led to an increase in learning, but above all it taught a young man to fend for himself in a dangerous and competitive world.

Exeter College was in its hey-day. It had been heavily re-endowed by Sir William Petre in 1566. Sir William could well afford to do so. He had been Secretary of State to four Tudor monarchs with all the profits such posts implied, and had been a large receiver of monastic lands at the Dissolution. He created a number of fellowships for appointees of himself and his son John. Bevill's brother Barnard came up from Cornwall to join him in 1612, and may have had hopes of a Petrean Fellowship, as such were called.

John Petre, having been created Baron Petre of Writtle in Essex, died in 1613, whereupon both Grenvile brothers wrote Latin verses to commemorate him: Barnard excelled by writing other verses to the widowed Lady Petre and Sir Thomas Bodley. That of Bevill is of course also in Latin but translated reads:

> 'Laments of the man of Exeter College:
> 'It displeased the Fates (for what does not displease them?) that you survived as a Rock for the House of the Muses; therefore, Petre, they cut your shining thread.
> 'Thinking that if so great a Rock falls, the House itself will collapse.
> 'However, I see they are mistaken in cutting Petre's thread: the Sacred House of the Muses is not going to fall.
> 'A second Atlas holds it up'.
> He concluded with the pious hope: 'Let Atlas sustain Bevill Grenvile, eldest son.'

The name Petre and the Latin word for rock, *Petra*, made Bevill's contribution a witty and apposite entry in *Threni Exoniensum*. Barnard became a Master of Arts in July 1619 but is not heard of again. I fear he died young.

Who, then, was the 'second Atlas' who would not only sustain the House of the Muses but also Bevill? The year before Lord Petre died a new Rector had been installed. He was none other than Doctor Prideaux, a man of great distinction, destined to be chaplain to both Prince Henry and to Charles I. The Prideaux family had been active in Cornish affairs for a century or more, and branches had become established in Devon. One branch had Bevill blood, and the family were regarded as cousins.

By the time Bevill had been up at Oxford three years, he wrote to his father saying he wished to become a Bachelor of Arts. Not all students bothered to take a degree, and additional expense was involved in doing so.

Sir Barnard wrote to him in reply:

> 'I would have you supply yourself thereby by your craving Mr. J. Fleminge's best help in furnishing you with any monies you shall want. On receipt of your letters I will repay him either there by the way of London, or in this country [Cornwall] at his pleasure. Not knowing what to send you. I like well of your proceedings, and I would not have you to be inferior to any in any ways — though I send you not monies at this time. Proceed in God's name etc., And so I pray God to bless you and do rest. Your loving father.' (Longleat MS, 21 February 1614).

Sir Barnard's letter was dated four days after Bevill graduated, so that his son's wish to do so seems to have been a last minute decision.

One gathers that Bevill was not a very serious-minded student from the letter he wrote his son Richard in 1640. Richard was then up at Oxford, and the letter forms one of a series designed to retrieve Dick (as he was called) from idleness and over-spending.

> 'I do no way dislike those other authors you name (whether poets or historians) but admire them, the one sort for their wit and learned allegories, the other (for their) eloquence and glorious examples of courage, mag(nified above) all other virtues, which may stir up an ingenious and active (spirit) to imitation.
>
> But these are so facile and pleasing studies, as (if) you fasten once upon them, you will never touch with the other more, and so lose the staff which would best support you hereafter: but if you will use those humane authors only for a recreation and refreshment 'til you have attained perfection in the others, you are then in the right, and shall please me, and profit yourself infinitely.
>
> I will say no more of it, having said enough heretofore, and methinks your own discretion should suggest no less unto you than I have often inculcated.
>
> I am myself in this very point a woeful example: I pray God you be not such too.
>
> I was left to my own little discretion when I was a youth in Oxford, and so fell upon the sweet delights of reading Poetry and History in such sort as I troubled no other books, and do find myself so infinitely defective by it when I come to manage any occasion of weight, as I would give a limb it were otherwise'. (Forster MS, 12 Jan. 1640).

Bevill presented a silver cup to his college, and thereby no doubt contributed to King Charles I's war-chest in the Civil War when all such gifts were melted down and turned into coin of the realm.

The new Rector, the Latin verse, the cup — all out-weighed the disadvantages of preferring poetry and history to logic and rhetoric, with the result that on 17 February 1614, at the age of 17, Bevill Grenvile became a Bachelor of Arts.

Events which would shape the world for Bevill outside the academic world of
Oxford were under way. One Sir Thomas Overbury, who had been a great friend
of the King's favourite Sir Robert Carr (now Earl of Somerset), had been sent to
the Tower of London in 1611. Two years later, on 15 September 1613, Sir
Thomas died of poison. Rumour had it that he had been poisoned by the administration of arsenic in an enema administered by an apothecary's boy on the orders
of the Earl and Countess of Somerset.

Since his marriage, the Earl had become over-bearing and difficult, and, one
must suppose, less accommodating. A new star was rising. Young George Villiers
was promoted to be a gentleman of the bedchamber. When the Earl sent a
constable to the Tower to seize papers required by the commission of enquiry
into Overbury's murder, with a view to destroying them, his involvement became
evident. In January 1616 Francis Bacon was able to advise the King that 'the
evidence upon which my Lord of Somerset standeth indicted is of a good strong
thread, considering impoisoning is the darkest of offences: but the offence must
be well spun and woven together . . .'. Further correspondence with the King
about Somerset's forthcoming trial was passed through the hands of Sir George
Villiers, as he had now become.

Sir John Oglander described Villiers as 'one of the handsomest men in the
whole world' and he was first seen by the King at Apthorpe in the summer of
1614, when he was at once installed as the King's cup-bearer. Oglander went on
to say, 'I never yet saw any fond husband make so much or so great dalliance over
his beautiful spouse as I have seen King James over his favourites, especially
(Villiers)'. Villiers was the King's 'sweet and dear child', and the King was
Villiers' 'dear Dad and Gossip'.

Endymion Porter had returned from Spain, where he had been in service
with the powerful Conde Olivares until 1612. The King's favourite had a
half-brother Edward Villiers who lived in Fleet Street and Endymion
joined his household. It was probably in late 1617 or early 1618 that Endymion left Edward and became Master of the Horse to George, now Earl of
Buckingham, and a Privy Counsellor, and on the point of rising to the Marquesate
of Buckingham and the post of Lord High Admiral. 'A prodigious ascent', to
quote Clarendon.

Porter, by making himself indispensable to Buckingham, opened doors to his
kinsman Bevill which might otherwise have proved impassable, and was to be his
channel of communication to King Charles I in later years. Bevill's father Sir
Barnard regarded him as a powerful friend at Court, and was in communication
with him until at least 1630. Sir Barnard, an outstandingly establishment figure,
could be relied upon to support the new Stuart King and his new friend
Buckingham, through whom all blessings flowed.

On leaving Oxford, Bevill found himself lodgings at Vreines House, behind
St Clement's church in the Strand, and within six months had fallen in love, or
had at least an ambition to get married. The object of his affections was the
daughter of JX, and I have been unsuccessful in establishing her identity,
although a number of clues exist in the letter his father wrote to Bevill from

Killigarth in answer to a letter Bevill had written seeking his father's permission for a match with the lady in question:

'She is of great birth that I much approve her person — a wise general in the wars will not put on upon any service but that he will first be sure to speed, or to cut off with honour. ... if you first attempt before you have hope of prevailing, and in the end be bitten with an honourable frown, it will be a corrosive — you have chosen well to work by that wise knight's advice, who and JX have long before this ... been very intimate friends. He hath great reason to love the off-spring of Sir R(ichard) G(renvile) ... or any other that you know can work powerfulest with JX and his Lady, and if by these, or your own merit, in the eyes of the young lady your hopes do give you an encouragement to proceed, promise anything of my estate ... and it shall be made good. I have heard that JX hath said (that) he had rather marry his daughter to a gentleman of a good family that hath a competent estate to maintain him, than to a great lord. This giveth me hope ... I like well your choice. A meaner hearth than yours hath obtained greater honour. Assure yourself there will be nothing omitted of my part that will further it. My chiefest desire is to see your prosperity in all goodness. I pray to God to bless you and so I rest your loving father.'

It was August 1614, and Bevill was only 18 years of age, but his father could not have been more delighted at the prospect of what was evidently a marriage into the nobility.

What Bevill was up to in London between August 1614 and March 1618 can only be surmised; only one letter covers that period of his life. But young men of good family with any ambition to prosper required access to the mandarins who circulated in Court circles.

His father had sold the great St Leger house, of stone and timber in the shadow of London Bridge, and the Grenviles had no other house in London. Armed with money supplied by Sir Barnard's agent, Mr. Fleminge, Bevill was able to pay for his lodgings and hold his own with his contemporaries.

His name may have secured his acceptance into Court circles unaided, but he had the further advantage of cousins in high places. Endymion Porter was in attendance on Edward Villiers in Fleet Street, the Arundels of Wardour were distantly related, springing as they do from that Cornish family, Sir Lewis Stucley was one of the first courtiers to be knighted by James I on his arrival from Scotland, and there were many others. One cousin, Sir Walter Ralegh, would have stood him in good stead had it not been for Robert Cecil's hatred of him. As Captain of the Guard, Ralegh had ridden out to meet the new King at the last possible moment from London. It may be that Ralegh hoped for the success of some other contender for the throne. The King had been well briefed on Ralegh by Cecil and returned his greeting with: 'Rawly? Rawly? And rawly ha'e I heard of thee, mon!' (that being the correct pronunciation of the name). It was at Windsor that his supposedly great friend Cecil approached Ralegh on the terrace of the castle and asked him to come inside and attend a meeting of the Privy Council. He left it for the Tower of London.

Down in Cornwall, Sir Barnard was carrying out admirably his duties as a Deputy Lieutenant. These included arming and training the Trained Bands (ancestors of our Territorial Army) for the defence of their county against a foreign invader. Musters were held from time to time, and armories located strategically at muster points inspected. Since Tudor days the Spanish threat had receded, and King James was anxious to pursue a pro-Spanish policy. But peace in Europe was precarious, and Algerine Moors and other pirates not only interfered with trade but from time to time carried out raids along the coast. Much of the armour and weapons collected in Tudor days was becoming obsolescent.

Bevill's father wrote to him in 1615:

> 'I also forgot to mind you to learn how I might be served with those pieces of armours that the country [Cornwall] want, as pauldrons, tassets, gorgets, and murrions, as well as whole armours. Let me know by your next . . .'.

Pauldrons were shoulder defences, the tassets the pair of plates which hung from the skirt or waist-flange of the breast-plate and covered the groins and upper thighs. Gorgets were collars or neck defences, usually well-padded because they bore the weight of the cuirass (breast-plate and back-plate). Murrions were open-brimmed helmets, and together those elements comprised a typical pike-man's armour of the period.

Sir Barnard also asked Bevill to concern himself in his uncle St Leger's business, the Munster plantations, and to obtain various items in London unobtainable in Cornwall. His advice to his son at 19 shows that his father expected him to stand on his own feet but to seek advice when he needed it.

Apart from his father's affairs, Bevill had personal matters in train. His pursuit of a daughter of the great JX proved unsuccessful, as he was at length obliged to admit to his father. Sir Barnard wrote:

> 'I am glad you resolve to make but small stay in London; I pray God you hold your resolution. Killigarth will be more safe and more quiet. If the Lady holds her strict perverse humour I well suppose it is to make a breach. I wish she might know, though, that there are many women as men in England.
>
> Howsoever it stand, I will ever honour that noble Lord and exceedingly love his virtuous wife while I live . . .'.

Bevill took his father's advice that there were as good fish in the sea as ever came out of it, and on his way back through Exeter called in on Sir George Smith at Madford.

Grace must have caught his eye as a *bonne partie* rather than as a great beauty. She was two years younger than Bevill, having been born in 1598, and was then aged twenty. The only portrait I have seen of her shows a plain dull looking girl, and we know she suffered all her life from ill-health. But she proved an uncomplaining and devoted wife, and was, of course, joint heiress with her sister Lady Monck to her father's properties in Staffordshire, Dorset, Devon, and Cornwall.

Sir Barnard not only knew Lady Smith but was able to address her as 'aunt' through her Bevill connection, and so at Bevill's request he wrote asking for Grace's hand in marriage. The Reverend Ralph Byrd, a life-long friend and companion of Sir Barnard's had prepared the way:

'Byrd did sing your affection to us so sweetly at his return from you as it hath armed me to slight all opposition and to signify unto you that my desire is so irremoveable to make your daughter mine, and my son yours . . .

And therefore will end with recommending my faithful service to you, and my hearty love to my pretty cousin, your daughter.'

This letter was dated 31 December 1618, from Killigarth.

Chapter Two

BEVILL GOES TO WESTMINSTER

BEVILL and Grace Smith were married in Exeter in the first quarter of 1619. Sir Barnard, now many years a widower, seems to have been delighted. The young couple set up home at Tremeer in the parish of Lanteglos, a few miles from Fowey and no great distance from Killigarth. I assume Tremeer to have been part of the Bevill Killigarth estate, as Bevill Grenvile described himself as 'of Killigarth' when he started his political career later the next year. Its present owner, Colonel Peter Shakerley, describes the building as a modest modern house of no apparent antiquity, so the young Grenviles' first home must have been pulled down and rebuilt. Roger Granville thinks the Reverend Ralph Byrd was the vicar of Lanteglos, and one hopes as Cupid he was allowed some part in the Exeter wedding.

Sir Barnard showed his approval of the match by settling Stow and the Manor of Kilkhampton, the Manor of Bideford, and the island of Lundy on his eldest son. But Stow, the principal house of the Grenviles, required many alterations and embellishments to become habitable. It, too, has disappeared. No-one now knows precisely where it stood. No picture of it exists. The ubiquitous Mr. Buck, who painted or sketched country houses, had not yet been born. Bevill was to make Stow his home in due course and loved it dearly; Grace never cared for it — the scene of so many traumas in her life.

So what does one know of the old Stow? It lay between the sea and Kilkhampton. The sea was an uneasy neighbour to have. Those who lived within sight of it had to be capable of self defence. Algerine pirates might land at any time and carry one off to slavery. Houses, at least of the gentry, were built to withstand attack, short of a regular siege. When it was pulled down by Bevill's son, Lord Bath, in 1679, a splendid classical mansion called Stow was built nearby: the old house was clearly beneath the domestic requirements of an Earl. No very big houses were built in Cornwall before the Stow erected by Bath. Those that remain from Bevill's time are mostly of moor-stone, granite from the tors of Bodmin. Granite boulders lay everywhere for masons to quarry and shape. Bevill, when adding a parlour to Stow, was to insist on having moor-stone windows, and healing-stones (or slates) were used on the roof. Apart from the chapel, the house contained a Red Chamber and a Chamberlain, and accommodation sufficient to house a large family and an appropriate number of servants. The garden contained fruit trees and herbs for salads. There was an orchard for the making

12

of cider and a hop garden for the making of beer. Nearby were trees sufficient to provide timber for house-beams and ploughs, and so presumably of oak. The stables are said to have been built or rebuilt by Bevill, and are said to be the nucleus of the present Stowe Barton farm-house which still stands, although sold by his descendant John Thynne a year or two ago.

In Bideford Bevill preferred, or perhaps was obliged (as his grandmother was still living there), to occupy a small house on the quay-side. The big house below the church was the home of his maiden aunts, and Granny St Leger would have preferred living with her daughters to living by herself at Annery up-river. The house between the bridge and the High Street is now the Gas Company's Show-rooms, having been a public house. Although extensively altered, the architect preserved a beautiful plaster fire-place attributed to Bevill, and showing him in civilian dress, on the first floor.

Bideford itself was very much the creation of the Grenvile family. Ten years earlier, in 1610, Sir Barnard had granted a new charter to the borough of Bideford, the previous charter, obtained by Sir Richard, being deficient (in the opinion of the townsfolk) for its lack of powers to make bye-laws. The town was becoming increasingly important, and its merchants were no longer content to live at the benevolent whim of a great land-owner. Quays were over-crowded and more were required. Their usage and all the incidentals of a bustling port required more immediate supervision than Sir Barnard could exercise from Killigarth in the next county. Port dues and manorial ground rents made Bideford a prime manor in the Grenvile estate.

Lundy, as we have seen, was St Leger property taken in payment of a debt by Sir Barnard. Surprisingly, it was worth £100 a year. Cattle were bred there, butter made, but above all it was a source of sea-birds' eggs, much prized as delicacies then as now. 'Egging' brought many visitors to that inhospitable shore. His father's generosity in settling his northernmost estates on Bevill made it possible for him to contemplate a political life in the House of Commons.

Life in the House was very different from today. Its members were elected by remarkably few people. Cornwall returned 44 members of whom 42 were elected by about 1,000 voters in the boroughs. Two members were elected as Knights of the Shire by all those who paid scot and lot, numbering perhaps twice that number. Devon only returned 26, while Dorset and Somerset had to be content with 18 each. Cornwall was favoured above other counties because many of its inhabitants were tenants of Duchy land. Monarchs dependant on the Commons for the wherewithal to govern England had to ensure a majority on fiscal motions. Some of the boroughs had less than ten electors, or the franchise was limited to magistrates and the like. This state of affairs continued from the reign of Elizabeth I until the Reform Act of 1832.

The Court party had election managers who put pressure on the electorate to vote for the nominees, and electors in many boroughs expected to be paid by those whom they elected. Prospective candidates sometimes stood for several constituencies, as Knights of the Shire or Burgesses (for boroughs) and, when elected for more than one seat, were allowed to opt for the seat of their preference. In disputed elections, and there were many by reason of fraudulent manipulations of the poll, much time was taken up at the start of each Parliament by committees appointed to decide who was lawfully elected.

Once elected, a Knight of the Shire or Burgess was required to attend. After prayers the roll was called, and absentees had to explain their absence, be pardoned for their non-appearance, or pay a fine, or in extreme cases, find themselves expelled from the House. One might get the leave of the House to be absent for illness, the funeral of a wife or near relative, or for some other pressing cause.

Deliberations of the House were secret, and decisions reached bound the Members as a whole. It was against the law to record proceedings in the House, as those who voted against the King's proposals needed to be protected against his vengeance. The House presented, through its Speaker, a united front. But the House included Privy Counsellors and members supporting the Court party who hastened to the King with details of whom had voted contrary to Royal policy, and what such members may have said in support of their opposition. Motions of the House, and decisions thereon, were inscribed by clerks in the Commons Journal, and one such, Rushworth, was known to be keeping a private record of proceedings. Sir Simon D'Ewes, a member of the House, also kept a careful diary of events, but no action was ever taken against either of them.

By 1620 King James had ruled England for nearly seven years without calling a Parliament. He allowed writs to issue returnable on Christmas Day 1620 for a Parliament to assemble on Tuesday, 16 January 1621. This decision had been reached reluctantly; the Royal revenues were insufficient to meet the expenses of government. To understand the King's predicament it is necessary to review the political situation of the day.

When James became King of England he had achieved his life's ambition. His new Kingdom was incomparably richer than Scotland, and if Ireland presented its problems, it was at least a third jewel in his crown. The two kingdoms he had inherited had been at war with Spain for some time. His predecessor, Elizabeth I, had allowed her seamen to prey on the 'flotas' bringing gold and silver from the Americas to Europe, and occasionally sanctioned raids such as that of Essex and Ralegh on Cadiz. Not only was the royal treasury augmented by the occasional, and sometimes very sizeable, treasure taken from Spanish ships, but the long drawn out campaign was extremely popular with her subjects. Of these, 90 per cent were bigotted Protestants, who regarded Spain and its Most Catholic Majesty Philip III as part of the Scarlet Woman of the Apocalypse. The gentry, enriched or created by the sale of monastic lands at the Reformation and Dissolution, were not only well represented in the Parliament of England and among the great nobles of Scotland, but could be relied upon to resist any return to that religion eschewed by Henry VIII. Any retrograde movement towards catholicism threatened their land-holdings.

Unattractive though King James might be, his mother had been a catholic, and he was well enough read to distrust extremism of any form. He was so far ahead of his contemporaries in some respects that he was able to perceive the flagrant injustice of burning witches on their confessions obtained by torture. Unbeknown to the general public, James became a pensioner of the Spanish Court. A gift of 50 million ducats on his accession was a powerful persuader, and it was not long before peace with Spain was sought and obtained, and raids on Spanish shipping declared piracy. It was clearly a term of any further Spanish subsidies that the penal laws enacted under the Tudors against catholics should be repealed or disregarded.

The Commons were totally opposed to peace with Spain or any relaxation of the harassment of catholics; they resented the rampant corruption among the King's ministers and loathed his favourites. Finding the Commons unwilling to vote him the money he needed, the King lived a hand-to-mouth existence, ever hopeful of tapping Spanish resources for more gold, and raising funds by selling baronetcies, a title he invented, for £400 a time. His favourites were allowed to dabble in patents and monopolies, from which great wealth could be achieved at the expense of tradesmen.

James's reign might have limped on from year to year, with just enough money to make ends meet, had it not been for his children. His eldest son, Prince Henry, a dashing young man adored by the populace, died of typhoid in 1612. His new successor, Charles, was not a patch on his elder brother. With a little wit, and the narrowest of minds, he was burdened with a stammer. James's only daughter Elizabeth married the Elector Frederick of the Palatinate in 1613. Any child she might have would succeed to the English throne if anything happened to Charles. She was much loved by everyone, and was known as the Queen of Hearts, but her strongest claim to the affections of the English was her husband's protestantism. Any child of hers could be relied upon to be a protestant, too.

It so happened that the childless Emperor Matthias abdicated in 1617, and Ferdinand, King of Bohemia, was elected Emperor in his place. Thinking Ferdinand had relinquished his throne in Prague for an imperial sceptre in Vienna, the Bohemians decided to replace him with a king of their choosing. A majority of the Bohemians were protestants, and Ferdinand had treated them harshly. Knowing the strength of Elector Frederick's protestant views, they invited him to become their king.

Frederick and Elizabeth reigned over two widely separated provinces in Germany, one on the Rhine, the other many miles to the east bordering the Kingdom of Bohemia. The temptation to promote himself from Elector to King and to aid his fellow protestants was a very real one. Elizabeth wrote home to her father for advice and King James was far from enthusiastic. It was clear the Emperor would deeply resent such a move.

In the end, Frederick succumbed to temptation, and the couple entered Prague in October 1619. The Emperor sent Frederick notice to quit Prague within the month. Frederick decided to stand firm, and sent round to other German Princes for help. None dared stand up to the Emperor.

To give King James I of England his due, he was prepared to help his daughter to the limited extent of his funds. Sir Horace Vere was then commanding an English regiment in the Netherlands. Its officers included Bevill's younger brother

Richard, the Earls of Warwick and Essex, William Waller, an old friend of the
Grenvile's, and Ralph Hopton, who was to play a leading rôle in things to come.
With some reinforcements this regiment was ordered into the Lower Palatinate
on the Rhine to defend it against the armies of Catholicism, those of the Emperor
and of Spain. By August 1620 the Winter King of Bohemia and his Queen of
Hearts had been driven out of all their possessions in what is now Germany and
Czechoslovakia, and the Queen and her children entered Holland for refuge.

If James was to achieve the restoration of his daughter to the Palatinate lands
he would be obliged to summon a Parliament to grant him the necessary funds
for a European campaign. This, then, was the true reason for the King having to
resort to his Commons, which gave occasion for Bevill — as one of the two
Knights of the Shire for Cornwall — to enter on a political career.

Sir John Greynevyle had been elected Knight of the Shire for Devon in 1388
and 1394, presumably being domiciled in Bideford; Admiral Sir Richard
Greynvile, Bevill's grandfather, was Knight of the Shire for Cornwall in 1529: his
son Sir Barnard, Burgess for Bodmin in 1597, so Bevill had some claim to a
political background for his name. But he never achieved the corridors of power.
He was essentially a back-bencher. I see no reason to doubt that with his background and up-bringing he supported the Court party at every division during this,
his first Parliament.

Bevill was now a young man of 24, red-haired and with ear-rings, a man-about-
town dressed in the latest fashion of his day.

Parliament sat on 16 January 1621. It soon became evident that its members
required substantial concessions of the King before voting him any supplies. The
basic problem was James's Spanish policy. The marriage of the heir to the throne
to a Spanish Infanta had been mooted for several years, and the prospect of such
a match was anathema to the country as a whole. The corruption of his Ministers
and Judiciary much offended James's faithful Commons, imbued as they were
with the new puritan morality.

In February a Parliamentary Committee of Privileges complained about the
wholesale issue of patents and monopolies and the indiscriminate use of the royal
prerogative: the complaints were valid, but the target aimed at was the newly
created Duke of Buckingham (as George Villiers had now become), who was busy
feathering his nest. Another committee of the House investigated complaints
against Sir Francis Bacon, newly created Lord Verulam, Viscount St Alban,
Keeper of the Great Seal, and Lord Chancellor of England.

Buckingham proved too powerful for the Commons to destroy, but Bacon, due
to Buckingham having adopted a new protegé, the Bishop of Lincoln, one
Williams, the Chancellor was left to his own devices. Without Buckingham's
support, Bacon knew himself lost. He took to his bed at Gorhambury. In Bacon's
absence from London the chairman of the committee, Sir Edward Coke, drew up
a list of 27 counts of corruption, alleging that the Lord Keeper had received
£100,000 in gifts from litigants over the previous three years.

Bacon replied to the indictment with a plea of guilty to each count, tendering
the Great Seal, and submitting himself to the judgment of the House of Lords.

Buckingham and Prince Charles suggested that no further action was required against Bacon providing he was no longer employed in office. The House met in May and fined Bacon £40,000, and ordered that he should be detained in the Tower of London during the King's pleasure, disqualified him from any office of state, and debarred him from attendance at Court.

After a decent interval Bacon was sent to the Tower on 31 May, but the King's pleasure was such that he was released on 4 June and allowed to return home. Neither was he ever obliged to pay the fine. His post as Lord Keeper, or as we would say today, Lord Chancellor, was awarded Bishop Williams, who expressed himself astonished by his appointment. Knowing no law, he let it be known he would only sit accompanied by two judges on his bench. But accept it he did.

These attacks on the establishment, with their evidence of power second only to the King and his favourite Buckingham, were highly instructive to any new member of the Commons. Bevill, as a new member, was not appointed to the committees who formed the spearhead of the attack, but he was given his chance to show his mettle as an administrator when, on 9 March, he was appointed to a committee to enquire into the requirements of Wadham College, Oxford. The widow of Nicholas Wadham, a gentleman of Somerset, had founded Wadham with money her husband had left for that purpose in 1610. The college was built on the ruins of a suppressed Augustinian Friary, outside the City's walls, and was completed three years later in 1613. Bevill was up at Oxford when Wadham was a-building, and might be expected to have some knowledge of the matter.

Committees of the House of Commons sat in the Star Chamber, the halls of the Middle and Inner Temples, the Exchequer Chamber and similar venues. The Wadham College Committee, under the chairmanship of Sir John Strangeways of Dorset, sat in the Exchequer Chamber. The sole issue was how so new a foundation could be brought within the scope of existing statutes governing the administration of other colleges. The problem would have best been left to the many lawyers in the House, and there is nothing to suggest that Bevill added anything to the debate. Nor was he ever called upon to sit on any other committee, although matters affecting a particular county or trade were delegated to named persons and the knights and burgesses of the area affected; hence, had he wished to do so, he could have taken part in a number of committees considering west-country affairs.

Ten days after his first committee Bevill became the proud father of a son, Richard, born at Tremeer on 19 March and christened at Lanteglos six days later. A daughter Elizabeth (Bessie) had been born the year before. Lady Smith would have certainly travelled down from Exeter to be with her daughter at the time, but Bevill was obliged to be in London. The House did not give leave of absence for a wife's child-birth, and would have been poorly attended it it had.

Up in London the King sent his Commons a request for supplies (as money was gracefully termed), and Sir James Perrot opened the debate by recommending the House to sacrifice its all for the preservation of true religion and the Palatinate estates in Germany. The motion to do so was seconded by Sir Robert

Phelips of Montacute and warmly supported by Sir Thomas Wentworth: all agreed that money should be voted on the condition that there was an end to religious toleration and that there should be rigid enforcement of the penal laws against Catholics.

On that happy ecumenical note the House voted its adjournment on 4 June until November 1621, Bacon was let out of the Tower of London and scurried home to Gorhambury, and Bevill set off on the long ride home to Cornwall, to examine his son and heir. Dick, as he was always called, was a promising start to a new generation of Grenviles. None of Bevill's brothers had married yet. Richard was gaining military experience under Vere, and Barnard was not heard of after 1619 and may be presumed dead; John, a barrister, wrote to his brother Bevill 'in Cornwall' from Lincoln's Inn on 18 July 1621. The vagueness of the address suggests that Bevill was already on the move. We know he was living at Stow within a year of Dick's birth, since all his subsequent children were christened (or buried) at Kilkhampton.

John's letter seeking his elder brother's instructions on how to deal with a creditor of Bevill's, with mention of the ubiquitous Ralph Byrd, and tit-bits of Court gossip, is the only letter of his that has been preserved. His last act was to witness a family deed in May 1622. By May 1626 Bevill was writing to Grace: 'If God send us a boy, I have a good mind to have him called John, for my poor brother John's sake . . .'. Bevill's affection for all his brothers, and particularly for John, is evident in all his dealings with them; it was able to comprehend and overlook the accusations of his brother Richard, whom he never forsook, even when opposed to him in Parliament.

John's messages to his 'sisters' would have been to Grace, his sister-in-law, and Gartrud. I give his letter in full:

'From Lincolns Inn July 18th 1621.

To my dearest brother Bevill Grenvile Esquire in Cornwall these:

Dear Brother: Mr Bonde making me acquainted with his return, I could not but let you understand of Wells the Barber's honest dealings with you. The matter is this, a few days before Mr. Byrd's departure, he raised unto him, and demands of him whether Mr. Byrde had any directions by Boge from you to be paid of his money, Mr. Byrd told him he had none, whereupon he swore you had done scurvily with him and said ere long you should hear of it, and again said he was basely abused by you, and since he was thus forced he would let the Town know of your dealings, and do you all the dishonour he could amongst the chiefest friends you have in London; nay further he said since you had so slighted him in this, he would forget you as well in greater matters; dear brother, I must needs confess I harkened to his talk with exceeding great impatience, when he had ended I told him those speeches became him not, and "what dealing there is between my brother and you I know not; if he have as you say injured you, I make no question but he will shortly give you satisfaction. But if you go about to scandalize him with such assertions as you say you will, I can assure you" (I told him) "you will purchase your railings dearly"; presently he went away and gave me no answer, and if I had known that he would have done you no displeasure in your business I vow before God he should have had cause to speak those words, or, if I might but understand how you take it, he shall soon perceive his speeches cannot be so soon forgotten.

My Lord of Oxford is sent to the Tower for a peremptory answer he gave the King upon a late examination before the Council. My Lord of Essex went lately to the Low

Countries, and is sent for back again, as it is reported. The King begins his progress this day. So entreating you to remember my best love to my sisters. In haste I remain your assured faithful brother

Jo(hn) Grenvile'.

The long summer vacation at Stow being over, Bevill returned to London for the second session of his first Parliament in November 1621. He probably lodged at the sign of the Rainbow between the two Temple gates, conveniently near his brother John and Westminster, in the Strand.

In Parliament, the King informed the House that his diplomatic activity on behalf of Frederick and his daughter Elizabeth had failed. Snide jokes were current in Europe that the King of England only fought for his friends with armies of ambassadors. In the Lower Palatinate, Sir Horace Vere and Count Ernest Mansfeldt still fought on against the overwhelming forces of Spain. The King asked his faithful Commons for supplies.

The House was agreed that, if war should be waged against Spain as in Queen Elizabeth's day, that if the anti-Catholic laws were enforced with rigour, and that if the King undertook to marry Prince Charles to a Protestant Princess, he could have all the money needed: in default of such undertakings the money would not be forthcoming.

James warned the Commons that if members persisted in meddling in affairs subject to his prerogative, they could expect to be punished. The Commons, he told them, held their privileges by the grace of their prince and not as of right.

To this the members adopted a resolution which read:

'That the liberties, franchises, privileges, and jurisdictions of Parliament, are the ancient and undoubted birthright and inheritance of the subjects of England: and that the arduous and urgent affairs concerning the King, State, and defence of the realm, and of the Church of England, and the making and maintenance of laws, and redress of mischiefs and grievances which daily happen within this realm, are proper subjects and matter of counsel and debate in Parliament: and that, in the handling and proceeding of those businesses, every member of the house hath, and of right ought to have, freedom of speech, to propound, treat, reason, and to bring to conclusion the same; that the Commons in Parliament have like liberty and freedom to treat of those matters in such order as in their judgement shall seem fittest; and that every such member of the said house hath like freedom from all impeachment, imprisonment, and molestation (other than by censure of the House itself) for or concerning any Bill, speaking, reasoning, or declaring of any matter or matters, touching the parliament or parliament business; and that if any of the said members be complained of and questioned for anything said or done in Parliament, the same is to be shown to the King, by the advice and assent of all the Commons assembled in Parliament, before the King gives credence to any private information.'

The Resolution was entered into the Journal of the House of Commons, and its content reported to the King at Theobalds. He came up to London by coach, sent for the Commons Journal, and tore the resolution of protest out. He next dissolved Parliament by proclamation, and on his way home to Theobalds on horseback, fell into the river 'so that nothing but his boots were seen'. He was pulled out of the river and put into a warm bed with all speed. A correspondent wrote with his tongue in his cheek: 'There came much water out of his mouth and body. His Majesty rode back to Theobalds, went into a warm bed, and, as we hear, is well, which God continue!' It was 8 February 1622.

Sir Robert Phelips of Montacute, Sir Edward Coke, and John Pym, having been most actively concerned in the drafting and acceptance of the Protestation, were thrown into solitary confinement in the Tower, where they remained for nine months. Sir Thomas Crewe, Sir Dudley Digges, and Sir James Perrot, as lesser offenders, were obliged to go to Ireland. The Opposition having been summarily dealt with, the King pressed on with his plans for a Spanish marriage for the heir to the throne.

The idea of a Spanish marriage had been mooted ever since peace was made with Spain in 1604. The principal attraction of the plan for James was his mistaken belief in the immense wealth of the Spaniards, and the likelihood of the Infanta bringing to England a dowry of commensurate size.

But Castile had enjoyed its great age of gold at the beginning of the 16th century; it was followed in the reign of Philip II by an age of silver, but by the time of Philip III (1598-1621) the Spaniards had been reduced to copper. Their economy was one of constant inflation and depreciation of their currency. Spain far outspent her income in the pursuit of her foreign policies. James's vision of a happy old age secured with Spanish gold and of independence from his tiresome Commons, was no better than a castle in Spain.

The advantage of negotiating an English marriage for Spain lay in the cessation of naval attacks on her treasure fleets as they sailed across the Atlantic. Queen Elizabeth had looked to Drake and Ralegh to augment her income by raids on the 'flotas', her successor had been so avid for peace with Spain that he made it the mainstay of his foreign policy, and sacrificed the ageing Ralegh on the scaffold to keep the Spaniards sweet. That judicial murder had been highly approved by Gondomar and Philip III.

King James's defence of his daughter Elizabeth's interests in Germany had failed diplomatically and militarily. Her husband's capital Heidelberg, fell to the Spanish Netherland Army in September 1622. James's pro-Spanish policy required that his son Charles should marry the Infanta and that the marriage contract would obtain the restoration of the Palatinate to Frederick and Elizabeth, and bring in some urgently required cash.

The Spaniards' policy was to preserve their annual injections of gold and silver brought by the 'flotas' from the Americas, without which nothing could be done to stem the rising tide of Protestantism in Europe.

King James of England had to be kept happy by the prospect of a carrot which he must never be allowed to attain, so that each time an agreement on the proposed marriage looked likely the stakes were raised: further concessions being required of the English King.

By August 1622 the terms had risen to include the repeal of the penal laws against Catholics, that the Infanta's Catholic church should be open in England to all worshippers, that her accompanying priests should include a Catholic bishop with extra-territorial rights, and that any children of the marriage should be educated solely by their mother.

These negotiations carried out in London through the Spanish ambassador the Conde de Gondomar, were handled by Endymion Porter for his master, the favourite, Buckingham. By September 1622 Porter was able to tell Gondomar that a fleet now lay ready to convey the Lord High Admiral Buckingham to Spain to bring the Infanta back to England.

Philip III having died, the Spanish throne was now occupied by Philip IV, a 17-year-old boy, and the country was effectively ruled by the Conde de Olivares. The King's sister, the Infanta Maria, was 16; she never gossiped or spoke ill of anyone, spent any money which came her way on charitable works, was deeply religious, and above all was horrified at the prospect of marriage to a heretic.

If Spaniards were bigotted in the sense that they regarded non-Catholics as damned and destined for Hell, the Church of England was no less so. For King James to believe he could steam-roller his subjects into a state of religious toleration showed an abysmal lack of judgement.

Bevill Grenville was a deeply religious man and Protestant to his core. The Parliament of which he was a member was committed to the withholding of supplies from the King while he persisted in policies so inimical to 90 per cent of his subjects. Parliament having been summarily dissolved by the King on 8 February 1622, Bevill was able to leave London and join his wife Grace in Cornwall earlier than he had anticipated.

That same spring Sir George Smith died. His very considerable fortune was divided between his two daughters, after a proper provision had been made for the life of his widow Lady Grace Smith. Grace Grenvile inherited a number of manors. There was then no equivalent of the Married Women's Property Act, and she and her manors belonged to Bevill. It is to his credit that Bevill conveyed her lands in trust to John Arundell of Trerice and John Prideaux of Treforder on 2 May 1622. The properties included 'Maydeworthy alias Madford' (in Heavitree, Exeter) and also a number of Cornish manors, Trethewell and Tregerean and many others. The deed was witnessed by John Coode of Morval; Elizabeth Coode had married Sir Lewis Stucley's son John and was thus a connection. John Grenville also signed the document, his last recorded act. And so did Sir Barnard and the Rev. Mr. Ralph Byrd. The decision to settle the Smith estates was carried out with due solemnity at Killigarth.

Bevill's younger brother Richard could not attend. He was still in Germany fighting a rearguard action for the King's daughter Elizabeth, Queen of Bohemia. He was in illustrious company, having as his companions the Earl of Essex, Sir William Waller, and Ralph Hopton, the future Lord Stratton.

Meanwhile, in London, Endymion Porter was sent to Madrid on 3 October 1622. The court was then at Theobalds, and his despatches were directed to Digby, James's ambassador in Spain, who had recently been created Earl of Bristol.

I cannot improve on Gervas Huxley's excellent summary of the political scene:

'It was unfortunately, to take more than Endymion's mission to shatter the illusions on which the whole edifice of the match was based — James's illusion that the Catholic

King of Spain could be induced to take up arms against the Catholic Emperor in order to restore the Palatinate to James's Protestant son-in-law; Olivares' illusion that the match could be indefinitely postponed, or even broken off, without a rupture with James: Gondomar's illusion that Charles had only to visit Madrid to be converted to the Catholic faith; the Pope's illusion that just as Henry VIII had turned England away from the true faith, so a Catholic King, converted by his consort, would now restore England to the fold.'

Such then was the position at the end of 1622.

Bevill, his wife Grace and children Dick and Bessie were at Stow. Sir Barnard was at Killigarth. Granny Mary Grenvile was at Annery or in the Grenvile town house below the church at Bideford.

The King was so displeased with his Commons that there was little prospect of a new Parliament in the immediate future, and the young Grenviles could look forward to a period of domesticity in Cornwall. It seems that much was needed to be done at Stow to make it an acceptable home for Bevill and his household.

Chapter Three

KING JAMES'S LAST PARLIAMENT

AMONG SEVERAL POSTS granted to Buckingham, his favourite, by the King, was that of Lord High Admiral of England. The King also made him Master of the Horse and Warden of the Cinque Ports, a plurality which was thought to weaken the defence of the Kingdom by entrusting so many defence posts in the hands of one man.

As Lord High Admiral, Buckingham had his agents everywhere along the coasts of the country. It was he who appointed Vice-Admirals (in return for heavy fees which went into his pocket) and they, in conjunction with the Admiralty Judges in each jurisdiction, and other officials, reaped a substantial harvest from the Admiralty Courts in which matters of prize, salvage, piracy and kindred matters were decided. In return for their pickings the Vice-Admirals had a duty to defend their coastlines against raiding Moors and pirates. A Vice-Admiral was himself both judge, administrator and captain. He pressed men for service at sea. A lion's share of all monies due to a Vice-Admiral had to be accounted for to the Lord High Admiral at the top of the pyramid.

One such was Sir Lewis Stucley, a first cousin of Sir Barnard Grenvile, who paid Buckingham £400 to become Vice-Admiral of Devon. Almost his first action in that post was to arrest Sir Walter Ralegh on his return from his disastrous attempt to find El Dorado up the Orinoco river in Venezuela. Ralegh had been let out of the Tower after 14 years' imprisonment and given a commission to seek El Dorado, with a stringent proviso to avoid any fighting with Spanish colonists in South America.

Some sort of incident arising from so provocative a move was inevitable. In a brief clash a relation of the Spanish Ambassador, the Conde de Gondomar, was killed. Shouting 'Piratas! Piratas!' the Ambassador rushed in to the royal presence to complain of the incident. Ralegh had been sentenced to be hanged, drawn, and quartered after a travesty of a trial for treason at the start of James's reign. The immense popularity of the old hero of Tudor times, to whom James's Queen and eldest son Henry were devoted, obliged the King to commute that savage sentence to one of perpetual imprisonment. His release from the Tower with the commission of an admiral enabled James to settle old scores.

Vice-Admiral Stucley, too, had old scores to settle. His father John must have often related how his pearl necklace from the Roanoke expedition had been taken from him by Ralegh at Plymouth. On their way up to London the King sent for Stucley and told him to 'Discover [Ralegh's] pretensions and to seize his secret papers...'. After conniving at Ralegh's escape by wherry down the Thames, Stucley had him arrested at Greenwich and his execution followed inevitably as night follows day. The judicial murder of England's great seaman, historian, and poet, raised a howl of execration throughout England. No one dared criticize the King or Cecil, and Stucley became the scapegoat. His fall from grace enabled Buckingham to dismiss his Vice-Admiral of Devon and appoint a new and promising young man in his stead. This was none other than John Eliot, Bevill's old friend from St Germans, who had been knighted at Whitehall on 10 May 1618.

John Eliot was to exercise so great a fascination for Bevill, and have so powerful an influence on his Parliamentary career, that no account of Bevill is complete without some account, too, of that complex character, Sir John Eliot.

The execution of Ralegh, on being reported to Philip III of Spain, caused that monarch to promise a personal letter of thanks to King James. But if no such letter materialised James could congratulate himself on having advanced his friendship with Spain and also his plan to marry the sole surviving son Charles to the Infanta Maria.

The new year of 1623 found Elizabeth, the refugee Queen of Bohemia, at The Hague. Her husband had achieved some reversal of their fortunes the previous year, when a victory over the forces of the Catholic League at Mingolsheim enabled him to sleep once again in his castle of Heidelberg. But lack of funds made his army mutinous for their pay, and he was soon reunited with his wife in exile. Early in 1623 Elizabeth learned that her much-loved younger brother, the Prince of Wales, accompanied by his father's favourite, Buckingham, had set out in disguise to pursue his courtship of the Infanta of Spain in person.

They travelled as Mr. John and Mr. Thomas Smith, each with a bushy black wig, and accompanied only by Cottington and Endymion Porter. Their adventures in Spain have no place in this account save for their effect on Bevill, but the suggestion that King James was normally heterosexual is hard to sustain in the light of the letters written to him by his favourite as they travelled across France: 'My thoughts are only bent on having my dear dad and master's legs soon in my arms'. In another letter he declared that once he had got hold of the King's bed-post again, he meant never to quit it.

In Germany the English regiment of 2,200 men commanded by Sir Horace Vere in which Bevill's brother was serving as a Captain under Sir John Burgh had tried to defend Heidelberg, Frankenthal and Mannheim. They were unpaid and badly supplied, and had had to face the armies of the Emperor and of Spain unsupported by the League of Protestant Princes. That Spring they surrendered, and Ralph Hopton, William Waller, and Richard Grenvile, and all the rest who had survived the campaign, were eventually allowed to return home to England.

William, third Earl of Pembroke, was Lord Chamberlain to King James I. On his recommendation Bevill was granted a pass by the Privy Council 'to travel into the parts beyond the seas for the space of one year, and to take with him one servant, their trunks of apparell and other necessaries not prohibited, with a proviso not to go to Rome'. The minute was signed by Lord Chichester, *inter alia*; Arthur Chichester was a younger son of the Chichesters of North Devon and had been created Baron Chichester of Belfast in recognition of his labours colonising Munster, and later went as Ambassador to the ill-fated Palatinate. It was a thankless task. Finding himself besieged by Count Tilly he complained at the lack of respect shewn to his rank. Tilly replied that he did not recognise his status as Ambassador. Chichester's rejoinder was 'Had my master sent me with as many hundred men as he hath sent me on fruitless messages, your general should have known that I had been a soldier as well as an Ambassador'.

Why then did Bevill wish to travel abroad? It was clearly no deferred honeymoon or grand tour. The pass was dated 2 July 1623, and Bevill was back in England in time to canvass his election to the Parliament which sat on 12 February 1624. It seems most probable that his journey, if it took place, was to the Low Countries to make it possible for his brother Richard to return home. Richard was constantly in debt and as constantly helped with money by Bevill. Chichester would have had news of him, having been driven out of the Palatinate himself. The Herberts were patrons of Bevill's. When the third earl died without sons, his brother Philip followed him in the post of Lord Chamberlain, and Bevill was to stay with him in due course at Wilton. There is no letter from abroad to Grace at home at Stow which has survived, and the journey remains something of a mystery.

Bevill's great friend Sir John Eliot, Vice-Admiral of Devon, was experiencing a traumatic event in his new post.

In May 1623 a famous pirate, Captain John Nutt, anchored his man-'o-war in Torbay. As a pirate he had friends in high places. One, Sir George Calvert, His Majesty's principal secretary, had established a colony in Newfoundland and had received help from Nutt in doing so. Calvert was shortly to become Lord Baltimore and the Governor of great estates in North America.

Lying alongside Nutt's ship was his latest acquisition, a Colchester ship, pirated by Nutt. The crew had been robbed and put ashore, but the Colchester master was still on board, a prisoner; her cargo was yet to be disposed of.

Sir John Eliot decided to cheat the pirate by tendering a royal pardon as bait and inducing Nutt to sail his ship and captive into Dartmouth. Once in Dartmouth harbour, the castle guns, installed by Henry VIII, would prevent him putting to sea again. Nutt had a wife and family living nearby, had made a considerable fortune as a pirate (or so it was rumoured), and was quite prepared to pay Sir John £300 for a pardon which would enable him to join them.

Eliot went to Torbay and sent a signal to Nutt to come ashore for a conference. Nutt replied that he would willingly comply were it not for his ship's company, who suspecting treachery were unwilling to let him land. The Vice-Admiral decided that as the mountain wouldn't come to Mahomet, he would be obliged to call on the pirate. A bizarre scene ensued in which the Vice-Admiral sat and wined with the pirate in his cuddy, while the master of the Colchester ship pleaded for his ship and cargo on his knees. Nutt dismissed the shipmaster's plea, indicating that if he was to fall in with the Admiral's plan, his entitlement to the unfortunate Colchester shipmaster's cargo was not to be questioned. It seems evident that Eliot took sides against the Colchester captain who, in effect, was told his cargo of sugar and timber was irrecoverable but his ship would be returned to him in due course.

Nutt sailed his ship and prize into Dartmouth after agreeing to pay an enhanced price for his pardon, £500. News of Nutt's surrender soon reached London, and Mr. Secretary Conway wrote to Eliot on 20 June that without regard to any pardon promised Nutt, Nutt was to be arrested and sent up to London for examination by the Lords of the Council. Five days later the Court of Admiralty sent to the Mayor of Dartmouth ordering restitution of the Colchester ship to its owners. The Mayor replied that Eliot had not only refused to deliver up the Colchester ship, but had also made off with their Lordship's letter and commission, so that the Mayor was unable to perform the service commanded.

Within a month, both pirate and Vice-Admiral were arrested and, although Eliot's biographer Forster claims that Sir John was an honest broker and his imprisonment was due to the machinations of Sir George Calvert, it is difficult to avoid the suspicion that Nutt and Eliot had indeed reached a mutually profitable agreement.

The Judge of the Admiralty Division in 1623 was one Sir Henry Marten. Marten was a creature of Buckingham's, but Buckingham was away in Spain putting forward the Prince of Wales' absurd claim to the hand of the Spanish Infanta. According to Nutt's evidence when questioned by the Council, Eliot had first advised him to put to sea, next that there were divers ships laden with goods and money from Spain lying in Dartmouth worth the taking. It was on this evidence of Eliot's incitement to piracy that Eliot found himself in the Marshalsea prison. Marten does not seem to have dared reach a decision one way or the other, confining himself to reporting the evidence and commenting on the inconvenience to Buckingham of having his Vice-Admiral of Devon locked up and thereby unable to contribute to his Lord High Admiral's profits. To give Marten his due, he reported on 4 August to the effect that he had found none of Nutt's accusations against Eliot proved and suggested Eliot's release from prison. But in Buckingham's absence in Spain, nothing was done save the release of the pirate Nutt on a petition to the council by Sir George Calvert. A more Gilbertian situation, with the pirate at liberty and the Admiral locked up in gaol is difficult to conceive.

In early October that other fiasco, the wooing of the Spanish Infanta, came to an end. The Duke of Buckingham returned to England with Prince Charles to find the whole of England in fiesta. Huge fires were lit and oxen roasted whole while barrels were broached in one great spontaneous celebration of their Prince's return unwed. Buckingham, who had actively contributed to the scheme from the first, now received a hero's welcome for bringing the Prince out of captivity. The whole enterprise and cornerstone of James's foreign policy had totally failed. The fleet assembled to convey the Princess back to England had cost money to fit out, as had the Prince's embassy in Madrid, where money had been splashed around in entertaining his Spanish hosts. King James I was harder up than ever, and no gleam of Spanish gold remained to cheer him.

The Spaniards alone had cause to celebrate. Their annual 'flotas' had continued to cross the Atlantic laden with silver and gold without interference by the English. The Infanta was relieved of the unpleasant duty to marry a heretic. The Protestant tide in Germany had been brought to a halt.

By November 1623 the Duke of Buckingham had managed to persuade his 'dear dad' to call another Parliament and ask for supplies, and had even talked him out of barring the opposition members, Phelips, Coke and Pym who had been released from the Tower: Crewe, Digges, and Perrot who were now allowed to return home from their exile in Ireland. Having achieved this major success, Buckingham then turned his attention to such minor matters as his Vice-Admiral in prison, and Sir John Eliot obtained his release.

Writs to elect members for a Parliament to meet on 12 February 1624 issued, and Eliot was able to start canvassing for a seat. Bevill, too, had every intention of sitting again for the County of Cornwall. His canvassing was necessarily interrupted when his grandmother, Mary Grenvile, the widow of the Admiral, died at Bideford 32 years after her husband's death off the Azores. The entry in the church register shows 'The Ladie Mary Grenvile, daughter unto the right worthie Sr John St Leger Knight, deceased, and wife to that famous warior Sr Richard Grenvile, Knight, also deceased, being in his life time the Spanniords terror. She was buried in the Grenvile's Ile in the Church of Bediford, the ffifth day of November Anno Domini 1623'. The old lady had little money, but she left some to the local poor.

Christmas and the elections over, Bevill was back in London at the sign of the Rainbow between the two Temple Gates in Fleet Street. When Parliament assembled he was re-united with a number of West Country friends. His fellow member for the county was William Coryton of West Newton, and Sir John Eliot was member for the borough of Newport in Cornwall. Although summoned for 12 February 1624 nothing happened until the 19th, when the King addressed Parliament in a conciliatory way, so shorn of his customary bluster that it is tempting to credit him with a sudden access of good sense. The truth is more likely to lie in the fact that he had only one more year of life before him: he was an old man, no longer strong enough to fight his rearguard action against democracy.

The Commons did not get down to business until 27 February, by which time they had elected Sir Thomas Crewe to be their Speaker; Crewe, fresh from his enforced stay in Ireland, must have viewed his monarch with a jaundiced eye.

This, the last Parliament of James I, had opened with a speech from the King in which he described how he had long been engaged in treaties by which he had hoped to settle the peace of Christendom, but that after many delays, and having even allowed his only surviving son to visit Spain, he had lost his belief in the efficacy of treaties with that country. He added, that contrary to rumour, he had never intended more than a temporary suspension of the penal statutes affecting catholics; an explicit admission of dishonest dealings with Spain.

A few days later Buckingham gave an account of affairs in Spain amounting to a thoroughly dishonest report of the proceedings there, and Prince Charles, by his presence at the side of Buckingham, gave tacit support to his lies. A version of the account given to the Lords was relayed to the Commons by the Chancellor of the Exchequer, and such was the general euphoria at the failure of the dreaded catholic marriage that the Commons passed a vote of thanks to the Duke.

Rudyard advised the House first to secure Ireland, perennially in revolt, and then to declare war on Spain as a diversion, while the country's real strength was directed to relieving the Low Countries, re-uniting Protestant Germany, and the recovery of the Palatinate for their beloved Princess, Elizabeth of Bohemia. Sir Edward Coke and Sir John Eliot were all for war. The House advised the King to break off all his treaties with Spain and a deputation of the Commons was sent to Theobalds to advise the King accordingly.

The King told the Commons that, such was his poverty, he would need £700,000 to declare war, and an annual payment of £150,000 to diminish his personal debts, pointing out that if Parliament was to assume his prerogative to declare war, then Parliament must pay for it.

Coke advised the House that the sums asked for were too high, and advised paying them by instalments. It was agreed to let the King have £30,000 as an earnest of their intentions, the money to be accounted for as it was spent to a committee of the House, the conduct of the war being left to the King. This was to prevent the syphoning off of monies designed for the war-chest to pay for the King's personal extravagances.

The popularity of war with Spain among the populace was demonstrated by bonfires in the streets of London, and much incivility shewn to members of the Spanish embassy.

Sir John Eliot, Vice-Admiral of Devon, had not sat in the Commons since the Parliament of 1614, when he does not seem to have opened his mouth. Now, 10 years later, his experience of imprisonment in the Marshalsea behind him, and his knowledge of the world enhanced by his dealings with the pirates in South Devon, this protégé of Buckingham's, and likely pillar of the establishment, struck a most discordant note.

He insisted on the correctness of the law set out in the protestation of February 1622 claiming freedom of speech for the Commons and the right to advise the King on matters claimed to be solely within his prerogative. It was a brave speech, but carefully phrased. Eliot had eaten his dinners at an Inn of Court.

The King could do no wrong. Any misunderstandings that might have arisen between the King and his faithful Commons in the last Parliament must therefore be due to misunderstandings or the inaccurate reporting of Parliamentary proceedings by members of the Privy Council, or perhaps ill-advised counsel. Nothing in the speech was treasonable. It was a model of discretion, and yet a forthright attack on the Stuart assumption of Divine Right. Eliot called for the King to accept the terms of the protestation he had torn from the Journal, but this motion met with a tepid response. Sir Robert Phelips thought it ill-timed, and Coke recommended the appointment of another committee to look further into the matter, and so it was shelved.

Eliot's undoubted ability as an orator and his growing experience of 'managing the House' would soon make him the acknowledged leader of the anti-Court party. Whether or not his radical views of the constitutional positions of King and his Houses of Parliament convinced Bevill of the rightness of Eliot's criticisms, Bevill became a staunch supporter of Eliot's, and remained so for the rest of Eliot's life. But Bevill was no orator, his contribution to the coming struggle would be in the division lobbies and by the lobbying of friends.

Nor can it be said that Eliot himself had acquired a reputation for opposition to the Court during that Parliament. Had he become the arch-opponent of personal rule in 1624 it is unlikely that Buckingham would have let him continue as his Vice-Admiral of Devon. Nor would he have served with Sir Barnard Grenville, Sir Reginald Mohun and Bevill on a commission appointed to deal with piracy in Cornish water, and in a similar Admiralty Commission with county worthies (which included Bevill as owner of Bideford and Lundy) of Devon, for that county, too. Both Eliot and Bevill were still willing to serve under Buckingham that last year of James's reign.

The previous Parliament had successfully attacked Francis Bacon, Lord Keeper and Lord St Albans, and if his sentence was never served, yet his public career had been ended. The present Parliament now turned its attention to another source of corruption in high places, the Lord Treasurer.

Lionel Cranfield was a London businessman who became a useful tool in the hands of Buckingham. Buckingham arranged for him to be ennobled with the title Earl of Middlesex, and appointed to the post of Lord Treasurer. Middlesex, it may be remembered, defrauded Sir Barnard Grenville out of the purchase monies for his Munster settlements, and then defrauded that other parvenue, Richard, Earl of Cork, when selling Cork the lands he had failed to pay Grenvile for.

The Commons now impeached Middlesex for extortion, accepting bribes, and for the malversation of his office. If Bevill remained silent throughout the proceedings so far as the records of events suggest, he can be relied upon to have voted for the impeachment. The evidence was so indisputable that Buckingham threw his protégé to the wolves, evoking the King's comment and warning: 'By God, Steenie, you are a fool: you are making a rod for your own breech!' Middlesex was fined £50,000, sent to the Tower, and disqualified from ever appearing at Court or in Parliament again.

Bevill lived as a grass-widower at the 'Sign of the Rainbow' in Fleet Street. There was occasional thought of letting his wife Grace join him in London, but it seems doubtful that she ever managed to get there. As early as March she wrote to him in London:

> 'My mother willed me to remember her(self) to you, and to tell you that she is much against my going to London. And that is very true, for you cannot imagine how vehement she is against it. I do every day wish that coach were come, that I might sooner be with you, and (tire) of hearing the persuasions that are used against it . . .

Bessy grows a lusty girl and I think eats more meat than I, for I have gotten a cold as well as Dick, and can neither taste nor smell with it; and before you went you know my hearing was somewhat defective, so you may well imagine you have a very (deaf) wife. But yet pray send for her, for if I were once with you I think to be sooner cured . . . than by taking any Physic, for had I not hoped to have come to you, I had been dead by this time.

So, Dearest, fare-well, and God give me life no longer than I am yours in all constancy . . .'.

Bessie was then aged about four, and Dick three. A daughter Grace was born in 1624, but she failed to survive. Poor Grace, being almost permanently pregnant, was most unlikely to have a coach sent to bring her up to London.

King James was 58 years old when he took to his bed in March 1625. The Duke of Buckingham's mother insisted on applying a plaster to the monarch and persuaded him to drink a posset, a mixture she had made of hot milk curdled with ale and wine, and spiced. The King's doctors watched disapprovingly and the lady's actions were carefully noted for future occasions. Notwithstanding the Villiers family recipes, King James I of England died on 27 March, Parliament was dissolved, and Bevill was able to return home to Cornwall, Stow, Grace and his two children.

Bevill's return to Cornwall proved no holiday. Ralph Byrd, his father's old friend and confidant, was pre-occupied with Sir Barnard's muddled financial affairs. Sir Barnard owed about £11,500 to a variety of people; to Byrd himself and to magnates in both Devon and Cornwall, to tradesmen both in London and in his neighbourhood, under judgment debts and in interest on mortgages. Much was owed to lawyers.

Bevill had incurred debts himself, on his father's account, amounting to a further £3,500, and their relationship was strained. Byrd and others persuaded Bevill and Grace to travel south to Killigarth to sort out Sir Barnard's affairs.

Sir Barnard enjoyed a life interest in his dead wife's estates. These were surrendered to Bevill as heir-in-tail to sell as best he could to meet the more pressing creditors. It was hoped that Killigarth — Bevill's childhood home — might be saved from the wreck, but that too was sold to Sir James Bagg in 1632, and the old gentleman had to spend the last four years of his life at Tremeer, a minor house on the Bevill Estate.

Sir Barnard had cut no great figure in London, and his debts — enormous in his day — were probably incurred supporting St Leger interests in Ireland. (*See* Appendix I, p. 151 for more details).

Chapter Four

KING CHARLES, AND HIS 'FAITHFUL COMMONS'

UPON KING CHARLES's succession to the triple crown of England, Scotland, and Ireland, he adopted a course guaranteed to antagonise his subjects. Within six weeks of his father's death he married Henrietta Maria, sister of King Louis XIII of France, and every bit as much a Roman Catholic as the Infanta Maria of Spain.

They were married in May 1625 on a specially constructed platform erected outside Notre Dame in Paris, rather than an allow an heretical English King sully the sanctity of that ancient cathedral.

One of the clauses of the marriage contract, kept secret from all but the King's closest circle of advisers, was to supply the French King with eight ships at any time on demand. Richelieu, the then power behind the throne, had inserted the clause to assist him in his difficulties with the Huguenots, who had made the free port of La Rochelle their base. The Spaniards, who were in dispute with the French at the time, where helping the Huguenots by sea, the port being encircled on land.

Charles's greatest friend was his Lord High Admiral, Buckingham, and in pursuance of Richelieu's request under the secret clause of the marriage treaty, he ordered Captain Pennington to hoist his pennant in the man-o'-war *Vanguard*, and to convey seven pressed merchant ships to sea. Various versions of their objective were given to Pennington and his seven merchant captains, but the truth, that they had orders to assist the French against their fellow protestants at La Rochelle, was only disclosed in mid-June. Pennington protested and delayed, but a warrant, signed by the King in person, obliged him to sail and place his ships under the command of the French. One merchant ship made off on its own, and the crews of the remainder deserted to a man. Nothing would induce the English seamen to attack the Huguenots. Leaving his unmanned ships in the hands of the French, Pennington made his way home overland.

Charles had not only inherited enormous debts from his father, but was also saddled with a more than usually absurd war against Spain, for which he and Buckingham were largely to blame. There being no money to satisfy either, it was necessary to apply to Parliament for 'supplies'. Writs issued for a general election and the new Parliament was ordered to meet at Westminster on 27 June.

That Spring the 'Election Managers', who stage-managed the polls in Cornish boroughs, arranged for Bevill to be returned as Burgess for Launceston, and Sir John Eliot a burgess for Liskeard. Others successful at the polls and who were to

prove critical of the government's record were Phelips of Montacute, Sir Edward
Coke, Thomas Wentworth, John Pymm, and Sir Dudley Digges. Bevill travelled
up to London and lodged again at the sign of the 'Rainbow' in Fleet Street
between the two Temple Gates.

When the new King opened his first Parliament on 27 June 1625, by reason of
an unfortunate impediment in his speech he stammered out an account of his late
father's debts amounting to £700,000, and asked for the means with which to
prosecute the war against Spain undertaken at Parliament's request. Had he
married a Protestant, all would have been well. All the Commons would vote him
was one year's 'tonnage and poundage', import and export taxes, normally
granted a monarch for his life. The grant was worth about £140,000, but to make
matters worse, the Lords refused to agree it, saying that such a grant being
without precedent was unlawful, with the result that the King got nothing.

Grace was staying with her mother at Madford and wrote from there on
4 July 1625:

> 'I heartily wish you home, both for my own content, and that you might take your
> part of a side of red deer that my cousin Ed[mund] Tremayne sent me this day. If you be
> not guilty of Sir Jo[hn] Eliot's sin (of) last year, you may have a share, for I vow to keep
> one pie till your coming; but if it offend your nose, the fault be yours.
>
> Your servant Will[iam] Way is gone, and is now servant to my cousin Dick Tremayne,
> out of a desire to go in this Fleet. My mother's servants are so few and mine none. Now
> he is gone I cannot send a message to Town. My sickness hath made me a poor woman in
> body and purse . . . I have been a borrower since your going.
>
> My mother commends [herself] to you, and the little crew are well, and I am better
> than I have been.'

The Fleet to which her cousin Dick Tremayne had gone, together with Grace's
one servant, was an expeditionary force gathering at Plymouth for an attack
upon Spain.

Meanwhile the plague, endemic in most of England's cities at the time, was
killing 5,000 a week in London. On 9 July the King acceded to a request from
both Houses of his Parliament to adjourn with a view to reassembling three weeks
later in Oxford.

The members made off for the country in such haste that Bevill was unaware
his wife was at Exeter, not having received her letter of the 4th, and reached Stow
to find her absent. From Madford she wrote to him:

> 'I do very much long to be at home with you, and am sorry it is not my happiness to
> have been home before you, but indeed it was not my desire that kept me back, but
> want of health.'

Sir John Eliot, too, travelled down to the south-west. His wife Radigund had
reared six children at St Germans. But he was unable to enjoy uninterruptly his
unexpected holiday. He was besieged on all sides by complaints that Barbary
pirates had appeared off the Cornish and Devon coasts in great numbers, seizing
ships, and carrying their crews off into slavery. Foreign trade was at a standstill
while the Muslims, in their long, light ships, well armed and manned, plundered

any shipping that attempted to sail in the south-western approaches. No fisherman dared set out to sea, and pirates were landing and making off with booty and prisoners at will. As Vice-Admiral of Devon, Eliot had to promise to try to remedy the situation.

The short recess over, Eliot, Bevill and the rest reassembled in Christchurch Hall, Oxford. Captain Pennington made his way there, too, and some said Buckingham prevented his reporting the La Rochelle matter to the Commons; but Eliot became fully aware of events within a short time, and all his friends must have contrasted the availability of their King's ships for action against fellow protestants in France with that for the protection of the island against piracy and Moors. Buckingham's competence as Lord High Admiral was questionable.

Sir Edward Coke headed the opposition in his criticism of the administration. He launched a violent attack on the government for creating new offices of profit, granting new monopolies, for lavish expenditure of public money on the Duke and his friends, the incompetence of the Duke as an Admiral, and blamed the latter for embroiling the country in an unnecessary war against Spain. It was a collision course aimed at impeaching Buckingham, but the King came to his aid by dissolving Parliament on 12 August. That was his prerogative, but Parliament had failed to vote him a penny for the conduct of the War.

Two days before the King dissolved Parliament, Grace wrote to Bevill:

'I am in much fear and grief to hear that the plague is in Oxford. Would God but grant you were home, 'til which my heart will never be quiet. Oh pray as you love yourself, your children and me, be careful of your health, otherwise we are all lost.

The sickness increases here apace and is much dispersed abroad in the City, and where it comes, it goes through the house and ends all. Wherefore I beseech you be not displeased with what I have done. You willed me to send the linen in your absence to Stow, but not to stir myself 'til you came; but seeing that the poor people would not be kept away, and that the servants went still into Town, and Exeter people come to us daily, so we are in as much danger as those of the City. Wherefore I have ventured to remove thither, also with the children, which I fear will not well like you, and which hath much troubled me and still doth. My dearness and care of the children hath made me adventure, and I hope your tenderness will be my best friend to persuade you not to dislike it.

My cousin D. Tremayn and Jo: are here and have brought horses for me. For myself my sister Dennis hath lent me her mare. And tomorrow we begin our journey.

G. Winslade came last week to Stow, and there upon this necessity will make a bad shift 'til you come, which pray let it be as soon as you can. Your beds are brought to Stow, but your linen you left with Geo[rge] Membry. My fa[ther-in-law] sent for it and had it away before they came.

Jo Gea[lard] brought back the money from Bydeford, for my aunt Ab[bot]: and my aunt Brid[get] held it until that my aunt Ursula should give that security unto which they themselves put their hands and seals, & drew a particular one for my aunt Urs[ula] to seal, which she did, and sent both acquittances also with a bond given by your father for securing the annuity, which if she should seal would be your security. Upon this necessity I have presumed to take £11 14s. out of your four-score, and I have left the keys of the trunk and cabinet with the key of the room, but nothing else. . . . Pray be not displeased for taking the money, for I will assure you it was for nothing but necessary ends. And in a strange place and to keep house I must needs say I disliked to borrow, and with what you left I have paid all reckonings.

God be praised we are all in health, yet you may the better excuse my removing because so many others do it. Mrs. Bampfilde is gone and her children, and Mrs. Isack with sons daughters and children are gone from Portlow, and all the citizens that can possibly get horses do remove. But my mother will by no means stir, which I am very sorry for. She hath given me a good bed and bolster, three pairs of pillows, two or three pairs of blankets and coverlets, some which she had of you; and she will speedily send another bed after me. I cannot get the bedstead chair and stools from Plimouth by no means.

Your case of pictures was loose and almost open before I had it, and the King's and Sir Jo[hn] E[liot's] hath received some hurt in carriage, but none since it came hither. I pray you to make haste and come home. So God keep you well, and be not angry with me.'

It would have been a harsh husband to have been angry in the circumstances. The plague became so bad that when, later in the year, the King passed through Devonshire he gave Exeter a wide berth to the disappointment of its citizens.

Meanwhile the expeditionary force at Plymouth was mustering. It was hoped to repeat the successful attack on Cadiz made by Essex and Ralegh some 29 years earlier. In 1596 (the year of Bevill's birth) an English Fleet had penetrated the inner harbour, a landing party set fire to and totally destroyed the city, while the inept Duke of Medina Sidonia set fire to his own warships and treasure-ships to prevent the English taking them in prize. An alternative object was the interception of a treasure fleet or 'flota' due from Mexico. Both King and Buckingham hoped to benefit from a sudden access of Spanish gold.

The Commander-in-Chief of the expedition was the Duke of Buckingham himself, but it was not intended that he should take any part in it. His deputy was Sir Edward Cecil, a brother of Lord Burghley's, who was appointed Lord Marshal and Deputy Admiral. The King ennobled him as Lord Wimbledon in advance of the expected victory. The new Lord Wimbledon was a competent soldier, but with no experience of ships or the sea. The gathering army referred to Wimbledon as the General and Buckingham as the Generalissimo.

The army consisted of 10 regiments of a thousand men each. The ninth regiment was commanded by Sir John Burgh who had seen much service in Germany and fighting for the Palatinate. Bevill's brother Richard Grenvile was an old comrade-in-arms and received his commission as Captain in Sir John's regiment.

Quite apart from Grace Grenvile's footman, who was clearly a volunteer, the majority of the soldiers were men pressed into service by their village constables. Another close relation of the Grenviles was also a volunteer.

To wish his expeditionary force God's speed, the King travelled down to Plymouth. The news of his coming west proved a great excitement in Devon, where all the gentry hoped to wait upon him and pay their respects to their new King. Among those who wished to show their loyalty by welcoming him to Devon was Sir Thomas Monck of Potheridge.

Although Monck's father-in-law Sir George Smith had died in the spring of 1622 little benefit seems to have come his way under Sir George's will. He had a number of unpaid judgement debts outstanding against him, and he dared not venture out of his house in the parish of Merton, North Devon, for fear of the bailiffs.

Monck sent his younger son, George, then a youth of 17, to square the under-sheriff of Devon to enable Sir Thomas to welcome the King without fear of arrest. The under-sheriff pocketed the bribe, but as soon as Sir Thomas appeared at the meeting place he was seized in front of the assembled company.

Young George deeply resented his father's loss of face and the treachery of the under-sheriff and set about the latter with a cudgel. An attack of an under-sheriff was a grave contempt of court punishable by imprisonment, and George was sent post haste to Richard Grenvile at Plymouth for service with the Fleet, to save his liberty. His uncle made him ensign in his company and the Fleet sailed shortly thereafter, on 8 October 1625.

It was an inauspicious departure, witnessed by Eliot, still the Vice-Admiral of Devon. Several ships collided as they made their way out to sea, and contrary winds sent others back into Cornish ports. Sir James Bagg, a prominent member of the Court party and a connection of John Drake of Ashe near Axminster, had been given the duty of victualling the Fleet. No funds having been voted by Parliament, insufficient food and stores had been placed in the ships.

The destination of the Fleet had been kept as secret as possible and it appears that the Spaniards were unprepared for its arrival off Cadiz. All should now have been plain sailing for a re-enactment of 1596. The English sailed into the outer harbour, men were landed and took the fort commanding the narrow Puntal passage leading into the inner harbour. At this point, the Rear-Admiral Lord Denbigh received word that the passage had been closed by four sunken block-ships. A council of war followed. The landing party having taken the fort were now allowed to broach some looted Spanish wine barrels and were soon in a state of drunken mutiny. This and the block-ships persuaded the General to call off the attack and attempt the interception of the 'flota' with its Mexican treasure. The fleet put to sea and after hanging about off Cadiz for some days, allowed the Spanish 'flota' to slip by in the night and enter Lisbon.

In a doggerel of the time the Fleet

'. . . which went to Spain
And when it got there came back again'

returning to Plymouth, having lost a thousand men, mostly from lack of food. Starving men were everywhere in the streets. Richard Grenvile and his nephew George Monck can hardly have enjoyed being part of such a fiasco, but no doubt both learnt a number of lessons from it which would serve them in good stead in the years to come.

The Fleet straggled back from Cadiz during the first three weeks of December 1625. James Bagg, a connection of Nicholas, who was Secretary of the Admiralty under Buckingham, had been knighted in 1624 and appointed Vice-Admiral of Cornwall. His commission from Buckingham was to victual the Cadiz expedition, but one returning Captain reported that the meat supplied the troops was less than half the prescribed ration and 'stank so that no dog of a Paris garden would eat it'. Neither was there sufficient money to pay the men off. Sir James, whom we shall meet again, was later accused by Mohun of embezzling £55,000, but as Buckingham's man he was immune from justice.

The Court Party hit upon two stratagems to cope with their difficulties; the first was to levy taxes on individuals and corporations by use of the King's privy seal; the second was to exclude the more radical members from any future Parliament that might be called, by appointing them to offices disqualifying them from sitting in the Commons.

The privy seal could be used for charters, pardons, and such like in anticipation of their bearing the great seal of England; minor documents such as discharges of recognisances and debts might bear the privy seal alone. It was now to be used, together with the King's signature, to demand sums arbitrarily assessed from all and sundry. Those connected with the opposition would be called upon for sums of about £40, those favourable to the Court party for half that amount. The method of assessment and collection seems to have been by way of Commissioners appointed for their adherence to Buckingham and the Court.

Before the latter means could be put into effect in 1626 a need for ready money to meet outstanding commitments obliged the King to issue writs for a new Parliament. The list of new High Sheriffs pricked by the judges was submitted to the King who deleted a number of names and substituted those of persons he supposed to be the leaders of the opposition. In this way Wentworth, Coke, Phelips, Sir Francis Seymour and others were disqualified from standing. Eliot and his friend Bevill were not then regarded as sufficiently dangerous to the royal cause.

Eliot was elected for the Borough of St Germans, his own village, and Bevill was back again for his old seat of Launceston.

On 2 February 1626 the King was crowned at Westminster in a splendid white robe. His Queen refused to attend the ceremony in a Protestant abbey. On the 6th was the opening of Parliament. When the roll was called Bevill was missing and was still absent on 5 April when in the words of the Journal: 'Mr. Grenevyle left to his own excuse at his coming'.

Why Bevill stayed at Stow is unknown; Lady Smith his mother-in-law was with him and one can only surmise that Grace was still unwell. He eventually set off for London (with Lady Smith it seems) in mid-April. He was at Madford on the 20th when he wrote:

'I have rested all this Thursday here and do intend tomorrow to go onwards in my journey. Your sister Smith hath you heartily remembered, and saith she will see you when you lie in [Grace was seven months pregnant].

Therefore I wish you to make as good provision as you can, and pray do not neglect to make speed in preparing a midwife.

Be careful of my business at home. I have desired of your mother to make what she can of the oxen and to send you the money. It were good you did quicken her a little with your letters for it for fear it were I doubt you will have need of it.

If you can see my cousin Thomas Arundell urge him to make what haste he can in paying the other £100 to R[eginold] Billing that he may return it to me.

I have willed Juell to call at Ar: B Colsons for a couple of cheeses that he gave me. If he bring them home [I] wish them be kept safe for me; and if he bring home also my civil picture, I would have the same care had of it likewise.

Dick Pomeroy I would by any means have my moorstone windows bespoken speedily, and in the same form we agreed of, but let him get a good workman to do them what shift soever he make.

I fear I have forgotten to take with me the acquittances which James Waller is to have from my father; if I have, pray send them on for me if you can. They may be in some of the black boxes in my study with windover or board. They are three in all, send all if you can, but be careful to hurt no edge of the board wherein are the writings of Treley. With that you must not meddle for I am sure they are not there. Be sure to send them by a trusty messenger [such] as my brother Denis if you can and for God's sake be careful to disorder none of the writings. The acquittances are one for £500 and the other for £1,500'.

The carving out of granite window pieces, the new picture of Bevill in civilian dress, and the pictures and glass sent down from London the previous year point to the embellishment of the old house at Stow and material alterations to it.

On his arrival in London he wrote again:

'My dearest; I am exceeding glad to hear from you but do desire you not to be so passionate for my absence. I vow you cannot more desire to have me at home than I do desire to be there. And as soon as I can despatch my business I will instantly come away. I am yet so new in the Town as I have been able to do nothing.

I hope you will not have child so soon as your fear; I will, as fast as I can, send down those provisions.

I have left no order with anybody for the moorstone windows but Pomeroy: I would have him to get them to be well wrought up against my coming down, and then I will take course for the fetching of them.

You shall do well to send to your mother for that money as soon as you can, for fear you want; and if you have need of more, you may entreat Nat: Gist to lend you some of my rent beforehand.

I would have the masons to go on as fast as they can about the stable, that if it be possible the walls be up and finished against my coming down.

I am afraid, as Allen is, that the ploughs will not be ready soon enough. To bring home the timber tell him to make what shift he can with that at home, but be sure he cut none elsewhere but out of the plot I appointed. They may take all that is there but spare the rest. Bid him to be sure to put in none but strong and sufficient stuff.

Have a care that the people want no provision and let my cousin Tremayne take up oxen and sheep enough to serve all the year, and make his bargain so as I may pay for it after my coming home, which shall carefully be performed. I would have some of my cousin Thomas Arundell of both sorts and allow for it in his expenses payment, but the £100 [due] now at Whitsuntide I depend on and he must not fail me of. I would have Mr Billings to take some course to return it speedily to me, but if it fall out that he cannot so early as he may be sure it will be with me before Whitsuntide, then do you receive it safe for me in your own hands, because I will come away before Whitsuntide if I can'.

To that he added a postscript:

'Make all the haste you can to thresh out your corn and for fear it be spoilt, and observe how many bushels it is. Let Charles the joiner make a board for the parlour as soon as you can; as plain and cheap as possible he can make.

Only two or three deal boards joined together and trestles to stand on, and so long as to reach from the bay window to the little door, but not to hinder the going in and out'.

The stable he built is said to have been converted later into the farmhouse which stands near the site of Stow today.

The lack of ready money is a recurrent theme in the Grenvile marriage. Sir Bernard and Lady Smith being both still alive, Bevill and Grace had to rely on their farm profits and the rent of tenanted land, windswept and marginal as it remains, around Kilkhampton. Additionally there were some 'old rents' and harbour dues from the port of Bideford, and something, one supposes, from Lundy.

Whether Bevill was fined for his late attendance on the House of Commons does not appear in the Journal; if his absence was due to his daughter Grace's death, as I suspect, the House would no doubt have been merciful. He was back on duty in London by 24 April 1626 when the Commons debated resolutions aimed at the Duke of Buckingham.

The Duke was accused in his capacity of Lord High Admiral of failing to employ the King's ships against the Barbary corsairs, of weakening the Navy by sending the *Vanguard* and merchantmen against La Rochelle to aid the French, and of antagonising the French by allowing Sir James Bagg, his vice-admiral, to seize the *Peter of Newhaven* with its treasure, the property of the French.

Other complaints included the sale of great offices, his conferring honours on persons of low degree, and his sale of peerages. An example of the latter was the barony conferred on Richard Robartes of Truro, a trader in wood and tin, in 1625. He paid Buckingham £10,000 for it. It was he who built Lanhydrock House near Bodmin in 1651, and notwithstanding his thirst for titles, a knighthood, baronetcy, and finally a barony, he was one of Parliament's most reliable supporters in the county during the Civil War.

Other, more general, complaints were laid at Buckingham's door, but the complexion of the particular matters complained of was Cornish. Sir John Eliot, still Vice-Admiral of Devon was turned against his master.

This attack by the Commons, either by accident or design, coincided with a bubbling over of resentment in Sherborne, Dorset. The Lodge, or New Castle, at Sherborne had been built by Sir Walter Ralegh. It was completed in 1594 and was a notable departure from conventionally designed houses of that date. Its great windows and sense of light and airness make it one of the first great houses built to live in rather than to take shelter in. Ralegh loved it.

Upon Ralegh's conviction for treason at Winchester in 1603 his estates were forfeit to the crown, but Cecil first arranged its conveyance to Lady Ralegh and then had that lady evicted in favour of the King's new favourite Robert Kerr or Carr, who had been created Duke of Somerset. When Carr in turn lost favour, the property was awarded to John Digby (created Earl of Bristol in 1622), and England's ambassador in Spain throughout Buckingham's adventures there with Prince Charles and the Infanta Maria. When Digby returned to England, the Court party feared that Buckingham's account of proceedings in Spain might not be preferred to that of the Ambassador, and Digby was ordered into what was virtually house-arrest at Sherborne. Lord Bristol had been angling for the Spanish match on behalf of the King since 1610 and no one knew more about the matter than he.

Becoming increasingly more angry as time went on, and seeking an end to his exile from Court, he decided to seek advice whether a peer could lawfully be prevented from attending the House of Lords when Parliament was in session. In

March a bill was laid before the Commons entitled: 'An act for the Restitution in Blood of Carew Raleighe, son of Sir Walter Raleigh Kt., late attainted of high treason'. The eminent re-emergence of the Ralegh family, Carew being the eldest surviving son, may have further influenced Bristol to fight for what he regarded as his right to Sherborne as well as his right to return to London.

Bristol appeared before the House of Lords where he accused Buckingham of High Treason. The indictment was based on Bristol's account that Buckingham had promised the Spaniards that the Prince would become a Roman Catholic if permitted to marry the Infanta Maria. The Commons were told of the charge on 2 May and immediately voted in favour of committing the Duke to the Tower of London. 225 votes to 106! A sizeable majority.

The King informed Parliament that he was aware that they '. . . do especially aim at the Duke of Buckingham — but can assure you he hath not done [anything] but by special directions and appointment as my servant'. 'I would', added the King: 'You would hasten for my supply, or else it will be worse for yourselves'. Buckingham counter-attacked by accusing Bristol of High Treason, and charge and counter-charge were debated in the House of Lords with the result that the complaints against Buckingham were found proved, and Bristol was exonerated. The King then sent the Lord Marshal Arundell to the Tower for supporting the case against Buckingham, and informed the Commons that they sat at his pleasure, and that if they failed to vote him supplies he would take the necessary measures and dissolve it. Both Houses were adamant. The King then gave way and said he would consider their enquiries about the Duke, and the Commons sent a message to the Lords asking for a joint conference to consider the Duke's impeachment. Articles of impeachment were introduced by Sir Dudley Digges and the Duke entered the Chamber to over-awe his opponents, but failed to do so. Eliot, in a powerful speech, supported the articles and compared Buckingham to Sejanus, a corrupt servant of the Emperor Tiberius. The speech was reported to the King who understood the allusion and said in terms: 'Implicitly he must intend me for Tiberius'.

The following day, Thursday, 12 May, the King went to the House of Lords where he stood beside Buckingham and announced that he had thought fit to take order for the punishment of some insolent speeches spoken to them yesterday and it behoved themselves to preserve the honour of the nobiiity against the vile and malicious calumnies of the House of Commons. He promised to give evidence himself in refutal of all charges against the Duke.

Meanwhile both Digges and Eliot had been called outside the door of the Commons on some pretext or other where they were arrested and taken to the Tower. The Commons was in an uproar as related by Bevill in the following letter to Grace:

'If my cousin Arundell be at Efford when you have child it will be very fitting she should be a god mother too, therefore, though it be a boy, entreat both her and my sister too. It is no more than we have done formerly.

My bro[ther-in-law] Den[nis] is the man, whether it be boy or girl, and I hope Sir Jo[hn] Eliot shall be there too if it be a boy, though the King hath lately sent him to the Tower for some words spoken in the Parliament, but we are all resolved to have him out again, or will proceed in no business.

And if the child chance to be born before my coming down, stay the christening 'til we here can hear from one another. I will write shortly to you again . . .'.

And two days later he was able to write:

'I have this week sent you a box of dried sweatmeats; as many sorts and the best I can get, saving only apricots, whereof there are but a pound, and those not very good, though the best that can be gotten too. There were few or none done last year because of the sickness, and that makes the scarcity. The note of particulars is herein (en)closed, wanting only one box of Quidiniock, which I have eaten.

I hope my Lady be now with you, therefore remember my duty to her.

We have Sir Jo[hn] Eliot at liberty again. The House was never quiet until the King released him.

If God send us a boy, I have a good mind to have him called John, for my poor brother John's sake: if it be a girl, Grace'.

Digges had been released from the Tower after only one day. The charge that he had inferred complicity in the King when Buckingham allowed King James to have his plaster and posset failed to stick. Upon his reappearance in the Commons the House turned themselves into a grand committee to consider the imprisonment of Eliot. The King sent word that he charged Eliot with things outside their jurisdiction, high crimes against His Majesty committed outside the House of Commons. The Lord Chief Justice Crewe and the Attorney General interrogated Eliot in the Tower, but finding no evidence of treason, the King was obliged to release him.

Summoned to the Lords, the Speaker bravely approached the King with a remonstrance from the Commons in his hand and begged the King to comply with a petition from the Lower House 'for the removal of that great person the Duke of Buckingham from access to your royal presence'. To this the King made no reply, and his commission to dissolve Parliament was then read.

King Charles, to whom not one penny had been voted, sent Bristol to the Tower, and ordered the remonstrance to be burnt. But the grievances of Parliament could not so easily be dispensed with. It was 15 June 1626.

Grace gave birth to a boy on the 23rd; his christening al Kilkhampton was delayed until 16 July to enable the godparents to gather. The child was called Bevill after his father, but only survived until the age of ten. Poor brother John, who one may assume had died of the plague in London, was to wait another two years for his name to be commemorated. The suggestion that the child should be called Grace is evidence that the Grenvile daughter Grace, born in 1624, had also died. Another of her name survived and married Colonel Robert Fortescue of Weare Giffard in 1644, but when she was born is uncertain.

Their effort to make Stow more liveable continued. In May Bevill had written from London:

'Your beds are amaking, and some Turkey work for stools and chairs I have seen, but not yet bargained for. It is very dear, but if money hold out, I will have them. I have lighted on a pretty commodity of damask and diaper and am told it is very cheap so cheap as I shall not meet with it so ordinarily, therefore I ventured a little money in it.

There is of broad table cloth damask 12 yards and three quarters in one piece, and of narrow napkin damask suitable, forty yards and a half in another piece ... forbear cutting of it till I come down that we may consider together. I hope it is good. Your shoes and the childrens' are amaking.

I would gladly understand how my work goes onward, how far they have brought the walls to the height, and how many beams be in etc. I hope my cousin Tremayne hath long before this sold my tops and rindes at Lancells, out of which money I would have him to be paid that roots them up. Tell my co[usin] Tre[mayne] he must make the fellow to fill the holes after the trees be [rooted] up. My cousin Porter is to pay £5 for the rindes he sold some for it. I have paid him his full money for the timber already — £30.

Send me if it be possible my co[usin] Th[omas] Ar[undell's] £100. I shall have great need of it. I shall not possibly come away before Whitsuntide, but will as soon as I can. I have bespoken four plumes of feathers for your bed: you must be careful to make ready the bedstead.'

In a postscript he added:

'Charge Postlett and Hooper that they keep out the pigs and all other things out of my new nursery and the other orchard too. Let them use any means to secure them safe for my trees will all be spoiled if they come in, which I would not for the world.;

Later he wrote.

'There is little hope of having any of the plate home as yet, but all that can be done shall be.

I am glad you have fetched some of the timber to keep Allen awork, for I desire the work should go on with all possible speed'.

The building work seems to have been progressing well.

By 27 May he was able to write, 'I am very glad the healing stones [slates] are home and no loss'.

Their Aunt Abbot was at hand for the accouchement, but Lady Smith had not yet travelled down from Madford. Bevill had a happy relationship with his mother-in-law: 'I do humbly thank her for her great token of salmon and lamprey pies. I pray God my Lady's saddle fit her, it is the best I could get for money'.

Stow seems to have been well known for its stud. Lady Bath had been obliged to write to Sir Barnard for a gelding back in 1603. In May 1626 Bevill wrote to Grace:

For my two mares, good increase. But if they be not put to the black horse before this comes to your hands, give strict charge that they come not near him or any horse 'til my coming down. For they, and all the mares I have shall have the stallion which I bring down, which is a goodly horse and as handsome a one as any is in England. For God's sake be careful hereof, but if they have had the horse already then there is no remedy.'

With no prospect of any immediate work in London, Bevill was free to enjoy the life of a gentleman at home in Cornwall with his wife and children around him. The events to cloud and sadden his happiness at Stow were even then brewing between the King and Buckingham.

Chapter Five

THE PARLIAMENT OF 1628

BY 1626 BEVILL had served in the House of Commons under two Stuart Kings, had fathered four children and buried one; and, with what was clearly the greatest and most loyal help of his sickly wife Grace, had somehow just managed to finance the alterations at Stow and his life as a politician in the Inns of London.

The Cornish and North Devon properties made over to him by his father carried with them the obligation to provide annuities for the three aunts at Bideford; and other relatives who found themselves in financial difficulties. They learned that Sir Barnard could not help, and regarded Bevill as a reliable source.

It seems clear that Bevill's mother left Sir Barnard a life interest in Killigarth and Treemeer and also made provision for her second son, Richard. We know he had the benefit of the tithes due to what had been the Benedictine Priory of Tywardreath before the Dissolution. But the St Leger blood carried with it a powerful strain of improvidence. Richard lived far beyond his means, and borrowed from all and sundry. His pay as a professional soldier was no doubt always in arrears.

Richard owned money to his cousin, Sir William Courtenay, and also to Sir Henry Spry, the latter having obtained Bevill's promise to restrain his younger brother from selling off his interests in land. Richard had been bailed out by Bevill on previous occasions as the following letter shows:

> I did hope that those former acts of mine might have wrought so good effects that you should not have been brought again to these extremities: as if you had husbanded them well this needed not have been. For my part, though I liked not the leasing of the tithes and advised the contrary, out of my fears only that thereby you would afterwards want means, which I now see proves too true. Yet, when nothing else would satisfy you, I gave way unto your will, and if you feel the want of it hereafter you cannot blame me . . . and lastly (which is the greatest reason of all), how will you do afterwards for means when this is gone? I know how small your estate will be then; and how great your mind and expenses are I would I could not have heard so much of.
>
> And for further help from me hereafter you must not expect it, for how willing soever I am, I know I shall be utterly unable to do anything more for you, for so great is the burden lying on me, as I pray God I may be able to find myself and young family bread hereafter.

Bevill refused to have any part in the sale of Richard's remaining bits of property until he had first repaid those creditors who had advanced money on their security but without, as it seems, formal mortgage.

'You cannot but remember how many times I have helped you to money for to pay your debts, and yet nothing is done. I will trouble you no further at this time but with the remembrance of my best love which you shall be ever sure of. I rest your unfeigned loving brother . . .'.

Richard wrote back and appears to have accused Bevill of improperly withholding deeds relating to Richard's property from him, and of being unreasonable in declining further help. Bevill replied:

'. . . I must come to your unkindness. You say that my reason is unreasonable in that I cannot join with you because of my word and solemn promise to Sir H[enry] S[pry] to the contrary. I am sorry you value those things so lightly as to think there is no reason for the keeping of them.

For mine own part I see so much reason in it as for all the wealth of the world I will not break one. . . . you must learn by my woeful experience that what you become bound for, you must account to be your own debt. For whether you will or no, you cannot avoid paying of it.

You should have done wisely to have disputed before you had given bond, but having done it, it is too late to plead conscience.

A third cousin of Sir Barnard, Sir George Grenvile, could not even plead St Leger blood, but having bankrupted himself and his estate of Penheale near Launceston, he had no hesitation in writing to:

'My honoured cousin Bevill Grenvile at Killigarth (!)
Sir, I have ever felt a sufficient penance and punishment in the affliction of my mind by reason of my misfortunes . . . otherwise I should have avoided the needful help of my friends, especially yourself, to whom I have been most, though unwillingly burdensome . . . I have no friend but yourself to whom I make known these my grievances or crave assistance and advice to save myself from the wretchedness I now suffer . . . I have written to Sir Barnard but I have received no answer from him . . .'.

If the Grenviles were short of ready cash, they were in august company. Neither of King Charles's Parliaments had resulted in money reaching the exchequer, and the King was faced with two alternatives. He could either give ground and concede some part of his prerogative, a course of action as unthinkable to Charles I as it had been to his father, or he could invite his lawyers to search for ancient precedents or other devices capable of raising money without the approval of Parliament. A longer term solution which might have to be resorted to would be an increased effort to obtain support in any future Parliament by fiddling elections and rendering dishonest returns from the polls, by bribing those of the opposition who managed to get elected with appointments to places of profit or with ennoblement, and by frightening and imprisoning the incorruptible.

Sir John Eliot, the burgess for Launceston in Charles's second Parliament, had emerged as a powerful and articulate voice against absolutism, and above all an outstanding opponent of his one-time patron the Duke of Buckingham. The Court decided to destroy him. Sir James Bagg, newly appointed Vice-Admiral of Cornwall, prepared a memorandum for his over-lord the Duke:

'The Commissioners think the best way to bring Sir John Eliot to account is to procure a commission out of the Admiralty Court, directed to gentlemen of worth, spirit, and integrity in the country who are well affected to my Lord (Buckingham): such as are Sir Barnard Grenvile, Sir James Bagg, John Mohun, Mr. Drake'

and others to be appointed by the local Admiralty Judge, Sir Henry Marten.

Bagg's next step was to attack Eliot's supporter, William Coryton. He suggested that the Duke should deprive him of his valuable post as Vice-Warden of the Stannaries, and appoint John Mohun in his place. 'The County of Cornwall has been backward in making contributions of money to His Majesty', wrote Bagg; 'None had been more forward to express their loyalty as Mohun and Barnard Grenvile.'

William Noyes was the Attorney General. Noyes put forward the view that Parliament had been neglectful in carrying out their duty to supply the King with the money he needed, and that the King had the right to demand 'free loans' from his subjects for the government of his realm, which sums would be repayable, without interest, from such monies as Parliament voted in the future. The collection of money by demands bearing the Privy Seal was falling far short of expectations. Commissioners appointed to collect money in this way included Sir Barnard Grenvile, John and Edward Trelawney, John Mohun, and Walter Langdon.

Eliot had retained his Vice-Admiralcy of Devon for seven years. He was dismissed and the post was awarded jointly to Sir James Bagg (who already had Cornwall) and the younger Drake brother of Ashe, a cousin of Bagg's and a grandson of Anne (or Amy) Grenvile.

Bagg lived at Saltram, between Plymouth and Plympton, and his letters show that Sir Barnard Grenvile, Sir Edward Seymour, John Mohun, Drake, and others — 'All of them thoroughly well affected to my Lord' — had accepted an Admiralty commission to look into Eliot's record, interview witnesses, and draw up an indictment which would achieve his imprisonment.

Bagg also reported Eliot as a recusant as early as October 1626. Those who neglected to attend Church of England services were liable to fines and imprisonment under Tudor anti-Catholic legislation. King Charles had promised not to enforce the penal provisions against papists when he married his Catholic princess, but their money induced him to break his word.

To win support from any future Parliament the King deported his Queen's French entourage, a Bishop and several priests among them. He sent to France for his seven ships loaned for use against La Rochelle, withdrawing them from their French service, and was content to allow his Lord High Admiral Buckingham to play the pirate on French shipping, one such incident having featured in the attempt to impeach the Duke at the end of the last Parliament.

Richelieu had every reason to complain of the conduct of Charles government, and he retaliated by placing an embargo on English ships loading claret at Bordeaux. To deprive the English of their favourite wine was sufficient *casus belli* for war to be declared in the spring of 1627. England was now at war with both France and Spain.

An Armada of over a hundred ships was mustered at Plymouth and six thousand soldiers empressed or recruited for service against the French. These men had to be billetted all over the neighbouring countryside in the farms and cottages of the peasantry. In theory the soldiers' reluctant hosts could recover the cost from the King, but no money was available for that purpose.

The 'free loan' commissioners, Sir Barnard Grenvile and the rest, wrote from Efford, an Arundell house outside Stratton in Cornwall:

> '. . . from the billets of soldiers one general common answer, that in their hearts they are most dutifully ready to subscribe to the said loan for as they may receive a portion of the monies due to them from His Majesty for the billetting of soldiers, otherwise they profess themselves utterly unable to lend the provisions directed out of the considera- tion of their disabilities, grown partly by the plague, which hath and doth yet reign in these parts and . . . through the great charge of billetting of soldiers'.

and asked the Privy Council for directions.

For Bevill the position must have been extremely embarrassing. His two great friends Eliot and Coryton being hunted by Bagg and Sir Barnard, and he, their loyal and faithful supporter, ignored by the Establishment, but only because of his father's support for all the things he opposed.

Bagg was able to inform Buckingham in spring 1627 that Eliot and Coryton had gone to London 'now or never to receive his award . . .' and both were imprisoned in the Gatehouse in June.

Bevill wrote to one of his friends in prison:

> 'I cannot but, out of the fullness of my grief, be very passionate at your long suffering, from which there hath not wanted the prayers of many good men to redeem you; but whence it grows that I am thus long left at home, when now of late also more of the honest knot are fetched away, drives me into wonder and amazement: no man hath more boldness declared his resolution in this particular than myself, which nor fire nor torture can divert me from while in my own heart I am satisfied that it belongs unto the duty of an honest Englishman so to do. I have much to say, but I know not how safely this may come to your hands, wherefore abruptly I present my service to you and my cousin Trefusis and my prayers to God for ye all'.

Grace was equally apprehensive on behalf of her husband and wrote:

> 'Sweet Mr. Grenvile: These letters I have received in your absence and did make bold to open Mr. Billinge's because I imagined I might find some news of the Pursuivant, of whose coming here I stood in much fear of, but I hope now we shall hear no more of this business and that I shall be so happy as to have your company here at home, though it be much against your will'.

With Eliot imprisoned, William Davyle was sent down from London to set up a Commission to try him in his absence. Sir Barnard Grenvile, Bagg, and Mohun were the most active members of it. Mr. Drake lived 80 miles from Sir Barnard, and the unfortunate Mr. Davyle spent the autumn riding between Ashe and Tremeer trying to get the Commissioners together; they eventually sat at Plymouth in October, when Drake wrote to London reporting that the evidence against Eliot 'falls foul on the Vice-Admiral's part, so foul, that if extremity be used, it will go near to touch his life in my poor opinion. When you shall see the full particulars you would think it impossible that any man that carries the face of an honest man, should do such things', he added.

While Eliot and Coryton languished in prison, the King's ministers issued a Royal Procamation calling upon the Sheriffs of Counties to support a 'voluntary levy' of 'four subsidies and three-fifteenths', a sum claimed to be that which Parliament would have voted had it not been for the 'disordered passion of some Members'. The privy seal was used on demands made for the voluntary levy and these began to issue in July 1627.

A subsequent decree ordered the collection of 'tonnage and poundage' and was made under the Great Seal itself. A Commission was appointed to enforce penalties against Catholics, and the City of London was ordered to provide £120,000.

On 22 September Bagg felt obliged to write to Buckingham and admit that neither Devon nor Cornwall had paid the sums for which those counties had been assessed. He blamed the 'Eliot faction' for the short-fall. But no names were mentioned, and with Eliot and Coryton out of harm's way, the silence about Bevill Grenvile's name must have seemed deafening.

By early October the King felt obliged to proclaim that all monies now called for would be regarded as a first charge on monies to be voted by Parliament in the future, but this had little if any effect on the country-wide resistance encountered by commissioners, who included Bagg and Sir Barnard Grenvile, seeking payment of the 'voluntary levy' and 'forced loan'.

Buckingham was determined on showing his ability as a military commander. Leaving the gathering of the sinews of war to the King and his other advisers of the Council, he arrived at Plymouth in late June. The expeditionary force was paraded and inspected and one unit with much experience gained in the Low Countries was the regiment of Sir John Burgh. His Sergeant-Major or second-in-command was Richard Grenvile, whom Buckingham knighted on 20 June, seven days before the fleet sailed. Young George Monck was commissioned as ensign in the same regiment.

The object of the expedition was to support the Huguenots besieged in La Rochelle by Richelieu's army. On the basis that the Cadiz fiasco had been caused by careless talk, security was so tight that the Huguenots were not told that the English were coming. The besieged Protestants had no cause to trust the Englishmen: seven English ships had been used against them by the English King's command, Not unnaturally, they refused to allow their new friends to enter their city. This rebuff to all his plans led Buckingham to land his men on the Île de Rhé, a nearby island commanding all approaches to the city. Richelieu had occupied the island and garrisoned the fortress of St Martin. An attempt to take it was made. The English were repulsed with heavy loss. Survivors made themselves dead drunk on French wine as had their predecessors before Cadiz. Sir John Burgh having fallen, Sir Richard Grenvile was promoted colonel, and the whole force returned homewards having achieved nothing. They were back in Plymouth by mid-November.

Buckingham returned to find that insufficient money had been raised to pay off his troops, that the wheels of government were grinding to a halt for lack of means, and it was clear that all other methods having failed, the King would have to summon his third parliament. It was thought that Eliot and his friends would have learnt their lesson, having suffered six months' imprisonment without trial, and they were released as writs for a new election, returnable on 17 March, issued in January 1628.

Between January and polling day the election managers, determined to secure the election of men to support the King and his council, did their very best to prejudice the result. The modern theory of universal franchise and 'one man one vote' was still some centuries away. It was particularly remote in some Cornish boroughs. Normally, those householders who paid taxes — 'scot and lot' — were entitled to suffrage, but variations arose. In some boroughs only freeholders of specific properties; in others the right was reserved to freemen of the corporate body; in others only those who were borough magistrates.

Eliot and Coryton stood as candidates to be the two Knights of the Shire for Cornwall, Bevill as prospective burgess for Launceston. A body of magnates, Deputy Lieutenants and Justices of the Peace, declared that they had been entrusted with the duty of nominating who should be the Knights of the Shire by His Majesty's Council in Westminster. This remarkable Commission then proceeded to nominate John Mohun and Sir Richard Edgecombe, and spread it about Cornwall that Eliot and Coryton were 'unquiet persons in disfavour with the King' and even went so far as to warn both Eliot and Coryton against standing for Parliament. The trained band was called out on election day to ensure no interference with the election of the nominated pair. The persons who had assumed such powers in Cornwall were: Sir Barnard Grenvile, Sir Reginald Mohun and his son John, Sir William Wrey, Sir Richard Edgcombe, John and Edward Trelawney, Richard Trevanion, and Walter Langdon.

Polling did not go at all according to play so far as the Establishment was concerned. Both Eliot and Coryton were elected for the County, and Bevill for Launceston. One of the few successes gained by the Court party was the election of Colonel Sir Richard Grenvile as burgess for Fowey.

Bagg reported to the Council that

'Bevill Grenvile, John Arundel, and Charles Trevanion had gone to the polls with five hundred men at each of their heels, and lodged in towns together, which in itself is not only unlawful so to give their voices and to assemble such a body of men, but they by their so coming through fear do constrain or exclude those that indifferently thought to give their voices'.

Elsewhere a certain Oliver Cromwell was elected for Huntingdon. Bagg had little trouble in being re-elected for his own borough of Plympton, but as a general rule, no one who had resisted the loans and levies failed to get a seat in the south-west.

The new Parliament mustered at Westminster in April 1628. Heneage Finch was elected Speaker, a weak choice of great timidity. Bevill and Grace had set out from Stow together and travelled together as far as Grace's mother's house at Madford. Bevill continued to London by himself and was soon back in his old lodgings at the Rainbow in Fleet Street. Sir Richard Grenvile does not seem to have accompanied them; one suspects that the relationship between the two brothers was strained.

As was customary, a Committee of Privileges was set up by the Commons and one of the first things brought to the attention of that earnest body was a letter addressed to the Speaker by William Coryton. In it was set out an account of the unusual Royal Commission in Cornwall and its actions with regard to Eliot and himself, and it must have been acutely embarrassing for both Grenvile brothers to hear their father impugned before the House.

Sir Edward Coke, that comparatively recent and for that reason most fervid convert to radicalism, inveighed against the Machiavellian tactics employed by the King's adherents in Cornwall. This brought an angry outburst from Sir Richard Grenvile who declared that the speeches of Coke and his friends were motivated by malice. Members incensed by the charge shouted: 'To the Bar! To the Bar!' demanding Richard's punishment. Sir Robert Phelips spoke up for him saying:

> 'Affection of a son may transport this gentleman, and ignorance of this place, having been a soldier. His own silence may hereafter, if you please, punish him.'

As was customary with new members, Richard was given his chance to show his mettle as a parliamentarian by being appointed to a commission set up to inquire into the finding of arms, the pressing of soldiers, and the regulating of the powers of Lords Lieutenant and their Deputies.

As he was never appointed to another commission, I assume his ability in committee was no greater than that of his elder brother. In the meantime the House ordered that Sir Barnard and his confederates should attend at the Bar of the Commons to explain their actions. Richard appeared before the Committee sitting in the Exchequer Chamber to plead for his father. He told the members that his father was

> 'Very unwieldy and sick. I hope [he] has not deserved punishment: if he have, I will be willing to submit my fortunes and life to any punishment, only that he may be spared'.

Richard struck just the right note. Barnard Grenvile's attendance was excused. Bevill took no part in any of these proceedings, nor does he mention them in the letters which passed between him and Grace that month.

Having parted at Exeter, Grace made her way back westwards to Orlegh Court to be with her sister-in-law, Gartrud Dennis, then expecting another baby. From thence she wrote:

> 'Dear Mr. Grenvile:
> I thank God I am come back well hither, and do long to hear of your health in London, which pray let me know of so soon as you can. I hear that our young crew at Stow are well. I came from Madford on Tuesday last, where I would willingly have stayed longer had it not been to have been with my sister at her lying down. I can get no hope from my mother to see her at Stow till Whitsuntide be past, and were it not to see my children, and that your occasions are such as will of necessity call me thither, I should not for some reasons much desire to see Stow till your return, for the place hath not been so fortunate to me as to draw my love much to it.'

She ends with an impassioned plea for funds, having insufficient money with which to keep house at Stow.

Bevill replied:

'I beseech you disquiet not your mind and use what means you can to preserve and
continue your health. I am sorry to hear you did remove so soon from Madford where
you might best have settled that: but if you have need, get Mr. Flay unto you with his
physic, and give him content whatever it cost.

I hope you will get in your money and follow my directions in my last letter concerning it. I desire to have all things paid at home if it be possible, and when Vanston hath
finished the house, let him make out the wall at either end for to keep the garden more
private: but let him be careful to carry it [out] just as I directed him before Chibbett,
and foot it with stone, just as he doth the house, the rest cob.

You must make a new bargain with him for the wall, wherein take some advice. If he
do not perfectly remember my directions for the carrying [out] of it then let him forbear
it. For I would not for a world have it done otherwise than I intend. But if they be sure
not to mistake me, I wish it were done with all possible speed.

If you be at Orlegh pray remember me heartily to the Master and Mistress there, and
to my aunts. I hope my sister is past her plunge. If she be not I do heartily pray to God
for her.'

One can imagine Grace's frustration at receiving such a reply! In the place of
ready cash, mere directions how she must raise it, and urgent calls for further
expensive building works at Stow. She was five months' pregnant once again,
and one could wish that Bevill had written home with some gossip about affairs
at Westminster.

Grace wrote again, asking for £50. As she said:

'Or else I know not what to do. Perchance you will blame me and think I take too
much, but your scores were so high before your going as all this, if I have it, will clear
them and not leave me £10 for all weekly expenses in your house and workmens' wages'.

In a postscript she added:

'If you please to bestow a plain black gown of any cheap stuff on me, I will thank
you. And some black shoes I much need.'

Sir James Bagg, the member for Plympton, was concerned on behalf of his
friend, John Mohun. As a member of the 'Royal Commission for Cornwall' he
was in jeopardy of losing his liberty. The matter was put right through Buckingham getting the King to remove Mohun to the peers. His barony of Okehampton
was dated 15 April 1628.

The Commons considered their grievances. The King was pressing them for
money. His secretary, Sir John Cooke, carried messages to the Commons no less
than five times in April asking for 'supplies'. A new expedition to relieve La
Rochelle was mustering at Portsmouth under the command of Lord Denbigh,
whose sole qualification for the post was that, as William Fielding, he had married
the Duke of Buckingham's sister and thereby been ennobled in 1620.

The Court was busy behind the scenes wooing individual members of the
opposition. Digges became Master of the Rolls, and Wentworth became a
Viscount. The King felt strong enough to send word to his Commons:

'Bidding you take heed that you do not force him (by your tedious and needless
delays) to make an unpleasing end of these fair beginnings'.

Refusing the Speaker's request to consider the Commons' grievances, the King reminded them that it was he

'who sat at the helm, and [he] whose exclusive business it was to guide it [the country]'.

and sought to allay fears by calling the Commons into the House of Lords and promising both Houses to observe the provisions of Magna Carta.

The King next sent word that he wanted 'action not discourse' reminding them that he had given his royal word. Sir Nathaniel Rich remarked that they had never received so many general promises to observe the law, and that the law had never been so ill observed as during his present Majesty's reign.

On 4 May Sir Edward Coke sent a Petition up to the Lords. It was a restatement of Magna Carta and had been thrashed out in a committee of lawyer members in Inner Temple Hall. It set out that there should be no taxes without the approval of Parliament, no compulsory loans, no charges on anyone under the title of 'benevolences', no imprisonment save after lawful trial by a man's peers. That the King's special command should never override an application for a writ of *habeas corpus*, and that there should be no billetting of soldiers on private citizens and that martial law should not be imposed in times of peace.

Bevill was back at Stow on 13 May. From there he wrote to his mother-in-law at Madford:

'my wife hath many times been my secretary; I am now her's. She hath stayed the messenger some days thinking to write herself, but some fits of sickness have (to my great grief) hindered her. Wherefore she entreats me to certify your Ladyship of both of it, and that [you] shall not fail of horses on Saturday.

Her sickness is a great pain of the spleen, which is accompanied with great vomitting, so scarce any meat will stay with her, and makes her very faint. But I hope there is no danger of [losing] the child, and I trust she will overcome it also quickly. We both thought good to acquaint you with it, and do think your company would do her much good. My wife says also that you need not to remove anything, if you so please, but may consider thereof at leisure.

She desires if there be any prunelloes that you would get her some and send them by the first messenger, and I will entreat you that one of your servants may bespeak some lamprey pies for me against I send.'

In Bevill's absence the King replied to the Petition in such a way as to dash all hopes of a compromise, and Eliot spoke of the condition to which the nation had been reduced by Buckingham, referring to the fiascos at Cadiz, the Île de Rhé, and La Rochelle. He advocated a Remonstrance to be addressed to the King, and the House agreed that course of action. All discussion of 'subsidies' ceased. To protect Buckingham the King told the Speaker to 'cease aspersion upon the state government and the ministers thereof', and on the message being read out it was met by prolonged silence. On rising to attack Buckingham the Speaker silenced Eliot saying he had been commanded to interrupt anyone who criticized a minister of the state. Alured's letter of 26 June said, 'Yesterday was a day of desolation among us in Parliament, and this day, we fear, will be the day of our dissolution'. Phelips, Coke and others wept. The House went into committee, thereby excluding the Speaker, and the door was locked. On hearing of it the

ANO·DNI·15 93
ÆTÃ·SVÆ
17

1. Elizabeth Bevill, the wife
of Sir Barnard Grenvile and
mother of Sir Bevill Grenvile
(reproduced by permission of
Sir Dennis Stucley, Bt.).

2. Bevill Grenvile. Possibly the 'civil picture' painted in 1626 when he was 30 (*reproduced by permission of Sir Dennis Stucley, Bt.*).

3a and 3b.   Views of a locket containing
a miniature portrait of Sir Bevill Grenvile
(*reproduced by permission of the British
Museum*).

4. The Lodge or New Castle of Sherborne built by Sir Walter Ralegh (*reproduced by permission of the British Museum*).

5. John, 1st Baron Mohun of Okehampton, by Hieronimo Custodis (*reproduced by permission of Desmond Fortescue, Esq.*).

6. (*left*) Sir John Eliot, an engraving from a portrait at Port Eliot, taken from Forster's *Life of Sir John Eliot*.

7. (*right*) Sir Bevill Grenvile, *c.* 1636, by Sir Anthony Van Dyke (*reproduced by permission of John Bowater, Esq.*).

AN·DNI·1636·
ÆTATIS·SVÆ
15

IOHN EARL of BATH
SON of SIR BEVIL GRANVILLE

8. Richard Grenvile, eldest son of Sir Bevill. The picture is wrongly labelled (*reproduced by permission of Sir Dennis Stucley, Bt.*).

9.   A plaster fireplace from Sir Bevill's house at Bideford, now the Gas Company showrooms (*photography by A. C. Littlejohn, A.M.P.*).

10.   Sir Nicholas Slanning; a drawing by W. N. Gardiner (*reproduced by permission of the Ashmolean Museum*).

11. View of Falmouth Harbour and Pendennis Castle (*reproduced by permission of the British Museum*).

Colonel John Trevannion.
A Drawing by W. N. Gardiner from the
Devonshire Clarendon.

12. Colonel John Trevannion; a drawing by W.N. Gardiner (*reproduced by permission of the Ashmolean Museum*).

13.   Ralph, 1st Baron Hopton of Stratton, by an
unknown artist (reproduced by permission of the

14.   Sidney Godolphin; a drawing by Harding (*reproduced by permission of the British Museum*).

15. Showing Radford Manor from whence Sir Walter Ralegh nearly made good his escape *(reproduced by permission of the British Museum)*.

16. Launceston Castle, a print from a drawing by Thomas Allan (*reproduced by permission of the British Museum*).

17.   Anthony Payne by Sir Godfrey Kneller (*reproduced by permission of the Royal Institution of Cornwall*).

18.   Sir William Waller; a painting attributed to E. Bower (*reproduced by permission of the National Portrait Gallery*).

19.   Cold Ashton Parsonage, now called the Old Rectory, where Bevill Grenvile died in 1643 (*photograph by John Stucley*).

BARNARD SON of
SIR BEVIL GRANVILLE

ANO · DNI · 1636 ·
ÆTATIS · SVÆ ·
· 9 ·

20.   John Grenvile, Sir Bevill's second son, afterwards 1st Earl of Bath. The painting is wrongly labelled (*reproduced by permission of Sir Dennis Stucley, Bt.*).

King sent word he would accept the Petition and great was the rejoicing. Bonfires were lit in the street and church bells rang. It was commonly thought that Buckingham had been sent to the Tower. A Bill for five subsidies was agreed and Parliament was prorogued until 20 October, but did not sit again until 20 January 1628.

The recess was not uneventful; Eliot himself had not been present during the events which led up to the prorogation of Parliament. He had obtained leave of absence from the House on 20 June, news having reached him of his wife's death in Port Eliot. Radigund had brought him wealth, being the heiress of Richard Gedie of Trebursey, and had six children alive at her death on the 13th. One, her daughter Elizabeth, was to be the wife of Nathaniel Fiennes, the Speaker of Cromwell's Parliament. But this was all in the future.

The prorogation of Parliament on 26 June 1628 came as a welcome surprise to four Cornishmen. Of the eight who had meddled with the Cornish elections, only four were brought to the Bar of the House of Commons: Walter Langdon, Sir William Wrey, Edward and John Trelawney. All four had been committed to prison for contempt of the Commons, but with Parliament prorogued, the King ordered their release and distributed favours. Sir Barnard was appointed 'Gentleman of the Privy Chamber', John Trelawney was made a baronet, and the Mohun family had already received their barony.

Eliot's friends started drifting away. Viscount Wentworth, the new Master of the Rolls, and shortly William Coryton himself would desert the cause. Only Bevill remained faithful to his friend Eliot until the end. His absence from the House was on account of Grace's indisposition as is evidenced by Bevill's letter to Lady Smith.

In August the Duke and Duchess of Buckingham travelled down to Portsmouth and took up their residence in a rented house. The King stayed with the Nortons at Southwick a few miles away. The occasion was the imminent sailing of another fleet to La Rochelle. (General Eisenhower launched an even greater fleet from Southwick in 1944.)

On the 27th, a naval officer called Felton, unable to obtain his arrears of pay, and disappointed at having been passed over for promotion, mingled with the throng in the Duke's rented house and with the words: 'May God have mercy on your soul!' plunged a dagger into Buckingham's heart.

The Duchess was so distraught she had to be restrained from leaping to her death from the gallery of the house, and when the news of the Duke's death reached the King he retired to bed in tears. The populace was delighted. But those who had blamed Buckingham for the maladministration of their country were to find that his death had in no way altered the King's policies at home.

Foreign policy was varied, however. Endymion Porter was despatched secretly to Madrid to negotiate an end of the war with Spain. Although it would be some time before the Spanish government could bring itself to take the necessary administrative steps, it was not long before Porter had laid the necessary foundations for peace, and was able to send home for a ship. The King ordered a ship to sail for Spain to bring Endymion home, but it was delayed by contrary winds.

Anxious to return home with all speed and report to his master, Porter took
passage in a Spanish vessel which ran aground and was wrecked in Lyme Bay on
the coast of Dorset. The villagers of nearby Burton Bradstock fell upon the surviving Spaniards and plundered them. They were quite unable to distinguish
between the King's confidant and his companions, and Porter too was stripped
of all he possessed. It was an unwelcoming landfall in December, but the local
squire was obliged to make him restitution on the King's orders.

Meanwhile the second expedition to La Rochelle had sailed. The late Duke's
brother-in-law had been superseded by the Earl of Lindsey, a soldier of some
experience. This new commander had in his force the regiment now commanded
by Colonel Sir Richard Grenvile. Nephew George Monck sailed with his men, but
the Colonel himself had been detained by business in the West and reached
Portsmouth too late to join the Fleet before it sailed. He hurried back to Plymouth, where he knew the Fleet would put in before venturing south into the
Bay of Biscay, but favourable winds carried the fleet faster than Sir Richard's
steed could take him, and he missed the boat again. His letter of apology was
accepted by the King without reprimand.

George Monck and his companions never saw a shot fired in action. After
surveying the defences prepared by Richelieu to welcome the English fleet, a
Council of War declared them impregnable. Without further ado the fleet altered
course for home, abandoning the Rochelloises to their fate. The Mayor of La
Rochelle decided it was better to deal with the King of France, who had the
capacity to take his town, than with the King of England who was unable to help
his allies, and decided to surrender. Of the twenty-thousand inhabitants at the
start of the siege, sixteen thousand had perished, mostly from hunger. Richelieu's
men entered La Rochelle at the end of October 1628. Peace with France was then
negotiated and achieved in April 1629.

The business which had called Sir Richard to the west country was maturing.
It had been noted on 3 November that he was interested in the cause of a certain
Lady Howard, then engaged in a law-suit against her late husband's relations.
She was the daughter and heiress of Sir John Fitz of FitzFord. He was a brutish
drunkard who had maltreated both her and her mother. When Mary Fitz was only
three her father had murdered a neighbour and fled abroad. His wife and mother
obtained a pardon enabling him to return to England, but no sooner back in his
own country he killed again. In a fit of remorse he stabbed himself to death. By
1628 she had already married three times men of good family but small fortunes.
She is reported to have been beautiful, but by now can have had few romantic
illusions.

Sir Richard was a good looking but penniless soldier. Having carefully put all
her properties into trust, she married him a few days later, on 24 November 1628.
Sir Richard's fury at finding that he was unable to make hay with his bride's
possessions may be imagined. Although she bore him a son, Richard and a
daughter, Elizabeth, the marriage soon deteriorated beyond redemption and the
lady was kept a virtual prisoner in her own house, and its management was
entrusted to his widowed aunt, Katherine Abbott.

To return to Stow: Bevill had been keeping Grace company since mid-May. His ailing wife gave birth to a healthy boy on 29 August. He was not christened until 16 September, by which time Sir John Eliot had sufficiently recovered from the loss of his wife to stand godfather at the font in Kilkhampton parish church. The boy was called after his sponsor, but Bevill probably had his late brother John in mind as well when choosing his name. Bevill did not spend all his time at Stow. After the christening, in November he went to stay with Sir John Eliot at Cuddenbeck, the dower house of Port Eliot. Eliot had used Cuddenbeck to entertain his friend Sir William Courtenay in July, a brave survivor of the first La Rochelle expedition, and was able to tell Eliot that the Duke of Buckingham regarded Parliamentary government as impracticable. Bevill was so hard pressed for money that summer that he wrote from Cuddenbeck to Grace at Stow:

> 'Pray watch diligently for my cousin Arundell's coming to Efford [John owned Ebbingford near Stratton] or [?Trerice] this week, and let him have this letter with speed, because it concerns his meeting of Sir John Eliot and me on Tuesday next at Caerhayes [the house of Sir Charles Trevanion], wherefore with your utmost speed let him have the letter. We are making a visit to Mr. Trevanion which will keep me a little longer from you.
>
> You must get in a little money and send me now, or I am spoiled. For God's sake do what you can in it. Get it either of Browning or Na[thaniel] Gist, or how you can, and send it sealed in a paper, not letting the boy know what he carries . . . and let the boy be with me tomorrow night here, or on Monday at Fowey.'

What it was that Bevill had to discuss with Eliot, John Arundell and Charles Trevanion can only be surmised. They were all active members of the opposition and no doubt wished to plan their strategy for the coming sitting of Parliament.

Poor Grace! She was a grass widow at Stow having the unpleasant duty of pressing her husband's tenants for advances of their rent. She was in constant ill health and disliked Stow, she had five children to attend to, and had buried at least one other. Lady Smith was with her, however, and her mother must have been a support.

When Parliament reassembled on 20 January 1629, Bevill was absent. He was engrossed in a lawsuit. Its precise nature is unknown, but was probably concerned with his late father-in-law's property in Devon. It was a long-standing feud. As early as March 1624 he had been told by Grace that her mother hoped he had not yet retained Sir Henry Yelverton, the Solicitor General, and would not do so without first consulting her. On 14 February he wrote to Eliot:

> 'I hope in the merciful court of your judgement I shall not undergo a harder censure for my so long constrained absence and neglect of duty in my attendance at the Parliament than in my own thoughts I do inflict on myself.
>
> None can acknowledge his fault more, nor shall blame me as much for it as I do myself.
>
> This is enough to so noble a friend, and my occasions have not been ordinary.
>
> I shall humbly beseech you to procure the Speaker's letter for me to the Judges of our circuit for to stop a trial that concerns some land of mine for this Assize, because I cannot attend it — and deliver it [the letter] to Kitt Osmond who will attend you for it. I think this is an ordinary courtesy for to be granted to a member of the House by the Speaker, but if you please to procure it, you shall much oblige him that hath vowed himself to be your faithful servant.'

Eliot replied on the 25th:

'Had not the daily expectation of your coming up prevented me, I had long ere this given you some sense of the unhappiness I conceive in that distance now between us, for as your assistance in the Parliament is some cause which I desire your presence for particular reasons do enforce it, as the object of my affection.

In your business I know not what answer to return to give you satisfaction. Your instructions are so short, though they give me hope of your request for the stopping of a trial, yet they have no mention of the parties in whose names it is to be, nor of the county where the scene is to be laid, so as I must confess though I presumed to move it in the general and had it ordered by the House a mandate should be granted, it exceeded both my knowledge and experience and all the abilities of the Speaker how it might be drawn.

Mr. Osmond was gone before I read the letter, and I can by no diligence enquire by whom to be informed, so as I must on this occasion render you only my good meaning for a service, yet thus much by another way to satisfy you if you please by your own letter at the Assizes, or by a motion of your counsel to intimate your privilege of Parliament, it will have the same operation with the other, and no Judge will once deny it.'

Eliot had been as good as his word, and the Journal shows that Bevill had been granted 'privilege' on the 23rd. The letter drafted by the Speaker and Eliot can hardly have reached Bevill in time to enable him to travel up to London in time to take part in the closing scenes of King Charles's third Parliament.

The House had proved no more willing to grant the King what he demanded than the King had shewn himself willing to grant the Commons' requests. Eliot rose to speak on 2 March 1629 but the Speaker told him he had the King's command to adjourn the House for eight days. The Commons regarded their adjournments as singularly their own affair and insisted on hearing Eliot speak. The Speaker thought he would bring the sessions to an end by leaving the Chamber, but Holles and Valentine laid hands on him and forcibly restrained him in his chair. The Sergeant tried to remove the mace, but it was wrested from him and replaced on the table. The doors of the Commons were locked. Black Rod arrived from the Lords and sought admittance but was refused.

Holles moved that anyone who sought to make innovations in the religion of the Church of England, who advised the King to levy tonnage and poundage, or as a merchant voluntarily subscribed to such a tax without the prior consent of Parliament, should be regarded as a betrayer of the liberties and as an enemy of England. The motion was carried by acclamation.

The King ordered the doors of the Commons to be broken open, but before his messengers could carry out their instructions, they flew open and the members poured out like a stream in spate, sweeping the messengers off their feet.

The warrant for the dissolution of Parliament was signed by the King on 3 March. Eliot, Holles, Valentine, Coryton, and five other members were summoned to appear before the Privy Council the following day. It was fortunate for Bevill that he took no part in the proceedings.

The King had now embarked on ruling without Parliament. His proclamation said he was obliged to govern without by reason of the behaviour of a few of its members, and promised their condign punishment.

Chapter Six

THE DEATH OF SIR JOHN ELIOT

ALTHOUGH NO ONE could have known it at the time, members of the House of Commons would not be called upon to serve again for 11 years. There was little point in summoning a Parliament for supplies of money when nine of its members were in gaol: experience had taught the King the impossibility of raising funds in such circumstances.

On 4 March 1629 Eliot and some of his supporters were arraigned before the Council in the Star Chamber and he was committed to the Tower. He was committed in 'close custody', as opposed to 'safe custody' which allowed only very restricted contact with the outside world and neither books nor writing materials.

The Lieutenant of the Tower, Sir Allen Apsley, was able to reassure the Privy Council that when Bevill and his companion, a Mr. Pollard of Devonshire, tried to visit Eliot in his cell, both were refused access. Bevill must have travelled up from Stow that March expressly to comfort his old friend and leader. One by one the other imprisoned members, including William Coryton, made their various submissions to the Council and were released or released on bail; by October only three remained in custody.

Bevill returned to London later, determined to do what he could for his friend. He was lodged once again at the Rainbow in Fleet Street and news that Eliot was now in only 'safe custody' must have percolated to Cornwall. This meant economy rather than kindness on the King's part, the King being obliged to provide food for those in 'close custody'. Grace wrote to Bevill:

> 'I will pray for your health and good success in all businesses, and pray but be so kind as to love her who takes no comfort in anything but you.

On 29 October 1629 Eliot, Holles and Valentine were taken before the Chief Justice in his chambers in Serjeants' Inn and thence committed to the Marshalsea prison in Southwark. This was thought to be an improvement on the Tower, and their friends hoped the move heralded an early release.

Bevill had left the Rainbow and was staying at Chiswick House, which then belonged to Richard Boyle, the 'Great Earl of Cork'. Lord Cork was an old friend of his father and of his St Leger relations.

On 26 November Bevill sent a letter to Eliot from Chiswick en route for the West. His messenger must have been told to await a reply.

'While I am deprived of my great happiness, the seeing of you; it will be my next to hear from you that you are well, which I covetously desire, and shall ever pray for as a public good. I know the unfitness of the time for any copiousness to pass between us, and therefore will use none, only I beg to know (as my greatest cordial) whether there be any more hope of so great a blessing as the seeing you shortly in the West? It is not fit to say more, as I cannot be quiet without saying something. Farewell — and love him that will live and die your faithfullest friend and servant.'

In a postscript he added:

'My best services I pray remember to your two noble consorts whose well being I shall no less pray for than yours. The noble master of this house kisses your hands, than whom you have not an honester or truer friend.'

Bevill was unaware that one of Eliot's 'noble consorts', Denzil Holles, lately member for Dorchester, had made his submission to the Council and had secured his release on bail. Only Valentine remained faithful in the Marshalsea. The guarded language of his letter shows how aware Bevill was that letters were opened and expressions of dissent dangerous in the extreme.

Eliot replied the same day to the effect that were he able to reconcile his principles with his wishes, he would answer the letter in person.

'My affection to be with you carries too much reason to be doubted. The times only are malevolent, and because I am not worthy, will not admit me to that happiness. My desires and wishes shall attend you in your journey (as the like services you have from my consort in captivity) while you remain with your noble friend —— when you are travelling my affection must still follow you. When that trouble is at an end and you arrive at the presence of your lady (that centre both of your felicity and rest) there shall I likewise meet you intentionally . . .'.

Eliot was fond of Bevill and Grace, and his affection for them survives the flowery language of the time. No word of recrimination for Holles appears in his letter.

Back at Stow, Bevill found Grace awaiting the birth of another child. Bessie was 10, Dick nearly nine, Bevill three and a half, and the two babies, Grace and John. Bridget (Biddy) was born on 30 January 1630, making the 'crew' at Stow six.

George Granville, Lord Lansdown (whose father had not yet been born), wrote to William Henry who succeeded as third Earl of Bath a letter dated 4 September 1710. In it he said:

'Stow in my grandfather's time till the Civil Wars broke out, was a kind of academy for all young men of family in the country; he provided himself with the best masters of all kinds for education, and the children of his neighbours and friends shared the advantage of his own. Thus he in a manner became the father of his country, and not only engaged the affection of the present generation, but laid a foundation of friendship for posterity, which is not worn out at this day.'

Some four days before Biddy was born at Stow, the trial of Eliot opened before the Chief Justice. Pleas of privilege were summarily dismissed by the Judge opening the proceedings with the statement that any offence committed in Parliament of a criminal or contemptuous nature were triable in other courts, and that all he was concerned with was to establish whether such acts had been committed.

Eliot was a thin slight man insufficiently robust to withstand prolonged imprisonment. His health began to fail towards the end of the trial, and consequently he was back in his cell when the Court found him guilt of conspiracy 'to resist the King's lawful order, to calumniate the Ministers of the Crown, and to assault the Speaker'. He was fined £2,000 and sent back to the Tower on an indefinite sentence of imprisonment. Holles was fined 1,000 marks and Valentine £500, the three friends being sent to three different prisons.

Eliot wrote to Bevil in June:

> 'I have been all this term kept by your countryman Arundell in hope and expectation of your coming up, and upon that, deferred my writing. But now being freed from that, and having a safe conduct promised me [for his letter] I cannot but tell you how much I joy in your absence from this town, though I grieve for the want of your presence to myself. There is nothing here to please you, nothing worthy of your view (the Court being not within the compass of your sphere) imprisonment is a favour, secluding the corruption of the time, which is so epidemical and common that it leaves almost no man uninfected, nor a safe retreat for liberty or virtue but the country. This is enough to commend the happiness of Devonshire, which is fortunately dissituate . . .'.

In August he wrote again on behalf of Sir Henry Bouchier:

> 'The present occasion that commands me is for the satisfaction of Sir Henrye Bowrcheir, who has much importuned me to know whether you would be pleased to depart again with Londey, either in fee or lease. He seems to have a great desire for it, and if you intend that way, I believe he will be drawn to a fair price.'

In a postscript he added:

> 'Present my service to your good lady and tell her though the perverseness of my fortune will not suffer me to kiss her hands at Stowe, yet I hope her sweetness does deserve so kind a husband as will sometime show her London, and then I may crave the happiness to see her.'

The Bouchier family then held the Earldom of Bath and lived at Tawstock in North Devon. That Sir Henry wanted to buy or lease Lundy underlines the fascination which islands have always had for some people. It consists of a granite slab rising sheer from the Bristol Channel to a flat table-land some 400 feet above sea level, three miles long by a half-mile wide. The island lies north and south and thus providing a lee from the prevailing winds. There was then no harbour, and visitors were obliged to land on an open beach and scale a steep cliff-side track to raid the many nests of sea-fowl which still frequent the island. For many years Lundy had been the haunt of pirates of every variety, French, Spanish, and Corsair. They preyed on the shipping of the Bristol Channel and were the despair of merchants everywhere.

Until 1639 Bevill had concentrated his interests, when not in London, on the additions and improvements he was carrying out at Stow. Although he was never to lose an opportunity to add to his garden and orchards, the cob walls to ensure privacy seem to have ended his building activity in Cornwall.

Bevill now became engrossed with his plans for Lundy. The letter from Eliot suggesting that he should lease or sell it, the no doubt innumerable complaints he was receiving from the merchants of his town of Bideford, and the occasional glimpses he caught of his island kingdom in fine weather all combined to stimulate his interest in this new project. His reply to Eliot has been lost, but its tenor can be sensed from Eliot's next letter:

> 'Your affection therein mentioned to that island you call desolate I cannot but commend. So far am I from the prejudice thereof and I confess the overture I made you at the request of others had in my intention but that end. By their estimation to endear it.
>
> But your design upon it I know not how to censure, there being many considerations in that work which must be first resolved on.
>
> ... My manner is not to object much where I cannot give my reasons, therefore in general I shall rest with this caution, and advise as Strato in Herodotus looked for the sun rising in the west. "Let your eye in this intention seek for the conclusion in the east".'

Or in other words: 'Do not by your actions excite the wrath of the King and his Council by overstepping some prerogative right which I will look into and advise upon in due course'.

It is clear that Bevill took advantage of fine weather that summer of 1631 to commence building a pier and to erect some sort of fort to protect his island from pirates. By September Eliot had read sufficient precedents to be in a position to advise Bevill further:

> 'Having received your papers and letters sent me by Mr. Ascot ... I have with that little judgement that is mine perused them to the utmost, and followed them with such considerations as a business of that nature doth require. First I have weighed your reasons and desires, then I have studied what in this time I might, to know the former use therein, whence you may see what latitude is before you, and then be directed by yourself.
>
> To build there is a free liberty to all men, but not to fortify without leave. All resistance to any enemy is safe where there is clear openess to the State. Leaving those words then, of fortification and inharbouring, I see not but you may perfect the works you have begun for the general good and benefit.
>
> ... and therefore let not your disbursements be too much, but with the public good, preserve your own interests and faculties.'

Eliot's advice could not have been sounder. 'Protect your possessions, but do not over-spend'. Eliot had attended an Inn of Court after finishing at Oxford and had been called to the Bar, but never practised as a barrister. Bevill wrote to the Tower from Stow:

> 'I am infinitely bound unto you for many noble favours, and not least for your last, wherein you have dealt so ingeniously with me concerning my late undertaking at Lundey, which I confess hath opened my eyes & given settlement to my resolutions.
>
> And I hope I shall walk with your caution in this affair, as you shall not have cause to repent your advice, wherein I will say no more till I may have the happiness to see you...'.

It is pleasant to discern that their political differences never induced Bevill to break off relations with his father. It was at about this time that he wrote to Sir Barnard:

'I'm glad the gull's [eggs] came safe to you and do humbly thank you that you are pleased to accept so poor a present. I willed my man to carry half of his gettings to you, but wrote not because I knew not what would be brought.

Mr Billing tells me you have a mind for some knotts'. There are some at Lu[ndy], but I could never yet light on them. I will try now again, and if I can you shall have them. However I doubt not of some salt-birds' for you, but I fear I shall not be able to send you a vast of any good butter from there this year, for since the departure of my old virgin, I have not had any from them that I liked. And though she was a black jade, yet she was the best about her dairy that ever I had, and I am now so destitute of a good dairy woman for that place as I would give anything for one.

I am going thither this week to see my great works finished, which I hope will be within this month.'

Sir Barnard himself had obtained little benefit from his ownership of Lundy and may have thought his son's expenditure there unlikely to benefit him. It may be that Sir Henry Bouchier had approached Sir Barnard in another attempt to secure the island for himself. At all events Sir Barnard visited his son at Stow with a proposition relating to Lundy, and had got up so early the following morning that he left the house before any of the household was astir: Bevill sent a letter after him:

'Sir, I am sorry I was prevented of taking leave of you before your return. You were so early gone that none in the house thought of it, and I for my part never knew it in two hours after you were gone. I have a little considered of that . . . proposition you made me concerning Lundey, and though my affection be much placed on it, and my future hopes are more than my present profit (though that be not unworthy the consideration also), yet notwithstanding if any such reasonable proffer may be made, as I may conceive how more to better my estate by parting with it, than by keeping it, I shall not be intractable, so these following considerations may go along with it.

The present value of the place is the thing least considerable in it, for the pasturage and other commodities that have used in former times to arise out of it, have not yielded above £100 a year. But I have lately made a quay and harbour there at my great cost, which the island ever wanted before, whereby an industrious man which will set on a course of fishing may as I think easily gain £500 a year by it. Moreover whosoever will convert the ground wholly to the breeding of a brave race of horses shall find it for that purpose the fittest place in the kingdom of Eng[land] and may make many £100s a year by it, beside the pleasure which will thereby arise. It hath all the properties which are fit for such work, both of earth, air, and water, in perfection, and that which is the special thing in the breeding of stone colts, namely the safe keeping them from mares, nowhere in the world can be safer if this course be taken . . . the best course herein may easily gain £500 . . . if he be careful to breed upon a good mare which I was never able to procure, and yet out of my poor jades, though the island were fully stocked with other cattle, I have bred divers horses which I have been offered a £100 a piece for.

I have had it in my hand but a short space, yet I discern several ways how to make great profit by it, which as yet I have not been able to put into execution. . . . there are acres of ground which are now bogs and barren which would with small charge be made as good land as any . . . and besides great hopes (and so it hath been long reported) of . . . and metals in the earth there, but as I can speak with no certainty . . .'.

'For these causes and many others which are too tedious to write, my value of it is £5,000 whereof I will not abate a penny if [I] part with it. And so you (if you please) may advertise any friend you have.

'I have so many reasons to be in love with it, as I shall never call it to sell or woo any man to buy it. But if any man be desirous of it that has my price or nothing and so I submit it and myself to your pleasure.'

And neither did he ever part with Lundy although no other land of his stayed unencumbered at his death. It proves a dangerous outpost to hold. The Pollard family (there were Pollards then at Horwood beyond Bideford) had a special relationship with the Grenviles. One accompanied Bevill to the Tower to see Eliot and another, christened Bevill Pollard, sent his namesake newsletters from the Low Countries. Then in 1633, Sir Barnard wrote to the Secretary of State:

'A great outrage has been committed by a Spanish man-of-war who on the 16th instant landed eighty men on the island of Lundy, when after some small resistance they killed one man called Mark Pollard, and bound the rest, and surprised and took the island which they rifled, and took hence all the best provisions they found worth carrying away, and so departed to sea again.'

England had been at peace with Spain since 1630. The Council ordered Sir John Pennington into the Bristol Channel, but the Navy arrived too late to catch the villains.

The next three years brought three additions to Bevill's crew at Stow; Bernard born in March 1631, George in August 1632, and Roger in November 1633. While infant mortality and then the fatality of most disease urged men to secure their posterity, Grace, with her difficult pregnancies, was to be pitied. Bevill's activities in those years may be glimpsed from the letters surviving from that period. As a Politician he was necessarily dormant. The King was making ends meet without the assistance of Parliament.

Eliot wrote at regular intervals from the Tower acknowledging letters and gifts sent him by Bevill and on occasions complaining that:

'If you consider how long it is since I had the happiness to see you, and that in all this time no paper intelligence came from you, you may pardon it without wonder that I presume thus now, which is but a formal way of begging, a petition for that favour which you were wont to grant me . . .'.

In July 1631 he wrote:

'I have a suit in law with Sir Richard Edgcombe of some value which comes to trial at Lanceston these assizes, wherein it is in your opportunity to do me a favour . . . You know the disadvantages I have if it depends on the judges, and what uncertainties, if not more, are implied in common juries, the presence and practice of my adversary with his solicitous adherents, and the reputation of their justiceships compared with my nothing, and that absent. It is not without reason that I seek the assistance of your arm to add some weight unto that number which must take the decision of our cause.

There are near you some of discretion and sufficiency returned upon the jury, whose integrities may counterpoise those dangers. My desire is that you will (though they attend not visually in such services) engage them to appear . . .'.

Bevill was to use his influence on the jury panel to secure a judgement in Eliot's favour. Edgcombe had been one of those who had tried to secure the election of court nominees as knights of the shire in the place of Eliot and Coryton, and had been obliged to make a humble submission to the House of Commons. There can have been little love lost between the parties.

In due course Bevill replied:

'I think I never gave any account of the service you commanded me at Lanceston since I received that letter, but I presume your servant hath given you notice of what passed, and of my readiness to serve you. . . . My neighbours I sent all forth, which did not deceive your trust, nor fail my expectation . . . such as for their honesties could not have been excepted at, and for my sake would not have been terrified or beaten from a good cause.'

The honest neighbours had, one may assume, returned a verdict to Eliot's satisfaction.

Bevill had accepted Eliot's horses for safekeeping and reported that his stud had met with a set-back:

'Divers of them have run mad and beaten themselves to death — amongst which your fair mare made one, whose loss grieves me [more] than all the rest. But she has left behind her a brace of lovely stone colts, which I hope will live to do you service . . .'.

Eliot's refusal to submit to the Council resulted in greater pressure being brought to bear upon him. He was moved to less agreeable quarters, cold and dark, and visitors were no longer allowed.

In early 1632 Bevill managed to smuggle a letter into him by a Mr. Newton of Barnstaple, an officer of the Admiralty, and mentioned having received one from Eliot by the hand of one Periman. Bevill had no liking for Periman who had caused him to pay nearly £500 during his sheriffwick. Bevill's Prideaux cousin being now High Sheriff, Periman had been deprived of his post. Eliot wrote from the Tower praying forgiveness for Periman, and Bevill arranged for him to be taken on again, a service undertaken for a friend rather than forgiveness of an enemy.

'Since that time', wrote Bevill: 'There have been rumours very rife in these parts of a Parliament. If it be so I wish you would let me have some timely notice that I may do you a service, which I more desire than any earthly thing besides, and I presume I have some interest in the affections of the people. But though you think me not worth the sending to, yet I have taken such course as you shall be sure [of] the first Knight's place whensoever it happens, but I assure you you shall not have your older partner, whoever be the other'.

Bevill had canvassed the freeholders to ensure Eliot's return for the County, and had placed his embargo on William Coryton. The latter, having reneged, could not be forgiven.

The last letter to pass between Bevill and Eliot was from Eliot, still in the Tower:

'The restraint and watch upon me bars much of my intercourse with my friends; wholly their presence is denied me, and letters are so dangerous and suspected as it is little that we exchange, so as if circumstances shall condemn me, I must stand guilty in their judgement, yet yours, though with some difficulty, I have received. And many times when it was knocking at my doors, because their convoy could not enter, they did retire again. Wherein I must commend the caution of your messenger, but at length it found a safe passage by my servants and made me happy in your favour, for which this comes as a retribution and acknowledgement. Your concession to John Periman adds much to the reckoning of my debt, though the obligation be the same: your interest in me formerly was such as it had no limit but my all, and I cannot give you more, which if I could this reason does deserve it that you have let down so much of yourself for him that it so un-worthy, who must confess the greatness of that courtesy. And I do hope the other will strive to merit it.

For those rumours which you meet that are but artificial or by chance, it must be your wisdom not to credit them. Many such false fires are flying daily in the ear, when there shall be that occasion, expect that intelligence from friends, for which in the meantime you do well to be provided, though I shall crave, when that dispute falls properly and for reasons not deniable, a change of your intention in particular as it concerns myself.

Represent my humble service to your lady and tell her that yet I doubt not one day to kiss her hands. Make much of my god-son — men may become precious in his time. To whom, with all your sweet others and yourself I wish all happiness and felicity and rest.

Your most faithful friend and brother ':

Poor Eliot! His ambition to kiss Grace's hand was to remain unfulfilled. On 27 November 1632 Sir John Eliot died in the Tower. His family asked for his body to bury it in Cornwall, but the King ordered it to be buried in the Tower. Charles had little generosity towards his enemies.

Bevill learnt too late that his old friend was dying. He wrote,

'Oh my dear Sir, such and so great is my agony and distraction at the reports which fly abroad and strike mine ears as I cannot express it, nor will tell what I would say, but sure I am it puts me out of my little wits and much beside myself: one while you are voiced for dead, another while sick, another while well, but all that's certain [the] author for either being but common fame, which I have ever found uncertain and lying. I dare not give credit unto any part of it. I must confess (that in the distemperature of my passions) I do fear the two first, for fear cannot believe the last, and yet I must also confess that the passion of fear hath seldom had power over me, and never any for my self. But this has put me beyond resolution, beyond constancy, and wholly from my self. For God's sake be so pitiful to me as to give me the certainty how you are and with speed too, or you cannot imagine what I shall give myself over unto, nor how I shall be abandoned.

It is lately reported that your physicians that country air would be a great preserver of you, and it hath long been reported that you may have your liberty, if you will but ask it, which, if it be so, I humbly beseech you (for your country's sake, your childrens' sake, your friend's sake, which respects the excellency of your wisdom and courage hath chosen to prefer above yourself, as the constancy of your sufferings both declare) I say, I beseech you be not nice, but pursue your liberty if it may be had on honourable terms. I will not desire you to abandon a good cause, but if a little bending may prevent a breaking, yield a little unto it. It may render you the stronger to serve your country hereafter. I do with great agony deliver these words while your life is called in question, but I beseech you think on it. You shall not perish alone. Pray afford me instantly some comfort . . .'.

This excellent advice never reached Eliot, but it is doubtful whether it would have persuaded Eliot to compromise, or whether a submission at that late stage would have resulted in his release. The vindictiveness with which the King treated him throughout, and his family thereafter, makes it highly improbable that Eliot would ever have been allowed to leave the Tower where he now lies buried.

Bevill was an executor of Eliot's will and was left a ring inscribed, 'Amore et confidentia'.

Chapter Seven

BEVILL IN HIS FATHER'S PLACE

THE MURDER of Mark Pollard on Lundy and the death of Sir John Eliot in the tower of London channelled Bevill's restless enthusiasm towards new targets. One Spanish ship had demonstrated beyond any argument the perilous nature of investments in off-shore islands. The very quay and harbour built at Bevill's expense had no doubt facilitated the removal of Bevill's cattle and horses from the island. Lundy does not feature in his letters again.

While Eliot lived, the intense loyalty Bevill felt for him kept him occupied with plans for his re-election as Knight of the Shire for Cornwall, in smuggling letters to him and keeping an eye on his interests in the West Country. As executor of his will he had his duties to perform for the benefit of Eliot's orphaned children.

With Eliot dead and buried, Bevill was released from supporting Eliot's political policies. His loyalty to Eliot's faction in Parliament was rather to Eliot himself than to the radical views of the reformers Eliot led. With his father and his brother Richard both committed supporters of the Establishment, Bevill must have regarded the collapse and surrender of the opposition to the King's personal rule as something less than an embarrassment.

Bevill's next venture was into the problems of the Stannaries. Tin had been mined in Cornwall since earliest times. The various taxes levied on that metal represented a significant part of the Crown revenues. In order to smelt the metal from its ore, the ore was heated with charcoal and bellows. But while tin could still be mined in increasing quantities limited only by man's ability to drain the pits, charcoal was becoming increasingly difficult and expensive to obtain. Trees grew mostly in southern combes, and large areas were and remain treeless. Charcoal had to be imported from across the Tamar at cost.

As Lloyd put it in his *Memoirs of Loyal Sufferers*, Bevill

'added to his other virtues a strict attention to whatever he regarded to be to the public service, and by a multitude of experiments showed, that it was both practicable and profitable to make use of coal instead of wood in the [s]melting of tin; and contrived likewise several methods to hinder the wasting of that metal in the blast. Which, having brought to perfection at his own private expense, he, from a principle of public spirit, communicated to his countrymen for their common advantage'.

Welsh coal was readily available and was being unloaded at Minehead in Somerset in 1642. There was no reason why coal should not have been unloaded at Hartland Quay or Bude, or further west at Padstow.

As early as 1623 one Doctor Jorden had asserted the practicability of using coal instead of charcoal, but had been unable to smelt with coal in practice. Bevill is said to have tried his hand at inventing a coal-fired smelting system, but with no greater success. This seems a more likely version, since it was not until 1705, a date coincident with the invention of Newcomen's steam engine for pumping water out of mines, that a Mr. Liddell obtained a patent for smelting tin with coal in iron furnaces.

Bevill had had to help out his brother Richard on a number of occasions in the past. He might be forgiven for thinking that his brother was no longer likely to be a financial burden on his meagre resources. Richard had been a success. The Duke of Buckingham knighted him in 1627 before the Île de Rhé defeat, when he was promoted colonel. A good-looking but penniless Colonel must necessarily find himself an heiress. Heiresses were not to be found in the provinces, and the Establishment set him up with the Borough of Fowey. As a burgess for that town he became a young man of good family in circulation in London.

As we have seen, Richard was absent without leave when his regiment sailed for the second expedition against La Rochelle, and managed to become Lady Howard's fourth husband by the time his men returned. Mary Howard, or Grenvile as she had now become, was believed to enjoy an income of £1,000 a year. This proved an over-estimate, but the £700 she did receive made her husband a relatively rich man. He bought himself a baronetcy and became a Justice of the Peace.

Sir Richard Grenvile's expenditure had always exceeded his income, and having fathered a boy called after himself, and a daughter, he found himself hard-up again. Mary had settled all her properties on trustees before she married Grenvile, and had sold long leases of some of her farms to George Cuttiford, her agent and (it was said) the father of one of her sons: she had won a law-suit against her brother-in-law Theophilus Howard, Earl of Suffolk, for a marriage settlement promised but unpaid. Neither had Suffolk paid up under the judgement she had obtained again him. The money, if it could be wrung out of Lord Suffolk, would accrue to Sir Richard's use, and Richard now went to law in attempts to execute judgement against Suffolk, and to evict Cuttiford, on the grounds that Cuttiford had obtained his leases by fraud.

In the words of Clarendon, 'Not being pleased with her fortune, [Sir Richard] became less pleased with his wife'. Having been kept a prisoner in her house with Richard's widowed Aunt Abbot of Bideford acting as chatelaine, Mary fled to Lord Suffolk's protection, reverted to the name of Howard, and opened proceedings for a divorce on the grounds that Sir Richard had fathered a bastard.

The peerage enjoyed certain privileges over others at law, and his campaign against Suffolk resulted in Richard being imprisoned in the Gatehouse as early as 1630. This did not deter Richard from calling Suffolk a 'base Lord' a few months later. Called before the Star Chamber in February 1632 Richard was fined £8,000 for slandering Suffolk, and having no money with which to meet such a penalty, he was sent to the Fleet Prison.

His nephew George Monck had sailed on the second expedition to Rochelle and, promoted to the rank of Captain, served with the English contingent fighting the Catholics in the valley of the Meuse. Bevill Pollard wrote to his right worshipful and his singular good master Bevill Grenvile esquire of Stow from his leaguer below the walls of Maestricht on 8 August 1632. After an account of the fighting, Pollard listed those who had been killed or wounded, noting that 'Cap[tain] Moncke had also a slight hurt'.

In October 1633 Sir Richard Grenvile escaped from the Fleet and fled to Holland, then to Leyden, and finally offered his sword to the King of Sweden. This move must have required money and it seems that Bevill had been obliged to come to his younger brother's help once again.

George Monck wrote from the Hague on 17 October that year:

'Dear Uncle,
    I must crave pardon of you for my long silence which I hope you will not impute it to the want of affection, but the want of communications, which is the real truth of it, or I shall desire you to be this far confident of me that there is no poor kinsman you have [who] shall be more ready to serve you to his power than myself.
    Sir, I am sorry I could not before now acquaint you with the receipt of the £30 which you gave me to be paid here for Sir Richard Grenvile, towards the payment of a debt which I stand in [person] engaged for, monies I have paid unto the party unto whom it is due. There is [sic] two payments more which is due unto the next party. The next £30 will be due the 1st January next . . .'.

If the summer and autumn of 1629 had been a period of family christenings and political planning for Bevill, his father was becoming less and less enamoured of his role as principal supporter of the King's policies in Cornwall. As a Commissioner he had the thankless task of levying taxes without the consent of Parliament and hence of very doubtful legality.

A letter he wrote to a fellow commissioner, Sir James Bagg, described the failure of his fund-raising efforts and complained that everything in Cornwall was out of order due to the 'foulness of sundry ill dispositions poisoned by that malevolent faction of Eliot' of which, of course, his eldest son Bevill was an enthusiastic supporter. All his fellow Deputy Lieutenants of the County were either fearful or unwilling to do as commanded by the Council, and he himself was weary of his Lieutenancy. As he added:

'Seeing I see it so much undervalued. The Lieutenancy is grown into such contempt since the Parliament began as there be [they] that dare countermand what they have on the Lord's command willed to be done. They have certified many [as recusants] but it is observed that nothing is done in it, therefore they put on greater liberty'.

A few days later he attended a muster at Bodmin where Tristram Arscott presented a petition, and, on receiving a frosty answer from Sir Barnard, returned with a number of adherents to demand a proper reply. Sir Barnard said he would send it to the King, from whom they would hear in due course; a threat which Arscott countered by saying he would seek the support of the Earl of Bedford.

Lord Bedford was Lord Lieutenant of Devon, where Arscott in fact lived, and had the reputation of being a keen defender of the liberty of the subject. Sir Barnard fearing trouble from that quarter wrote again to Bagg giving his version of the affair and concluded that having been a Deputy Lieutenant for two or three and thirty years 'He [had] never met so ill affections as at the present time', and begged Sir James to let him relinquish his post.

A 20th-century Englishman is so conditioned to accept the rightness of what is called a Constitutional Monarchy, with all real power vested in the House of Commons, that it is difficult to appreciate the awe and reverence then felt for the Lord's anointed, or to feel sympathy for those who found it difficult to accept the concept of a people's sovereignty.

Sir Barnard Grenvile was such a one. His appeals to Byrd and Bagg to obtain his release from his duties as Deputy Lieutenant and Commissioner were not founded on any philosophical dislike of absolute monarchy. He was an old man for his times, about seventy years of age, and he was appalled by the unpopularity which had greeted his loyal endeavours.

His last surviving letter of that year is dated from Tremeer. His old friend Ralph Byrd is thought to have been vicar of Lanteglos-by-Fowey nearby which may explain why he elected to move there from Killigarth.

That Spring he wrote to his 'father-in-law' Endymion Porter expressing 'strong fillial regard to him and his honourable mother with affection to his pretty brothers' soliciting the cause Ralph Byrd had been invited to press on his behalf. It seems strange that a man of his age should address one 20 years his junior as his 'father-in-law', when such connections as there were between the Porters and Grenviles were at most distant cousinhood. Yet Buckingham's brother addressed Endymion as his 'Loving uncle' and other members of the Villiers family, including the Duchess, implored favours of him in similar terms of self abasement.

Endymion had become a very great man, indeed. Sir Warham St Leger, President of Munster in 1627, wrote in facetious vein that he had told the Great Earl of Cork not to visit England, where he was a party to a law-suit, without first presenting Endymion with a douceur of £1,000 and making a present to the Duke of Buckingham of between £3,000 and £4,000. By 1632 Huxley says he was the most trusted of the King's personal attendants.

When in Holland, Endymion bought the King his first Van Dyck, 'The story of Rinaldo and Armida', for £78, inclusive of packing and transport. He also bought a number of pictures by the same artist for himself.

The more recognisable Porter cousins lived at Launcells next door to Stratton and just south of Stow. Bevill had occasion to write to one of them in no uncertain terms:

> 'Sir, I have ever wished you well, and shall still do so unless I find great cause to the contrary. I am informed of base and lying speeches delivered to me which I cannot endure and will acquit myself of the injury or die in the cause. And although I can be kind, yet I will not be trampled on. I am engaged the beginning of next week to ride from home again, but after my return I shall take time to talk with you. Resting now hastily your well wishing kinsman — B.G.'.

Bevill had had dealings with one of the Porter family over the rinds (or bark) of felled trees. His letter must have caused some alarm and despondency in Launcells. Bevill was clearly no man to malign with impunity.

If Bevill's relationship with his father was strained at times, he was always a dutiful son. It may have been Richard who leapt to his feet in the House of Commons to defend his father's actions, but Bevill it was who sent him butter and sea-birds' eggs from his beloved Lundy. The death of Eliot made it possible for father and son to sink their differences; in a letter addressed to his Cousin Arundell, presumably John of Trerice, Bevill wrote:

> 'I received a message from my father that he would be with me in the middle of this week, wherein nevertheless he hath failed by some occasions . . . He hath promised not to fail being with me next week'.

The process of reconciliation seems to have begun even before Eliot's death in the Tower. It was in 1633 that Sir Barnard co-operated with Bevill seeking naval help in defending Lundy. It may have been that occasion that first heralded Bevill's change of attitude towards the King's government.

It was in the eighth year of King Charles's reign, 1633 or 1634, that Admiralty Commissions issued for Devon and Cornwall, and Bevill featured in both (owning land in both counties). The list of his fellow commissioners would have made poor Eliot turn in his grave. Those appointed included Sir Edward Seymour and Sir James Bagg, joint Vice-Admirals of Devon, and Sir Nicholas Slanning (Bagg's son-in-law). For Cornwall were John, Lord Mohun's father, Sir Reginold, Sir John Trelawney, Slanning (again), John Arundell of Trerice, William Coryton, John Trefusis and others.

Bevill's last letter to his father reveals the distance he had travelled since Eliot's death:

> 'Sir, I humbly thank you for your kind letter by Mr. Trott, which came in my absence so I saw him not, but met it after my return. Sir, the necessity of my sending him to London that I did, it was not only a money business (though I sent a great sum) but some other affairs that he was proper for and acquainted with, which I sent, otherwise I should not have been unwilling to make use of Mr. Trott, whom I shall use in what I find him fit, and already have some courtesy to for your sake, and so shall still.
>
> I did not send Jo[hn] Gel[ard] up purposely about my business, but he, having some of his own that carried him up, I sent a despatch by him to my other servant that was there before. It is true I find him too much given to drink and cannot for my life reform him though I have endeavoured it, and it doth much displease me. And were it not for my wife's sake, whom I desire to do good unto, I should not endure it. But I must also say that though he be too faulty therein both to God and himself, yet I never found him false in what I have trusted him.
>
> I met at Exeter the news of the new Lord Treasurer and of my Lord of Essex his parting with his lady; but she deserved to be cast off if the report be true, and I am sorry for his unfortunateness in wedlock, for I honour the man'.

Bishop Juxon had been appointed Lord Treasurer on 6 March 1636 and Lord Essex separated from his wife at about the same time. (Bevill radically altered his views on Lord Essex when the latter commanded the Parliamentary armies in the Civil War: he then referred to Essex as the 'Great Cuckold'.) Bevill's letter to his father continued:

> 'My journey to Exeter was to meet Sir James Bagg as he appointed me by his letter, and there I found both his son-in-laws and divers others expecting him, but he came not.

Neither have I heard of him since. I pray for his happiness, and with my service to Mr &
Mrs B(yrd), I crave your blessing . . .'.

That Bevill should be keeping appointments with the 'bottomless Bagg' (as
Laud had called him) would have caused Eliot even greater distress in his tomb.
Of the sons-in-law, Sir Nicholas Slanning was to become a life-long friend and
companion in arms, and Sir Henry Cary of Cockington will appear again on
Braddock Down dressed as a woman.

Sir Barnard Grenvile died at Tremeer in the company of his good friends the
Byrds on 16 June 1636. Ralph Byrd sent a messenger to Bevill with the news.
Bevill replied:

> 'I do with a much grieved heart receive your sad news, and shall endeavour myself to
> return you as good an answer as the distemper of my passion will permit, which, if it be
> imperfect I shall entreat you to impute it to the overflowing of my grief, which (as I hope
> for heaven) I vow doth exceed all ordinary bounds.
>
> My hope and desire was great that we might have lived longer comfortably together,
> and I have taken some comfort in his late loving expressions to me than ever I did in any-
> thing in my life. But I learned long ago to submit myself to the will of God, and though
> the familiar acquaintance I have had with misfortune and unhappy accidents had so
> prepared me against all chances as I did think myself prettily fortified against all
> accidents, yet I must confess this touches me near.
>
> But God's will be done to Whom, as I heartily prayed for his health and recovery, so
> I shall no less petition Him to send us a joyful meeting in another world. His body I shall
> desire (as I have already acquainted you) may rest here [at Stow] among his ancestors
> such as the war hath spared, where I hope myself, with others of his posterity, may lie
> by him if it so please God.
>
> It was reputed an honour in the Old World for those ancient saints of God which then
> lived to be gathered after deaths to their fathers. And I conceive it to be the last honour
> I can do unto my good father to gather him again to the poor remainder of his family.
>
> This is my last request unto you for him. I shall also beseech you to acquaint Mr.
> Davies that I desire him to use the means of his art for the preservation of his corpse
> till I may prepare myself with most decency to fetch it away.
>
> This is as much as the time with mine own sorrow will permit. Let my best service and
> my wife's be presented to good Mrs. B[yrd] with my unspeakable thanks for all your
> loving care and good respects to my dear father, both in his life and death; for which I
> beseech God to reward you all.'

Sir Barnard was buried at Kilkhampton 10 days later. The contents of his will can
be guessed at only from the following letter, written possibly to Sir James Bagg:

> 'It hath pleased God (to my great grief) to take my good father out of this world by a
> short and painful sickness . . . I expected no worldly goods from him and therein I am not
> deceived, for neither to myself nor any child he had, hath he given the value of a penny,
> which (for my own part) I am rather glad for than sorry, that my love may appear to him
> for his own and not for any worldly sake. And my mind hath ever despised all muddy and
> mercenary considerations. But in the loving and kind expressions he now at last made
> unto me, with the hearty bequeathing of his blessing and good wishes, I take more
> comfort than in all the wealth of the world.
>
> But leaving this subject (which I cannot touch without passion) I shall make bold to
> trouble you with a word or two in another business. It pleased my father when he found
> his disease and danger to grow upon him, to send hastily for me, and I posted to him all
> night. He made many requests unto me concerning several persons, which I granted all,

and at last, concerning myself, he told me he had one earnest request unto me which I durst not deny him. I answered him he should never speak to me in vain neither would I deny him anything. He then told me it was concerning his Regiment and Deputy Lieutenancy, that I would accept of it and execute it, which I had often before refused; but he hoped that now I would not deny the request of a dying father. He added for reason likewise that seeing those places had ever been in the hands of my ancestors ever since the first institution of them, and that the Regiment lies about my habitation, and in the heart of my estate, it were unfit for me to suffer a stranger to come in.

I confess I could not answer his reasons nor deny his request, and yet I remonstrated mine own unfitness with my resolution not to intermeddle with the affairs of the commonwealth, and the disproportion between my disposition and the course of the time, but nevertheless he persisted and I promised. In conformity whereunto I make bold to address myself unto you, beseeching you to acquaint my noble and ancient friend Mr. Oldisworth that if I may be thought worthy to succeed my father therein, I will thankfully accept it. But I will not write to him beforehand, because (though I will accept it, yet) I will not sue for it . . .

Your faithful friend and servant . . .'.

The Mr. Oldisworth to whom the indirect approach was directed, was secretary to the Earl of Pembroke, Lord Chamberlain. He had long been a friend as a letter written him by Bevill in January 1628 showed:

'In a season of so much infelicity when the sense of both public and private misfortunes hath almost broken my spirits, I have not found any other so great or reviving a consolation as this; that so noble a friend as yourself doth suffer me to live in your memory and think me worthy of a salutation from you.

I confess that my ambition (being strongly wrought on by the apprehension that you were turned courtier and I clown) did not soar [to] so high a pitch as to hope for such an honour.'

The foregoing had been written when Buckingham's failure off La Rochelle had led to great popular outcry and concern for the state of the nation. Bevill's political chief had been reluctantly released from prison, and canvassing was going on with a new Parliament due. Sir Richard Grenvile too was a friend of Oldisworth's, and letters were sent to Oldisworth for Richard to collect when in London.

This reluctant application to join the establishment as colonel of the local trained band and to become a deputy lieutenant of his county was another step away from the ranks of the opposition to monarchical rule. Bevill was now the head of his family, the owner of substantial property in Devon and Cornwall, and the father of 10 red-haired children. Joane, the most recent addition, had been born in September 1635.

Bevill also wrote to Sir William Wrey regretting that Sir Barnard's funeral could not be delayed sufficiently to enable Wrey to attend.

'I found after my coming to Stow that the negligence of the embalmer had been so great as I could not delay the interment a jot, but was forced to despatch the funeral the next morning with great haste and much inconvenience.'

Sir William was, of course, the man who had joined with Sir Barnard in that unsuccessful attempt to exclude Eliot and Coryton from being elected knights of the shire.

The great Mr. Oldisworth visited Cornwall, but stayed with William Coryton. In January 1632 Bevill had assured Eliot in the Tower that Coryton would not be re-elected having deserted the opposition cause. But Bevill now wrote to Coryton complaining that he had not been invited to meet Oldisworth saying with some lack of candour:

'I have no suit or ends upon him, but only a zealous desire to observe the laws of friendship . . . and therefore I cannot choose but (in the liberty of a friend) [to] tell you I take it a little unkindly, yet will remain your faithful kinsman and servant'.

He wrote to Oldisworth — possibly by the same messenger —

'I did solace myself with the hope of reviving our ancient friendship, which these distances and mists that have been between us (I feared) might a little obscure'.

Towards the end of 1636 or very early in 1637, Bevill and Grace had themselves painted. Their portraits used to hang at Wellesbourne and were attributed to Van Dyck. That painter had returned to England in the spring of 1632 having been abroad for the intervening 12 years. He had a house and studio at Blackfriars and the King provided him with a room at Eltham Palace and a pension of £200 per annum. The pension was never paid, and by 1637 was £1,000 in arrears; additionally, when as Court Painter Van Dyck sought payment for his many pictures of the King and Queen, Charles invariably reduced his bill by half. Not that his fees were excessive. Van Dyck charged £20 for a small picture, £100 for a full life-size portrait, and £200 for a large family group. He had been introduced to the King by Endymion Porter, and Porter may well have persuaded Bevill to patronise his protégé. Additionally there is an excellent portrait of Bevill identical to the above but showing only his head and shoulders at Prideaux Place, dated 1636, and a gift to his eldest daughter Elizabeth Prideaux no doubt.

Bevill wrote from Bideford on 29 March 1637 'Let me hear whether the picture came home safe and did escape the wet'. In the same letter he told Grace he had put three tunns of white and claret onboard a barque, with sack to follow, not wishing to overload the horse sent to collect the wine. One supposes the barque to have put in at Bude, although Hartland Quay was then a possible alternative.

Overlooking Falmouth Harbour or Carrick Roads on a promontory from which Pendennis Castle could be seen, lies the village of Trefusis. The squire, John Trefusis, was a fellow magistrate with Bevill. Bevill, when writing to Slanning the governor of the castle, added a postscript to his letter:

'You are, Sir, environed with many rare felicities, and I wish them centupled, but I only grudge you one which is neighbourhood to my ancient most dear and noble friend of Trefusis, because I cannot share it with you'.

As magistrates, these old friends became seized of issues which would not trouble magistrates today. Bevill wrote from Bodmin in April 1637, having been ordered by a missive from London to unravel a problem at Bodmin, that he had tried, with Trefusis, to reach a compromise between the mayor and burgesses of that town without success. He had perused their charters, examined the particulars of their petition and the articles exhibited therewith, and could not obtain agreement between the parties. The dispute seems to have been over who should be mayor of Bodmin.

In May, the Star Chamber, accepting Bevill's recommendation, ordered that Stapp should continue mayor but that he should do nothing without the consent of the majority of the council, and that Perryman, 'seeing himself not beloved by many of them, should voluntarily declare that he would no longer interfere' with the business of the town. One Hoblyn, who had not been elected by a majority should stand again.

Bevill may not have been a lawyer, but he had learnt a great deal about electoral law as events would prove.

He was much concerned with the education of his sons: 'I do much desire that you would not let the boys lose time from their schooling', he wrote. Richard was now 16, poor little Bevill had died in 1636 aged 10, but John was nine, Barnard six, George five, and little Roger four. Dennis was born in February 1637 and was too young yet to join his brothers at their schooling.

Richard was now of an age to leave home and attend a University or the Inns of Court. One would have expected him to follow his father into Exeter College where the distinguished Doctor Prideaux was still Rector after a quarter of a century. In his pursuit of uniformity within the Anglican Church, Archbishop Laud had reason to complain that not only had three Oxford divines attacked Laudian principles in defiance of the King's instructions to the contrary, but that Doctor Prideaux had failed to discipline the three errant preachers. It may have been this hint of nonconformity which made Exeter less attractive as a college to the new recruit to the establishment, Bevill Grenvile.

In the 13th century the Benedictine fathers had established a huddle of buildings far to the west of Oxford's wall and remote from the temptations of the city. The foundation was suppressed by Thomas Cromwell at the Reformation, but its ramshackle little row of houses became the 'mansions' of Gloucester Hall, now known as Worcester College; and at the time of which I write, the Principal of Gloucester Hall was a westcountryman called Wheare.

Mr. and Mrs. Wheare were well known to the Grenviles. The Grenviles regarded them as entirely trustworthy, but they were very conscious of the St Leger blood recurring in their son and heir, Bevill's letter is of considerable interest since it paints his own portrait as much as that of the undergraduate life of his times.

'It is my purpose to commit my eldest son wholly to your trust. I intend he shall depart hence the next week after Easter. I will say nothing to your better judgement by way of direction, but commit him wholly to your care, only beseeching you to conceive (as I do) that it is a greater trust than if I committed my whole estate into your hands.

I only will acquaint you with my desire, but the way and manner I leave absolutely to yourself.

I desire to have him a good scholar, and kept strictly to those courses that may conduce to that end. I have been as careful to have him well grounded as I can that he may be the fitter to be wrought upon.

I will allow him a competency to maintain him like a gentleman, but not to invite him to excess or prodigality.

I am not unwilling he should use decent and gentle recreations, as well for exercise and health as for gracefulness, as fencing, dancing, etc., but I would have them used as recreations, and not hindrances to his study '.

A few days later the unfortunate Mr. Wheare was the recipient of further instructions fron Cornwall.

I have at length sent you my son, humbly beseeching you to go on with the work I have begun in making him a scholar. Let no indulgence or connivance hinder it. I am serious in this purpose, so far as I shall think myself injured by you (whom I trust above all the world, and with more than all the world else is to me) if you fail of your endeavours and he for his part loses all the interest of a child in me.

It is a strong vow I have made. I am unalterable in it.

I do with grief find my own defects, and feel an infinite maim by the want of letters. I am desirous therefore to have it supplied in him.

He is (unless I am abused by those I trust) conveniently prepared for a country scholar. I have been strict in bringing him to it. I kept him longer to school than most of my friends were willing, because I would take off all objection that a tutor might make, now at his coming up, so as if I fail in my expectation, the fault must be so great either in his tutor or himself, as it will be inexcusable, and for the boy he is irrecoverably lost, and must never see my face again.

It is but the spending of three years that I desire, not for my own good but his, and for it I will be but his drudge in the meantime, and give him all that I have in end.

I confess I have been severe to him, but it hath been only to this end, and I saw his nature needed it, or he would not have gone the way I wished. I am willing to have the same course continued, and yet not his spirits suppressed or killed.

I debar him not from gentle recreations or fit exercise. I know these necessary. But I would not have him make studies of them. Let him use them as whetstones to increase an appetite to his studies, and so he shall find benefit, and I comfort.

But I beseech you withdraw him (as much as you can) from the infection of that general contagion which hath spread itself not only over the University but the whole Kingdom, and which I can with sad experience say was the ruin of divers hopeful gents there in my time. You may guess what I aim at. I will not name.

There was a nation of ancient seniors (and I doubt not but there is a succession of them unto these days) who, having gotten a convenient stock of learning in their youth to make them good company, did employ their parts to nothing but the increase of good fellowship, and changed from the better study to the worse. They were my destruction and many others in my time.

I am willing to prevent a mischief, and yet I am far from being stoical or rigidly severe. I debar no fit or sober liberty only I would prevent the abuse, and have him study this short space that he may thereby know how to govern him[self] well and to use pleasures aright; and then he shall do what he will. My zeal to a good work, and my confidence in your worth, makes me boldly tedious; but I hope you will pardon it, knowing whence it springs.

He hath some imperfection in speech and a body nothing strong. I know that industry may somewhat amend both. I desire that he should attain to a fluent Latin tongue and not lose his Greek. I will say no more, and when I have all said, I commit the whole work to your trust and better judgement.

I will allow him £80 a year, whereof I would have him to bestow £10 a year upon his servant, and to be at no further charge with him. The other £70 I desire you would take into your custody, and order in such sort as it may serve his turn to live in as good quality as he can with it, but by no means to exceed that proportion, for more he cannot have.

And I beseech you to direct his habit and garments in such sort as you think fit. I have now sent with him £50 which I would have thus disposed: £5 of it I have given him to put in his purse, £10 I would have bestowed in a fair piece of plate for your Hall. The rest all (except what must defray their expenses[coming] up) I have entrusted Mr. Sharsell to deliver unto you, and I beseech you order it as you think best for him, and so the rest of his exhibition which I will send quarterly unto you; for he will not yet be fit to govern money.

In a postscript Bevill added:

'I expect that the £70 should defray his diet, his chamber's rent, his clothes, his tutor, and all other charges whatsoever. For more he cannot have.'

On 30 April 1638 Bevill wrote his first letter to his son Dick at Gloucester Hall. It is only too clear how great a disappointment the boy had been to his father. 'I have been so affectionately large in my discourse unto you at your departure, as I shall say little . . .' but then continues to comment on 'some passages at Exeter' where the boy had no doubt stayed with his grandmother Lady Smith at Madiford.

'I know no need you had to make alteration in your clothes there, which I am sure well enough fitted before your departure. Neither needed you to bestow such a price in a new saddle, for that which you had was not old nor much worn, but sufficiently able to have done service, and of stuff and trimming of the richest sort. Besides, in Oxford you are not to make use of saddles.

I say this to let you see your vanity and weakness, which I wish you to reform. Be wise and conform yourself to the quality of my enfeebled fortune. I do (to show my affection) strain myself beyond my power in the proportion I have allotted to you. You must not exceed it. If you do, you are undone.

Bevill advises him that his three years at Oxford are not for Dick's pleasure but for his profit; warns him that the Forest of the World contains many wild beasts lying in wait to devour youths by depraving their manners. That the sight of other students wasting their time should not be allowed to divert him from his studies. That a general in the war can err but once when all is lost, and that he too has one chance left and only one chance. That if he fails to make good use of his time at Oxford it will be the end of him. 'I am herein serious and unalterable and God is witness to my vow'. But 'if you carefully apply yourself to follow my advice you shall find me ever your very loving father'.

Three other letters followed. That Dick did not destroy them is evidence that if the flesh is weak, the spirit was at least willing. His father wrote:

'Pray begin in time to fall upon some considerations of providence and thrift. It will be necessary after such wasteful predecessors as we have succeeded. And if you neglect it, the poor remainder of the fortune which is left for us will hold but a little while . . . I am told you take too much time in pleasures. If it be so you are a lost man. You have better things to fix upon. I require you to avoid those nocent things which will be hindrances unto the good work which I have designed you for . . .'.

Letter number three warned him not to

'swerve from those profitable rules that I have prescribed unto you. Do not think you can delude me with fair shows unless your heart be right. Truth will not long be hid, nor can my jealous eye be blinded which is watchful over your welfare as my heart is wholly intentive upon the pious work of establishing you in the perfection of learning and good manners'.

Bevill complains about Dick's poor hand when writing a letter, and advises him as to form:

> 'I wish you would contract your sentences into a little shorter form. Methinks the short sentences (if they express the full sense) are ever the most elegant . . . Shun drinking houses and drunken companions are poison. If you do not you are utterly lost in my opinion for ever, and be careful to keep within the compass of your exhibition, for more you cannot have.'

The last in the series started on an optimistic note: 'I do believe you have bestowed your time better since I parted from you heretofore' and continues to advise less attention to Virgil, Homer or other historians, and to concentrate first on Logic and Philosophy.

Dick's mother too added her pen to the barrage of advice: 'If you serve God as you ought, and follow your father's precepts, you cannot do amiss' and warns him that he cannot hope to deceive his father should he be tempted to stray.

Poor Dick. Events were to prove him neither the great scholar his father wished him to be, nor the successor of a martial race. His studies were to be interrupted by the very selfsame dangers his father had foreseen but dared not name. The invasion of Lutheran thought in opposition to the high Anglican tenets of Archbishop Laud.

Chapter Eight

THE FIRST BISHOPS' WAR

THE YEARS 1633 to 1639 saw religious discord in both England and Scotland. Lutheran ideas had been rapturously received on both sides of the border. In Scotland the boy King James VI had been compelled to declare Calvinist worship the national religion in 1580. But he managed to persuade succeeding Assemblies of the Kirk to accept the return of episcopacy, confirmation by bishops, and the taking of the communion kneeling. These concessions had been obtained partly by bribery, and partly by leaving those noblemen who had seized church property in possession of their spoils.

King Charles was, as usual, experiencing great difficulty in raising money without the authority of Parliament. He was obliged to lend a spurious legality to his exactions by obtaining verdicts favourable to his views of his divine powers from both bench and pulpit.

William Laud, the son of a Reading tradesman and described as a 'little, low, red-faced man', irritable and opinionated, served admirably in this context. He was called in when Bishop of Bath and Wells to help the King over the Sibthorne affair. Doctor Sibthorne wrote a treatise extolling the supra-legal position of Kings and asserting their right to tax their subjects at will. The Archbishop of Canterbury, George Abbott, was told to publish the book under his seal of approval, and refused to do so. The Archbishop was rusticated to Kent and his powers exercised by a Commission of amenable bishops, one being Bath and Wells.

Laud was promoted to the see of London in July 1628 and, after Buckingham's murder, he became an intimate friend of the King's. When poor George Abbot died in 1633, Laud, Chancellor of Oxford University and the man selected to christen the young Prince Charles, caused no surprise when he was appointed Archbishop of Canterbury.

Laud was a high churchman who saw the Anglican doctrine as the true Catholic faith, deploring the errors of Rome, but abominating the Germanic heresies giving rise to Puritanism. His ideal was a church, rigidly and efficiently organized, with the whole population gathered together in one docile flock. This vision matched the King's.

Laud advised reforming the church in Scotland as early as October 1633 when orders issued to conduct services in the Chapel Royal at Holyrood using a Laudian form of service. Charles I never visited Scotland until the ninth year of his reign (1634) when he went through a Coronation Ceremony using Laudian ritual and attempted to give the Scottish Archbishop precedence over the Lord Chancellor. This caused great offence among the Scottish nobility, as did the appointment of Bishops to vacant places on the Privy Council. The great Lords of Scotland became fearful that if Bishops held sway, their lands would be in jeopardy, and the Ministry of the Kirk opposed to Bishops and Ritual were actively supported by Noblemen, most of whom had no particular views on religion at all.

By September 1634 the King had signed Laud's new prayer-book for Scotland, containing liturgy and canons to be imposed on the Scots by regal and episcopal authority, without the consent of the Scottish Parliament, or of the General Assembly of the Kirk. No one had the courage to issue it. Meanwhile the King, with his usual lack of tact, sent to his Scottish bishops word that they should celebrate those saints calendared in England, and only observe the feasts of such Scottish saints as boasted royal blood. The Bishops, with their replica of the Court of High Commission in England, showed themselves willing to conform in all things.

In 1637 three Puritans, William Prynne, Henry Burton and John Bastwicke, for their published attacks on the bishops of England, were sentenced to have their ears cut off in the pillory and imprisonment for life. Prynne had been sentenced to lose his ears once before, but the executioner had left enough for the sentence to be repeated. These savage sentences of the Star Chamber raised fears in Scotland that a similar court of law might be added to the High Commission already established there. No National Assembly had been called in that country since 1618.

The new prayer book still awaited distribution. It was prefaced by a royal command directed to all ministers in Scotland that they each had to purchase two copies and use them in their kirks or suffer outlawry. The Scottish Privy Council advised delay, but the King would not allow procrastination beyond 23 July 1637. But he reduced the number of places into which the prayer book had to be introduced to those churches in and around Edinburgh.

No sooner had the Dean of St Giles' in Edinburgh opened the new prayer book than the poorer members of the congregation, and particularly the women, started clapping and shouting against its use. The Bishop went to the pulpit to preach, thinking he would pacify the tumult, and within a short time someone threw a stool at his head.

The provost and bailiffs eventually restored order by ejecting the noisy members of the congregation and securing the doors against them, so that the Dean was able to continue with the service notwithstanding the uproar outside, the rapping on the doors, and the throwing of stones through the windows. There were shouts of 'A pape! a pape! Antichrist! Pull him down!'

On his way home the bishop was knocked off his feet and might have been trodden to death had rescue not been at hand. This demonstration was repeated everywhere that the new prayer book was aired. The nobles of Scotland had combined with the ministry and the Calvinist majority of the citizens to demonstrate their hatred of their King's 'wind of change'. It was the nobles who now formed the 'Tables' and led the revolt. The 'Tables' were committees set up by

Lord Balmerino and others to receive complaints and information from the people and to decide things accordingly. These soviets were decreed illegal in February 1639, but by then they were well established and no one paid any attention to their illegality.

The 'Tables' decided to publish a Solemn Covenant between the people of Scotland and the Almighty to defend their reformed religion to their death. On 1 March St Giles was thronged with covenanters of all classes and from all over Scotland. They wept and shouted aloud in their exultation and religious dedication, and on their dispersal spread their enthusiasm throughout the land. By the end of April the Catholic minority were threatened with expropriation, if nothing worse, and almost every protestant had signed the Covenant.

For 10 years England had been at peace, the King not having had the money to fight a war in any event. Soldiers from both England and Scotland had gone to Germany to fight Catholicism, some with official approval, and more without. The Anglican clergy were fully alive to the risk of Calvinist infection, and the Bishop of London thought it necessary to issue directions with regard to whom might be appointed chaplains of English regiments serving on the Continent. One Scot, Alexander Leslie, had risen to be a Marshal of the Queen of Sweden's army in Germany. Returning for a visit to his native land he passed through London on his way north and apprised of the position in his homeland, organized an Army of Covenanters, before returning with copies of the Covenant for signature by Scottish mercenaries in Germany. Not every Briton in Germany was a Covenanter, for though many Scots returned to defend their faith, there were others, such as Sir Richard Grenvile and his lieutenant George Monck who were only too happy when a change in policy enabled such exiles to return home, the Star Chamber sentences against them having been set aside.

Gradually the King came to admit that the Scottish trouble was likely to become dangerously associated with the widespread Puritan opposition in England. Both King and Archbishop Laud believed that severity was needed. But first it was necessary to keep the Scots in play while means for their retribution were gathered.

The King decided to send a Commissioner to Scotland to that end and against Laud's advice, selected the Marquess of Hamilton. Hamilton had been Charles's page and was now a pompous ponderous man in his early thirties. He had tried to fight for the Protestants in Germany, but had never achieved the leading of his men into battle. He held a high opinion of his own martial prowess, nevertheless.

A National Assembly was ordered to convene at Glasgow in November 1638. Hamilton sent on ahead to his supporters to muster on Clydeside to overawe the Covenanters. They were prevented from doing so. The Scottish Council proved sulky and un-cooperative, being either in sympathy with or in fear of the Covenanters; at Hamilton's suggestion the King had offered to re-issue his father's Confession of Faith of 1580 in order to gain time. 'Flatter them with what hopes you please', wrote the King to Hamilton. 'Till I be ready to suppress them. I will rather die than yield to these impertinent and damnable demands'.

The stratagem of re-issuing the Confession of Faith took the Covenanters aback at first, but the nobles side-stepped the trap and soon had their mobs of supporters crying, 'Away with any Covenant but our own!' After a week of un-fruitful effort in the Glasgow Assembly, Hamilton ordered its dissolution in the King's name, and left the scene. The Assembly having gathered refused to disperse and continued to sit illegally. In Hamilton's absence they agreed to do away with bishops, vestments, and ritual. There emerged as leader in everything but name of the Covenanters, the Earl of Argyll, one Archibald Campbell, a devious and complex personality, indeed.

By Christmas 1638 all prospect of peace had vanished. The proceedings in the Glasgow Assembly after Hamilton left were equivalent to a declaration of rebel-lion. On his return to England, Hamilton sent word to the King's Council in Scotland that His Majesty would be at York at Easter, when he would make his wishes for Scotland known.

The peerage of England were now called upon to perform their antique duties of raising such retinues as were appropriate to their ranks and lead them north, or compound their inability to do so with cash payments into the Exchequer. A great number sought to excuse themselves on account of their age, poverty, or both.

Lords Lieutenant and their Deputies were ordered to raise their trained bands and muster at York. There was little love of Puritanism in Cornwall, but as one Cornishman wrote: 'Bishops put out by a general consent cannot be set up again without being guarded like castles'. When 13 guns and 100 men were shipped round from Pendennis Castle to Cumberland, there were complaints that Cornwall was being left without defences against pirates. As a Deputy Lieutenant, Bevill and his fellow Deputies met with some opposition when they set their constables to press the 1,600 men required of them for service against the Scots, and in collecting the necessary 'coat and conduct' money required for each pressed man. There were complaints that bereft of men the Cornish tin mines would flood and harvests be left to rot.

Sir John Trelawney saw no reason why Bevill should himself leave Cornwall to fight the Scots, and urged him not to risk the happiness of Grace and their children.

He replied,

'Most honoured Sir: I have in many kinds had trial of your nobleness, but in none more than in this singular expression of your kind care and love. I give you also, and your excel-lent Lady humble thanks for your respect unto my poor woman, who hath been long a faithful and much obliged servant of your Lady's; but, Sir, for my journey — it is fixed.

I cannot contain myself within my doors when the King of England's standard waves in the field upon so just [an] occasion, the cause being such as must make all those that die in it little inferior to martyrs. And for mine own part I desire to acquire an honest name or an honourable grave. I never loved my life or ease so much as to shun such an occasion, which, if I should, I were unworthy of the profession I have held, or to succeed those ancestors of mine who have so many of them in several ages sacrificed their lives for their country.

Sir, the barbarous and implacable enemy (notwithstanding His Majesty's gracious proceeding with them) do continue their insolences and rebellion in the highest degree, and are united in a body of great strength, so as you must expect if they be not prevented and mastered near their own homes, they will be troublesome guests in yours and in the remotest parts ere long.

I am not without consideration (as you lovingly advise) of my wife and family, and as for her, I must acknowledge she hath ever drawn so evenly in her yoke with me as she hath never pressed before or hung back and behind me, nor ever opposed or resisted my will. And yet truly I have not in this or anything else endeavoured to walk in the way of power with her, but of reason. And though her love will submit to either, yet truly my respect will not suffer me to urge her with power unless I can convince by reason. So much for that, whereof I am willing to be accountable unto so good a friend.'

Bevill took the precaution of making his will. It was dated 8 April 1639. The King was already at York, having set off with Endymion Porter and the rest of his court on 27 March. His will shows Bevill's deep religious convictions:

'First I commend my soul into the hands of Almighty God, my Maker and Redeemer, in full assurance that all my sins are washed away by the precious blood of Jesus Christ our Saviour, Who is the Lamb of God, that taketh away the sins of the world, and that at the last day I shall be presented to him without spot, and received into His Kingdom of glory, there to live evermore.'

A confident assertion indeed!

His attitude towards Grace is made equally clear:

'And forasmuch as Grace my wife hath always been a most loving and virtuous wife unto me, her deserts far exceed any requital which my fortune can afford.'

He left her a life interest in Stow and all its contents.

Of the surviving children, Richard his heir was to have £100 per annum until all debts and annuities had been paid, John, Barnard, George, and Denys £20 a year until they attained the age of 17, and thereafter £50 per annum. Poor little Roger had died. As for the daughters, his eldest, Elizabeth was to have £1,500, and the remainder, Bridget, Joane, and Mary £1,000 each on attaining the age of 20, until which time 40 marks per annum each (£26.66). Grace, who was very much alive, was omitted. She could hardly have so disgraced herself by the age of 12 to merit disinheritance, nor was she under any apparent disability, since she married in 1644 and had issue. It may be that her mother intended to do something for her in her will, but in the outcome she only obtained a 'jewel or picture' as did her sister Elizabeth.

Bevill only mentions interests in the manors of Bideford, Kilkhampton, Wydmouth, Woodford and North Leigh: the bartons of Stow, Dinsmouth, and Wolfston; lands in Stratton, Cleve, and Colworthy, and three livings.

The trustees of his Will with one exception came from Devon. That exception was cousin John Arundell of Trerice. The rest were Sir John Acland of Columbjohn (now Killerton by Exeter), Sir Arthur Bassett of Heanton-Punchardon (a farmhouse near Braunton), Antony Dennis of Orlegh, Richard Prideaux of Thuckborough, and William Morice of Churston.

Having ordered his affairs, Bevill set off for Oxford with servants and retinue armed and mounted at his personal expense. Richard his eldest son had by now spent exactly one year as an undergraduate at Gloucester Hall, and was just 18 years of age. It was unthinkable that a Grenvile should lead his men into

battle without any adult son to squire him. Poor Richard, with weakly body
and impediment of speech was to be subjected to the ultimate proof of manhood,
the test of battle.

Others, too, were on the move. Richard his brother had returned to England
and held a commission in the artillery. Nephew George Monck was there as well;
both, one supposes, being that rarity in the King's army, soldiers serving at the
King's expense. Also present at York were Endymion Porter in close attendance
on His Majesty, and Sir Edmund Verney the King's Knight Marshal and Gentleman of the Privy Chamber in Ordinary who received a summons to present
himself there on 1 April as a 'Cuirassier in russet arms with gilded studs or nails
and befittingly horsed'. He had felt obliged to comply, and set off from Claydon
in Oxfordshire with the greatest reluctance, not only sick in body and mind, but
with a son strongly in favour of the Covenanters.

The gentlemen of the King's army were having the greatest difficulty in
equipping themselves. There was a general shortage of weapons and armour.
Endymion wrote from Durham as late as 1 May:

> 'I thank you for remembering my gauntlets — and send them to me with the pistols,
> if Mr. Courten have as yet procured them . . . these pernicious rebels are very insolent,
> but the English are not afeared of them'.

Even at Berwick, Sir Edmund Verney had not managed to kit himself up
completely. He wrote thence:

> 'I believe there is never a long gauntlet sent: let Hill [the armourer] make one with
> all speed he can possibly: for it will kill a man to serve in a whole cuirass. I am resolved
> to use nothing but back, breast and gauntlet. If I had a pot for the head that were pistol
> proof it may be I would use it, if it were light'.

A day or two later he wrote:

> 'I have received all the arms that you have sent. Pray haste away my pot, and take care
> it be wide enough, for this is so much too little that nobody but a madman could have
> been so mad as to mistake so grossly. This will come upon no part of my head it is so very
> little'.

Bevill had had himself painted in cuirass and with a sword in 1636 — so one hopes
he and his son were better prepared for war than the others. The Earl Marshal had
advised arming the men who lived along the border with Scotland with bows and
arrows, and an expert had been sent up to the northern marches to instruct men in
their use. Swords had been ordered from Holland, but were of indifferent workman-
ship, and some of the belts were described as being made of brown paper.

The King had appointed his commanders back in January. The Marquess of
Hamilton was given command of the fleet to the fury of Northumberland, the
Lord High Admiral. Hamilton had no experience of war at sea or on land, but one
supposes the King thought a Scot more likely to achieve an unopposed landing in
the royal cause. In the outcome Hamilton was unable to land even his sick or send
parties ashore for water.

The commander-in-chief of what was essentially a feudal array rather than an
army was Lord Arundell, hereditary Earl Marshal, with Lord Essex, an experienced

soldier, second in command, but on the Queen's insistence the cavalry were put under the separate command of that notoriously frivolous, haughty and incompetent Henry Rich, Earl of Holland. It was a recipe for military disaster.

Riding northwards from Oxford, Bevill and his son were venturing farther north than either had travelled before. How many troopers rode with them in the white and blue Grenvile livery can only be guessed at. All one knows is that Bevill had borrowed from one Millard and no doubt from others for ready cash with which to finance the venture, and that Bevill was one of very few such gentlemen to be rewarded by the King for his service. His must have been a sizeable contingent, and it came under the command of the Lord Chamberlain, Pembroke.

Both Bevill and Dick fell ill at York, but Dick was in some way held to be to blame for his indisposition. Both seem to have recovered in time to march with the King's army when it set off for the north on 29 April. The King himself slept at Raby Castle, which belonged to the Treasurer of his Household, Sir Henry Vane, and also at Durham, before ending up at Newcastle. From Newcastle survives a letter containing all the latest news known to Bevill which was sent with a covering letter to his wife and other relations in Cornwall. It was copied by someone not specified, presumably not by Dick whose handwriting was little admired by his father. Antony Payne, Bevill's henchman, was literate, and seems the most likely person to have been entrusted with the task.

The surviving letter was addressed to William Morice, and in part says:

'I have made a collection of the truest news that is here stirring among us, and have sent you a copy of it, which though it be not very noteworthy, yet because it carries the badge of truth with it, and may contradict the false rumours that run about the country, I present it to you, and for expedition (in the copy) I am forced to use the help of another hand.

. . . for my part I go with joy and comfort to venture a life in as good a cause, and with as good company, as ever Englishmen did: and I do take God to witness, if I were to choose a death, it should be no other but this. But I cannot be larger at this time. Expect to hear from me again after some memorable action, if I survive it . . .

My last shook hands with you at York, and gave you an account of such collections as I could gather there; in which course I shall proceed rather to correct the various and uncertain reports which you daily meet in the country, than to give you any notable news from hence, where hitherto nothing more than ordinary is to be observed.

The ninth day after my arrival at York, the King removed with the regiment of his household in two days to Durham, the rest of the troop to Newcastle in Northumberland, being twelve miles farther, and the week following his Majesty removed thither also, where we are all yet.

The town full with as many as it can hold, the rest billetted in the country about.

I cannot yet give you a certain list of the army, for besides the regiments already here, divers others are sent for; and no doubt but there will be need of them, for our army is not yet very strong, not such as will become the Majesty of so great a Monarch to march with into a country, where he is sure to meet blows.

It hath been thought impossible that the Scots could be so impious as to lift their hands against him: but it is now taken for granted that nothing but force can reduce them to obedience; for they are guilty of this aggravation to their offences. The King sent a proclamation lately into Scotland to pardon all offences past if they would yet submit, but they have slighted it, and not a man comes in, but rather are confirmed in their insolence by his graciousness, and continually some fall off from the King to them, as of late some great ones near his person.

When news reached the King that the Marquis of Huntly had been persuaded to sign a modified form of the Covenant he was astounded. The great strategy on which he relied was the appearance off Aberdeen of Hamilton with his fleet and five thousand muskets where a link-up was to be made with Huntly and his three thousand Gordons. Leslie would then have a powerful force at his rear.

Unfortunately for the plan, the Earl of Montrose with his Covenanters entered Aberdeen before Hamilton arrived off that city, and Huntly had orders to do nothing until Hamilton arrived. Huntly was then persuaded to sign a modified form of Covenant, notwithstanding his being head of the catholic clan Gordon, and then, relying perhaps on that document, he entered Aberdeen with his two sons and was immediately taken prisoner. His eldest son, Lord Aboyne, by breaking his parole, managed to reach Newcastle with a report of proceedings for the King. The King varied Hamilton's orders to a blockade of Leith and expressed himself aghast at Huntly signing such a thing.

Not everyone agreed, and some demurred at the condemnation of Huntly. The King thereupon called for each nobleman in his company to take a new oath of loyalty and obedience in the coming struggle. Both Lord Saye and Lord Brooke refused to do so, and were placed under arrest. Upon Lord Saye's release five days later he took himself off with all his retainers, pointing out that they were his personal retainers and not soldiers of the King. It underlined the essential weakness of a feudal array. It was clearly to the defection of Lords Saye and Brooke that Bevill referred.

Bevill's news-sheet continues:

> 'The Marquis of Hamilton was sent a good fleet of the King's ships and some five thousand land soldiers to lie about the coast of Scotland, and being lately desirous to refresh some of his sick men on the shore, he was forbidden by them, and had the cannon threatened to him if he did attempt to land; so he must endure the sea 'til we meet.
>
> Our army is governed by two several and distinct policies, having divers generals without being subject each to [the other]. My Lord of Arundell is generalissimo, and commands the greater part of the army. But the King's household, with all his servants both in ordinary and extraordinary, are of a body apart and designed for the guard of the King's person, which are all under my Lord Chamberlain's command, who is our absolute general without subjection to any but His Majesty himself, and we consist of divers troops of horse, but the most glorious in the world, whether we consider the quality of the persons, or the bravery of arms, apparel, horses, and furniture.
>
> There is also a regiment of foot also appointed for the guard of the King's person, in which Sir Nicholas Slanning hath a company, and is sergeant major of the regiment.

Philip Herbert, Earl of Pembroke, was then aged fifty-four. Besides being Lord Chamberlain he was a Privy Councillor and a man who concealed his natural craftiness under a mask of buffoonery; he was a bad-tempered, overbearing man who boasted of being illiterate. He retained the King's favour partly because of the good hunting he could offer and partly because his eccentricities amused the King. Slanning was of course a son-in-law of the bottomless Bagg. Bevill continued:

'The Marquis of Huntly, who was reported at York to be absolutely revolted, is said not to be so now. But though he gave way to some things, yet he opposed them in others, and is imprisoned by the Covenantors. Thus you see we have uncertain reports here as well as you in the country.

We are not certain of our abode here in this place but as soon as things can be made ready we shall march to Berwick, where we are threatened with bad entertainment in a very barren country. And the last news is that Leslie is marching with a goodly army to welcome us upon the frontiers as soon as we shall appear there, and that they have three armies in readiness consisting of three score thousand men in all. Thus you see I am forced to pick up petty matters for want of better news, which, when it happens, you shall have your share of'.

On 16 May Doctor Denton wrote to Ralph Verney from Newcastle with the news that:

'The King goeth towards Berwick — and intends to entrench himself within five or six miles of it, but on this side of the Tweed. I hope that the King doth not intend to fight this summer, but thinks, by drawing his forces so near to them to tempt them to bring out their forces in a body, and by that means to exhaust them. But I fear he will be cozened, for I believe them to be as cunning as they be wicked'.

A day or so later Sir Edmund wrote

'We have had two of the coldest days here that ever I felt, and I fear if it continues it will kill our men that must lodge upon the ground without anything over them ... tomorrow the King removes'.

The army reached Berwick on the 28th, the King on 30 May, when the royal party went under canvas. The following day Lord Holland led two thousand horse to Duns, some 15 miles to the west and into Scotland. Rumour had it that the Scots had six thousand men quartered there. None could be found save towns-folk, who greeted the soldiers with loyal shouts of 'God bless the King!' and with tankards of good scottish ale.

On 2 June news reached Arundell that some 1,500 Scottish soldiers were at Kelsey, only six miles from the King's camp. The following day Lord Holland set out into Scotland again. Accounts differ as to his force; cavalry being described as one or two thousand and foot soldiers two or three thousand. The English army, discounting the garrisons of Berwick and Carlisle and the five thousand foot under Hamilton, amounted to 19,614 foot and horse 3,260. Holland's expedition was little more than a reconnaissance in strength. I think it unlikely that Lord Pembroke's household regiments took part in it.

The very cold weather of May had given way to hot and sultry June: Holland's foot shewed little enthusiasm to hurry forward in their invasion of Scotland, for which few if any had much inclination; and the cavalry insensibly drew ahead. Soon three miles separated the horse from the infantry; the cavalry gaily advancing without picquets to scout out the land ahead, and the whole body of horse suddenly came face to face with a small body of 150 mounted Scotsmen.

Lord Holland sent a trumpeter to bid the Scots retreat; but the trumpeter returned with advice to be gone. Of a sudden four thousand foot appeared on either flank from behind hedges and little hills. Some put the number as high as ten thousand! With no foot at hand and heavily outnumbered, Lord Holland had little option but to accept the advice he had been given. The English retreated to their camp with their tails between their legs.

On 5 June the Scots advanced to within sight of the King himself. Great was the consternation of the English. 'Have not I good intelligence', said King Charles, 'that the rebel army can encamp within sight of mine, and I not have a word of it!' Leslie's army was well armed, adequately provisioned, officered by men who had seen service in Germany,, and above all, consisted of men determined to fight for their brand of religion.

The Earl Marshal Arundell was sent for. He blamed the Scoutmaster, who being a catholic, was naturally suspect. It was fortunate that the Scots were no more eager to invade England than the English were to invade Scotland. The English soldiery were unimpressed by their commanders after so many fiascos, and their morale was low; they had little interest in forcing bishops upon the alien Scots, and above all, their biscuits were mouldy and it was difficult to find enough to drink. As Verney wrote:

> 'The truth is we are betrayed in all our intelligence, and the King is still made believe in a party that will come to him [from Scotland], but I am confident he is mightily abused in it, for they are a people strangely united.'

If Bevill reported all these proceedings they have not survived; in truth they would have made sorry reading after such high hopes of knight errantry and glorious enterprise. While the Grenvile brothers and young Richard followed their martial bent at Berwick, poor Grace in Cornwall was only too aware that soldiers needed money to survive and fight, and with a penniless King it fell on her to raise the necessary funds.

She wrote from Stow on 30 May:

> 'O my dearest, I have received yours dated 15th May from Newcastle, bringing me the glad tidings of your recovery, before I heard of your sickness, which I thank God for, and shall long to hear the same of Dick, whose sickness being so foolishly gotten I fear may prove dangerous, and must confess till I hear again shall remain in much doubt. I am both sorry and ashamed he should err so much to his own prejudice having had so many warnings, but I shall and do beseech God to restore him and bless him with judgement and grace to serve God truly and obey your precepts.
>
> I must beseech you, though at this distance, that you will pardon ordinary errors in him, hoping that by degrees they will be reformed, though not so instantly as our desires are.
>
> Since I wrote last, Mr. Prickman was here, who showed me a writ and told me it was to be delivered the Sheriff to extend both your lands and goods for Mrs. Herewyn's money, which he says is £500, that is behind of the statute.'

Sir Barnard had given Jacob Herewyn a bond of record, that is to say a deed under his hand and seal authenticated by the Sovereign's seal. Such a bond enabled a creditor upon any payment becoming overdue under the bond to obtain a so-called 'pocket-judgement', one which required no proof of the facts in any court of law, and to require the Sheriff to distrain on the debtor's lands or goods to satisfy the debt. Bevill had failed to repay the £1,700 due.

Grace's letter continues:

'I entreated him to consider how impossible anything was to be done to give them satisfaction now in your absence, desiring they would forbear any extremity of law, and [that] I well knew you would perform justly on your side.

Whereupon he promised me that there should be nothing done in it for the present, or by him at all in your absence, and that he would use his best endeavours to pacify Mrs. Herewyn, and her agents, though he pretends they are already jealous of him on your behalf, and that now his forbearance would make them much to differ in a very unkind way.

He says he cannot undertake for Mrs. Herewyn though he will do his best, and he knows it will be for some short space that she will forbear, and will then employ some stranger that will bear no respect unto you.

He hears that you have put away some part of Stratton Manor, and he wishes and believes she would willingly take land on indifferent terms, but withall, he says, he believes you are willing to keep your statute afoot for other reasons, but certain he is that something must be done, for it will not be long foreborne.

He wishes the statute might be laid on Killigarth and that some friend of yours, paying Mrs. Herewyn her money, might have the statute assigned him, and believes you, by such a way, may redeem Killigarth for the same price you sold it. He hath written to the effect and desires to know your mind at full.

And he also tells me of Millard's debt, which is likewise in his hand against you. £600 at least, he says it is.

For Christ's sake duly consider what is to be done, and both write to him about these several particulars and also direct me what is to be done. If I should be vexed with these law's extremities God knows they are businesses as far beyond my capacity, as power to compose. And though now to my infinite sorrow and misfortune we are so divided, yet consider my position with pity I beseech you, for I labour under an insupportable burden of cares and fears. Were not God's mercies great unto me in the midst of my affliction, for the cares, though they are many I value not, but the hazardous way you are in is my daily tormentor.

I had almost forgot to tell you that I paid Mr. Prickman £20 — due to him from you as appears by a bill under your hand, which I have taken up, though I was so much out of money then as I was fain to borrow it. Yet I would not refuse to do it, doubting a greater shrewd turn if he were put off. But he makes as large protestations now as ever of his great respects and service to you, and I hope it doth not displease you that I paid him.'

It seems to have taken about twelve days for a letter to travel from Berwick to Stow and Bevill's news-letter was enough to make any wife nervous for her husband's safety.

Up in Northumberland the King found himself in an unenviable position. Arundell having urged him on to punish the rebels seems to have been alone in wishing to invade Scotland. Both Laud and Wentworth urged him to be cautious. Save for a few hot-heads (among whom Bevill must be numbered) the vast majority of the King's army had gathered most reluctantly to do his bidding. His generals had proved themselves incompetent and so touchy about precedence that the Earls of Holland and Newcastle had challenged each other to a duel. Across the Tweed lay a far better organized and much more resolute army which might, at any moment, cross into England and put him to flight.

It must have been a considerable relief when Leslie sent a trumpeter to the King's camp to ask that commissioners be appointed to meet the leaders of the Covenantors in order that misunderstandings might be resolved and the peace preserved. On 18 June the King signed the treaty of Berwick in which both sides agreed to disband their forces, the Scots to return those forts and castles they had occupied in Scotland, the King to hold a Parliament and an Assembly of the Kirk in Edinburgh in August. Had the King kept his word, that would have been the end of the matter, but in the event, this first Bishop's War was followed by another.

Meanwhile, those gentlemen who had mortgaged their estates to show their loyalty to the King, had to be rewarded in some way which would be of no expense to the King.

Bevill wrote to Grace on 25 June with the news that he would soon be travelling southwards and looking forward to seeing

> 'Lincolnshire and Cambridgeshire as I return, where I have not been [before as] I came upwards through the middle of England. I have this morning sent Dick away to Oxford in the conduct of my brother and some servants.
>
> The King hath been gracious to me both in words and actions, yet one thing I wish had been forborne, but it cannot now be helped. I see it was a plot between my Lord General [Arundell] and my Lord Chamberlain [Pembroke] before I thought on it. As I was on Saturday last in the privy chamber among divers others, upon a sudden my Lord General (being within in a inner room with the King) came to the door and called for me by name. I went to him and he took me by the hand before all that were present, and led me in where the King was, and he, after gracious words, upon a sudden drew my Lord General's sword and gave me a dubbing. I value all his favours very preciously, otherwise I should have wished this forborne, but it cannot now be helped. My Lord Chamberlain hath made me promise to spend a week or two with him at his residence of Wilton as I return'.

The letter was addressed in the fashion of that day to 'my best friend the Lady Grace Grenvile' in anticipation of the modern media usage in the press and on television. A postscript relates that John Heale and James Thynne, the eldest son of Sir Thomas Thynne, had also been knighted. Sir James was to marry Isabella Rich the daughter of Lord Holland but they had no child to follow them at Longleat.

There had been a new look with regard to knighthoods since James I came south from Scotland. He had dubbed so many that some wit of the day would ask 'Is he a gentleman or only a knight?' King James had invented that peculiar title of baronet which he sold for the benefit of his privy purse. His son King Charles carried the matter still further. He issued writs to the sheriffs of England and Wales to proclaim that all persons in receipt of £40 per annum over the three previous years should by 31 January 1626 present themselves to receive the order of knighthood. In 1638 we find a magistrate, William Coke Esquire, having his fine for not doing so reduced from £25 to £5 in consideration for his services to the King. It would be unwise to assume that Sir Bevill, as we must now call him, escaped some expense as a result of his elevation.

Chapter Nine

THE SECOND BISHOPS' WAR AND THE ELECTIONS OF 1640

THE TREATY between the King and his Scottish subjects was a humiliating outcome for the King himself, and a considerable anti-climax for those like Sir Bevill who had plunged heavily into debt and interrupted his son Richard's education at Oxford for the vision of a Grenvile leading his men into battle.

Philip, Lord Pembroke had achieved one minor gain for his master. He must have known full well by reason of his secretary Michael Oldisworth's friendship with Eliot and Bevill that Grenvile was a fish worth catching in the King's cause. His five hundred or so retainers in their blue and white livery was a useful token of the political power wielded by the Grenvile clan in their native Cornwall. Sir Bevill could ensure the election of whom he wished as the two knights of that shire and pick his own borough to represent in Parliament. To wean even three seats from the opposition and fill them with supporters of the King was worth the candle. Having despatched poor Richard (presumably by now recovered from his 'so foolishly gotten sickness') with his uncle Colonel Sir Richard and some servants to Oxford, he remained to accompany the royal household on their southward journey.

For his part Sir Bevill, having been picked out by his Sovereign for particular praise, and with an invitation to stay with the Lord Chamberlain at Wilton accepted, the full strength of his devotion and loyalty, once focused on Eliot, transferred for all time upon the King. Pembroke may have been illiterate, but he knew a good bargain when he came across one. His splendid collection of pictures painted by Van Dyck are evidence of that.

The end of June was not perhaps the best time to hunt, roe buck may have given sport then in the New Forest, but a considerable time passed before Bevill rejoined his wife and 'crew' of youngsters at Stow. By October he was offering his cousin Edmund Tremayne at Collacombe in Devon the use of his barbary stallion. The stallion was no saddle horse, and Stow having no suitable walled paddock, Tremayne was welcome to it. Stabling must have been at a premium; we know that he had a number of colts thriving in May, from Grace's letter. Bevill was back in Cornwall that autumn.

The Berwick expedition had been an appalling strain on his finances, never in a particularly sound state, and for ready money to finance his contingent to the Royal Army he had had to borrow money against the security of his land from Sir Ralph Sydenham of Youlston, and his kinsman Mr. Roe. The latter was asked for more time to pay monies due to him on 2 November that year, secured, I believe, on the Manor of Bideford. At the same time he was writing to Sydenham. Sir Ralph had married the widow of Chichester of Youlston, and the Chichesters were able to find money for several mortgages at this time.

> 'Sir', wrote Bevill, 'I lived in hope to have seen you and your noble lady in this poor place ere now . . . and now that tempests have so sudden drawn Winter [I am] altogether in despair of it . . .
>
> 'And now Sir I shall trouble you with a word or two about our old business concerning the money which you may expect from me at this time. I have been delayed by my Lo[rd] of Ar[undell] for that great sum which is between us ever since his departure, and cannot be satisfied till his return.
>
> But I was lately so staggered by a letter which Sir James Ba[gg] brought me signed with his name of Ar[undell] and Surr[ey], and of my lo[rd] Ma[ltravers] his son, and dated in the end of July, that I verily believed that he had been returned, for the letter did imply no less, and declared that in the beginning of Mich[aelmas] Term all things should be ended between us. Whereupon I was confident that he was returned; but finding it contradicted by everyone I was something troubled at it, and sent to Sir James Ba[gg] to understand this riddle to me . . . [I] know not how therefore to pay in [time] . . . [rather] than you should suffer I will sell anything in the world. And what interest is due. So let me know; it shall be speedily sent.'

Enclosed in the letter were those he spoke of, from Lord Arundell and Sir James Bagg, for Sydenham to read and return. It seems clear that Bevill had been persuaded to lend Lord Arundell some large sum of money repayable at Michaelmas, 25 September, and this being overdue, Bevill was more than usually in straits.

That November saw the return to England from Ireland of its Lord Deputy Wentworth. The old colleague of Bevill's in Parliament, another follower of Eliot, had travelled far since the murder of Buckingham. He and the Archbishop, Laud, were by far the most intelligent of Charles's counsellors. Both in the northern counties of England where he was Lord President and in Ireland he had ruled with a tight rein but an even hand. Even the Irish were quiescent, savouring the advantage of fair treatment for a change. The Irish Parliament had voted monies with which an army of eight thousand well armed men had been raised and stood in readiness for service in Scotland. Fully committed to supporting the King's policies and manner of Government, Wentworth, and to a lesser extend Laud, had become the arch-villains on the contemporary stage in many people's eyes. It was not that Wentworth had replaced Buckingham. Wentworth had none of the Villiers' charm. He had a coldly logical mind, great competence, an abrasive manner, and was generally hated by parliamentarians for his apostasy. Laud was hated for his love of high church ritual and blamed for the King's tolerance towards Catholics.

Wentworth was warmly welcomed by his King, and before he returned to Ireland had been made Lord Lieutenant of that island, a Knight of the Garter, and Earl of Strafford. In return he made the King a parting 'loan' of £20,000.

The King regarded his retreat to London a necessary interval while new forces were raised to punish his Scottish subjects. They for their part had not disbanded, and Leslie was still very much their general. Both sides made what preparations

they could for a resumption of hostilities the following year. Not everyone saw
things in that depressing light. The poet Cowley wrote:

> Others by War their conquests gain
> You, like a God, your ends obtain
> Who, when rude chaos for His help did call
> Spoke but the word, and sweetly ordered all.

Meanwhile Inigo Jones was busy preparing a masque for the entertainment of the
Queen Mother, the royal children, and a distinguished gathering of ambassadors
and courtiers. The production came off in February 1640 and showed the King
and Queen descending from the clouds to vanquish the furies of rebellion.

Dick, after his Christmas vacation, was back at Oxford. His father wrote to him
from Stow on 12 January:

> 'You persuade me that you constantly bestowed the forenoon since we parted in
> Logic and Philosophy: I am glad of it if it be so, and would not wish more, for so many
> hours of a day spent therein would very sufficiently effect what I desire. But take heed
> do not abuse me whereof I doubt, for if you say true, neither could you be so defective
> therein, nor your tutor have cause to complain.
> This is enough hereof, and you have had enough of me also in other points. I beseech
> God to open your eyes and guide your heart aright. Then you shall with comfort enjoy
> what I with care and pains have preserved for you, when it was upon the brink of a gulf
> to have been overwhelmed everlastingly; wherein my toil has not been small.
> There rests farther of your part nothing to be more seriously thought of than thrift.
> You are to succeed so many wasteful predecessors, as if your discretion guide you not to
> hold a little, we are gone in an instant, and you will see in your days the woeful end of a
> family which hath (without dishonour) endured the heats and colds of many hundred
> years . . .
> I have also now, for an encouragement while you do well, sent you a supply larger
> than is due or you can expect, and you shall not want what I can help you, if you make
> good use of your time.
> But above all things be sure to keep out of debt . . .'.

His mother wrote by the same post imploring her son to follow the excellent
directions of his father and urging him to write to his cousin Dick Prideaux and
to keep his father informed of the doings of other cousins at Exeter College.

Their son and heir was not shaping as the Grenviles would have wished. One
wonders if Bevill included himself in the category of Richard's wasteful predecessors.
For the moment the creditors seem to have been satisfied, Mrs. Herewyn
perhaps paid, and from the increased allowance paid Dick it might be inferred
that Lord Arundell had paid up.

Meanwhile, the new Earl of Strafford had been summoned to return again to
England and serve as Lieutenant-General in the army destined to march into
Scotland later that year. The Marquis of Hamilton had orders to provide shipping
for transporting the Irish army across the sea to land on the west coast of
Scotland. The King had hopes of money from Holland to fund the campaign, and
was full of high hopes and dreams of crushing his rebellious Scottish subjects.

On the advice of his council, the King had issued writs for an election. There
having been no Parliament for 11 years and Eliot being dead and buried in the
Tower of London, it was hoped that a new assembly of members would vote him

money required to prosecute a campaign against the Scots. Bevill and Ambrose Manaton were returned as burgesses for Launceston. The hustings drew him as always. From Hayne he wrote to Grace:

'You know what I am going about and how it concerns me. I know not what kind of security he will pitch upon. I will tender him what he please of mine own estate, *or yours*. But if he accept yours then he cannot be well satisfied without view of your deed, which, whether your mother will venture out of her hand or no I know not. I leave it to your wisdom to consider what is fit to be done in this case.

If the deed be sent me, I will bring him safe again, and he shall never be out of my hand.

I leave it also to yourself whether you will acquaint your mother with the reason or no. But if you send the deed, be sure to pack him safe with wool and paper, and seal the box and take care to prevent the wet. He must be with me here tomorrow night if at all'.

In a postscript he added: ' I have no news of the footman. If he be come home he may be fitted to be trusted with the deed.'

One has to admit that Bevill was being less than honest with Grace, and was quite prepared to jeopardise his mother-in-law's life interest in the Smith properties to save his own, and to do so surreptitiously. His casting the responsibility for the decision on Grace was less than worthy of him. In his defence one can only surmise that his financial affairs were in such straits that he no longer knew where to look for funds.

Grace would have none of it. She had battled bravely throughout her married life to raise the funds her husband needed, either to embellish the house at Stow, or to provide the wherewithal for his political life in London, or latterly to equip him for his martial role at Berwick. None knew better than she that the Grenviles were better at spending money than gaining it. Her only real security in life was the property left her by her rich father subject to Lady Smith's life interest. Once Bevill had been allowed to raise money on the Smith estates, neither Grace nor Lady Smith would be able to sleep in peace. Her reply to Bevill's letter has not been preserved, but one can guess its contents from the letter written by Bevill 10 days later:

'I have with sadness received your last two letters because with so much passion and sharpness you do fall upon me, while I conceive I did not deserve it. 'Tis true I expressed in my former letter grief that you should distrust me, and that you should think I would so endanger you as to leave a necessity upon you that should force you to sell your land.

Truly, love, I have no such design. I have had some conferences with you to contrive what may be best for our estate, and some resolutions we have fallen upon; which, seeing you dislike, I will never press more.

You need not exercise your pen so much to satisfy me; I am no way displeased, nor can be with you. I have nothing in the world pleasing, delightful, or contenting to me but yourself. In you my love did begin and must end . . .'.

He ended with a postscript to this letter he wrote at Bodmin: 'I will stay the election here so it may be late ere I come home'.

His preoccupations over money are underlined by the letter he wrote to Mr. Acland:

'I find an unconscionable conspiracy among all monied men to ruin those that must make use of them. They know my necessity and the danger my best manor stands in, and therefore by a general consent and agreement among themselves will not offer by £2,000 as much as the land which I tender to sell is worth. I would therefore take a little more time if I might, which may well be done if Mr. Crew will spare that money. Pray [let me] know what security will content him, for he shall have satisfaction.

I will engage By[deford] or what he will which will be disengaged by the help of his money. Mr. L has been with me to treat for St[ratton] but sticks just on the rate of other men, yet hath promised to send speedily to his brother Cr[ew] and father-in-law to further the other business.

I will be bound to give £2,000 more for Stratton seven years hence than I will now take for it. I doubt not but by some means that I may use I shall be enabled to it — I will say no more.

I beseech you continue your noble goodness and help to me in this my dangerous distress. I must else lose one of the finest manors that this part of the Kingdom hath . . .'.

He added: 'I am told casually by some that seem to know, that Mr. C[rew]'s money is all in his father-in-law's hands and not in his power to dispose, that there is much doubt he may fail me. I beseech you consider what a rock I may be cast against!'

Parliament assembled on 13 April 1640. Alas for the King! Another had assumed the mantle of Sir John Eliot. He was John Pym, the member for Tavistock and a politician who knew better than anyone how to manipulate the Commons. By the 17th he had set out a list of grievances which he said should be remedied by the King before any monies should be voted to him. Various committees were appointed, one to look into the prosecutions of Eliot and Denzil Holles with a view to impeaching the judges concerned, another to investigate the case against Hampden for his failure to pay Ship Money. The fiction that the King was in no way liable for the matters complained of was upheld with the explanation that the advice of evil counsellors had led to the various abuses arising. The King was told by his faithful Commons that they would only consider his requirement for money after they had discussed their grievances. Nothing had altered since March 1629. Nor was the King any readier to sacrifice what he regarded as his prerogative powers. In exercise of one such he dissolved Parliament on 5 May. It was to be the last time King Charles would be able to do such a thing.

He explained his reasons in this way when addressing the Lords that day:

'These ill affected members of the House of Commons have taken upon them[selves] to be guides and directors in all matters temporal and ecclesiastical, and in an audacious and insolent way censured His Majesty's government, traduced his administration of justice, and endeavoured to render his Ministers of State odious to the people, and have introduced a way of bargaining and contracting with the King as if nothing ought to be given him but what he purchases off them, either by quitting somewhat of his Prerogative, or by lessening his Revenue.'

The Short Parliament having lasted only three weeks and its members having failed to get any of their wishes met, or the King lawful taxes, Pym and others of like mind determined on revolution, despairing of reform.

On 9 May a poster was stuck up in the Royal Exchange calling on the apprentices in the City of London to sack Archbishop Laud's Palace of Lambeth. Five hundred beset the Palace at midnight on the 11th, but were beaten off and the ringleader was hung drawn and quartered for treason on the 23rd. The King's government still had the means of maintaining order and might have continued to do so had the King not committed himself to teaching his Scottish subjects a lesson.

To raise an army without money the King was obliged to send for his attorney general, Sir John Bankes. A Commission of Array copied from a precedent of 1404 was sent to the Lords and Deputy Lieutenants of each county and their Sheriffs for use as circumstances might require, and the King set off for the northern counties. On his way he issued a proclamation dated 20 August addressed to all those persons holding their lands 'in capite', that is to say as tenants directly of the King, or by other feudal tenancies such as by Knight's Service, to muster with horse and arms at Newcastle before 20 September. Before anyone could reasonably be expected to obey this latest command, the Scots invaded England, crossing the river Tyne on 27 August 1640.

Sir Edward Seymour, a grandson of the Protector Duke of Somerset, then lived at Berry Pomeroy Castle in Devon. He was a friend of Bevill's and had political aspirations. After staying with the Grenvile's at Stow he wrote a most appreciative bread-and-butter letter saying:

> 'My dear honoured brother, the comfort I lost when I left you, cannot be repaired but by you. I am now extremely sensible of my unworthiness in leaving Stowe . . . I believe I shall digest all the meat I shall eat this twelve month — I cannot long live without your society in which there is so much cheerfulness as it sweetens all misfortunes, and makes them none where you are.
>
> I make no question but you have heard of the Proclamation which hath struck with such amazement all our gentlemen here in Wiltshire which hold "in capite". What effect it works in other countries I know not. My Lord of Herbett received a letter from His Majesty very lately to repair to him with all the forces of the County of Wiltshire, as well as traine[d] as other able men. What event, this general distraction will produce is yet uncertain.

The Crossing of the Tyne had come about in this way. The two armies had encamped within sight of each other, separated only by the river, and so continued peacefully enough for several days. Unfortunately, an English soldier fired his piece and killed a Scottish officer watering his horse at the river. The Scots then bombarded the English lines with their cannon, the raw levies deserted with earthworks and at low tide the Scots waded their horses across. While most of the English fled in panic, Sir Richard Grenvile and a few other officers and men of the cavalry contested the Scottish charge across the Tyne and refused to return until the retreat had been sounded. His nephew George Monck, now an officer in the artillery, also achieved distinction in the fighting. The so-called Battle of Newburn ended in an ignominious retreat by the English to Durham. One casualty in the skirmish was Cornet Porter, the son of Endymion, who was killed.

From the King's point of view nothing had gone right. The Marquess of Hamilton failed to take any step to embark the Irish army and land it on the west coast of Scotland. The gentry of England who had mustered with some enthusiasm the previous summer barely put in an appearance this time. And the Scots he had intended to punish had swept all before them and were now occupying large tracts of northern England, and even held the city of Newcastle. Most people in England respected the Covenanters and held religious views not far removed from theirs. The second Bishops' War was an even greater defeat for the King's policies than the first.

Back at York the Earls of Bedford, Essex, and Hertford with nine other peers presented the King with a petition setting out a list of complaints

> 'for remedy whereof they beseeched the King to call a Parliament, whereby these and other their grievances may be taken away, the authors and consellors of them punished, and the present war composed by His Majesty's wisdom without [further] bloodshed'.

The City of London added their petition to that of the peers, and the gentry of Yorkshire faced with having to pay their trained bands to defend their county added their pleas for another Parliament, too. Stafford pointed out that the English army was already a fortnight in arrears for its victuals, and needed £200,000 to maintain it in arms.

With no realistic alternative, the King announced at a Council of Peers assembled in the Dean's house at York on 24 September that 'he desired nothing more than to be rightly understood of his people, and to that end had resolved to call a Parliament'.

Commissioners were appointed by both sides to work out a treaty between the Scots and the English, and by 16 October the English had agreed to pay the invaders £850 a day to cease hostilities and ease the burden imposed on those in occupied territory.

October 1640 was memorable for the elections held to find members for a new Parliament to meet at Westminster on 3 November. Both Cornwall, and to a lesser extent Lancashire, as royal duchies, had acquired representations in Parliament out of all proportion to the number of their inhabitants.

Cornwall, like most other counties, had a right to return two Knights of the Shire. These were normally elected by the 2,000-odd freeholders of the county. The family connections and general popularity of Sir Bevill could always ensure him one of the two places available. But by far the most important political aspect of Cornwall was its innumerable boroughs. Twenty-one such, each returning two members, contained between them just over a thousand entitled to vote.

Nowhere in England was electoral corruption so rife as in Cornwall. Bossiney, which had the aliases of Trevenna and also Tintagel, came within Bevill's sphere of influence by reason of his having purchased a freehold in that borough. His wholesale sale of the estate he had inherited from his parents had left him with no other borough in Cornwall which he could call his own. And even at Bossiney he was in competition with his old friend William Coryton who, as the principal agent for the Court Party in Cornwall, was determined on the election of only those persons whom the Lord Chamberlain, the Earl of Pembroke, sent down for election. It must be remembered that in 1640 the concept of 'rotten boroughs' had not yet been invented; but few boroughs were more rotten than those in Cornwall.

Coryton was Mayor of Bossiney, although there is doubt that Bossiney, being charterless, was entitled to one. He himself stood for and was elected the member for two boroughs, Launceston and Grampound. This was a device often employed by Parliamentary candidates to ensure their election. Then, having two to choose from, the successful candidate could elect which be preferred. In medieval days the borough electors were obliged to put up the money required to send members to Westminster. Some boroughs neglected to exercise their right on occasions to avoid the expense of doing so. By the 17th century prospective candidates were clamouring for borough seats, and were prepared to pay for them.

Grampound, one of Coryton's boroughs, had few electors, but each required a sizeable sum of money. The successful candidate handed over a lump sum to the mayor who then paid off the freemen of his borough. It had the distinction of being the only borough in England ever to be disenfranchised for corruption.

So far as Bossiney (or Tintagel) was concerned that October 1640, John Pym, through his agent Lord Robartes, was determined to have Sir John Clotworthy elected; he was also put up for the borough of Maldon in Essex to ensure his entry into the Commons. Although described as of St Andrew's, Holborn on the writ, he was one of the leading land-grabbers of the Ulster plantation and came from an old North Devon family. He was a great opponent of Strafford's government in Ireland and was to serve as a voluble witness against Strafford when impeached.

Lord Pembroke was the principal fixer of elections on behalf of the King. Coryton was his agent. Coryton put forward Sir Christopher Yelverton for Bossiney. He seems to have been elected by the dubious practice of allowing only those in favour of the candidate to vote at his election.

The third contender for Bossiney was Sir Bevill Grenvile, but not for himself. His candidate was Sir Ralph Sydenham, a fervent royalist but not, it seems, on Lord Pembroke's list. Sydenham had married a Chichester widow and lived at Youlston in North Devon; his daughter married Bevill's cousin Thomas Stucley, but one has to admit his principal ground for preferment was the large sum of money owed him by Bevill and which Bevill could not pay.

The advantage of standing for small rotten boroughs was that the smaller they were, the less money it cost to be elected. It seems to have been that which Edward Seymour had in mind when he asked Bevill to help him win a borough seat. Sir Edward was aged thirty. His grandfather had built a fine house within the curtain walls of Berry Pomeroy, one of the few impressive castles in Devon. Edward Seymour was a baronet and great-grandson of the Protector Somerset. But Ralph Sydenham had precedence in Bevill's programme, and consequently he wrote to him in the following terms:

'Glad I am to hear from you again, and shall ever account it amongst my greatest happiness that afford me your company and next to it, your lines . . . Sir, I am wretched, for I fear I shall not be able to serve you as you desire, for by God, I am not sure of a borough in all the county, they are so taken up by lo[rd] 's letters before I knew of the Parliament. And such base means have been used by some ill members in the county as all places were forestalled before I knew of it.

A town or two hath sent to me that will choose me if I will serve myself, but will not give me leave to put in another, and on my faith there is not one borough in all my own land, but they abound in the poor towns of the Stannary, where I have nothing to do.

Though my power in boroughs fail, yet I doubt not but to make whom I please Knights of the Shire.'

Bevill's polite but unaccommodating letter may not have caused Seymour much concern. He managed to be elected as Knight of the Shire for his home county of Devon in both the Short and the Long Parliaments of 1640; he was eventually disabled to sit by his colleagues for his royalism in January 1643.

William Coryton, as Mayor of Bossiney, was charged with the duty of making an honest return to the election held in his borough. There were, in fact, two parallel polls in that hamlet. One organised by Coryton to elect two candidates sponsored by Lord Pembroke, the other by Bevill to secure the election of his friend and creditor Ralph Sydenham. The hand-picked few who were allowed to vote in the first elected those for whom they had been paid to elect, the Grenvile organised election that followed elected Sir John Clotworthy, Lord Robarte's nominee, and Sir Ralph Sydenham. Sydenham does not seem to have been present or to have faced the electorate at the hustings, because Bevill had to write to tell him the good news of his success.

> 'That I am willing to serve you I hope I need not now to tell you, as the following discourse shall be an argument of it. Yet at best I can but embark you in a brabbling title. Truly, Sir, if all the power I had in the world could have served you better, it should. But by this you may perceive how difficult a thing it is to effect such a business.
>
> I attempted many places for to procure buroughs, but found not hope but in a poor burough in the parish of Tintagel, and you must understand that in all my estate there is not one.
>
> In that place I found the inhabitants [ag]grieved at a course that was held, wherein nine or ten did take upon them to be the only choosers of the borough; whereas they conceived that the rest has as much right to do it as they.
>
> And I well know that the opinion of Parliament House hath ever been that all inhabitants, being free men, have voice; and so I have known it often adjudged. Whereupon I urged them to give me their voices for you, and I would try the title to put them in a right way.
>
> Mr. Coryton's power is great there. He continues himself mayor divers years and supports the former custom of choosing by a few, because they are mostly at his command. I gave him to understand that I was willing to join with him if he pleased, whereby my Lord Chamberlain would be sure of one [seat], if he would let me have the other, but he was absolute, and would have all or none.
>
> Robartes is powerful there . . . [and would] have carried both against Mr. Coryton if I had not interposed. Nevertheless, he, in a private and unlawful way, having gotten the writ into his hands, went into the election calling none but were at his disposition. But the others learning of it, went in and declared for whom they were.
>
> So there are two elections made; one by Mr. Coryton's men, and another by all the freemen who are, we hear, three to one again him. And they have chosen you and another called Sir John Clotworthy on my lo[rd] Rob[arte]'s recommendation.
>
> . . . I am confident your election must stand.'

In this Grenvile was in part mistaken. Coryton's conduct as Mayor of Bossiney led to his expulsion from the Commons on 18 August the following year. Sydenham represented Bossiney until 1642 when he was 'disabled from sitting' for his royalism. As an 'election manager', Coryton had put forward 16 court candidates for the Short Parliament and all but one had been rejected. For this, the Long Parliament, no court candidate was successful. Bevill suspected that his new friend Lord Pembroke would take umbrage at his interference in the Bossiney poll. Accordingly he wrote to Sydenham:

'Now, Sir, one task I must impose upon you to prevent my Lord Chamberlain having a misconceit of me: he is my good co[usin], and I have special relations to him. I believe he will be informed that I oppose[d] him, which truly is not so, for I offered to join with Mr. Coryton — which he refused. And if I had not interposed, my Lord Robarte's agents would have carried both by that way of election.

'I shall not be up [at Westminster] at first sitting. Pray hasten in your petition as soon as you can that you may be first heard. Advise with some of experience, and take your no[ble] co[usin] Mr. Edward Sydenham's help to keep in right with my lo[rd] Chamb[erlain]'.

Bevill seems to have acted quite fairly towards Coryton. His desertion of Eliot had caused a breach in their old standing friendship, but now, in effect, they were both back on the same side again.

Bevill wrote to him at the time of the Bossiney affair:

'I am become by purchase a freeholder within that borough of Trevenna [Bossiney]. I therefore have some reason not to suffer it to be abused by any undue course.

Moreover, most of the inhabitants, and other gentle neighbours which have freehold do complain of the wrong and desired my assistance to redress it, which I will endeavour to do. You know as well as I what the opinion of the law hath ever been in the point of election[s]. You will find that all who pay scot and lot, and which are suitors to the town court, have voice in all elections. So I have known it adjudged many times, and I will try it here.'

He signed himself 'Yours affectionately' but there is a steely ring in his declaration of intent. As we have seen, Coryton was disabled from sitting for either of two boroughs which elected him to Parliament, but he was to change sides once again. On the outbreak of the Civil War he 'became sensible of his errors' and took the Oath and Covenant.

Having attended to some personal affairs, almost certainly measures to keep his creditors at bay, Bevill rode up to London and lodged at the Hatchett behind St Clement's church in the Strand. This new Parliament, the Long Parliament as it is known in history, differed from its predecessors in its determination to establish its sovereign power and end King Charles's personal rule. Many thoughtful men had pondered the unsatisfactory state of affairs which had led their monarch to attempt rule without recourse to Parliament. The King was resolved to retain his prerogative powers inherited from his father and bestowed upon him by God at his coronation. Parliament had striven unsuccessfully to date to become an executive rather than a consultative body. The King had the ace of trumps. At every previous Parliament the King had been able to order its dissolution when its demands became intolerable to him. He had managed by dint of resurrecting antique laws researched by his Attorney General William Noy to raise sufficient funds to govern England, and through Thomas Wentworth, Lord Strafford, to govern Ireland, But when faced by rebellion in Scotland, his lack of money and dependence on medieval methods of raising an army emphasised the impotence of personal rule in the 17th century. Neither Charles nor his father could intervene in Europe with forces exceeding a division. Yet neither could bring themselves to realise that if the house of Stuart was to continue, as Kings of the three countries, concessions had to be made to Parliament, and those called upon to pay taxes allowed some say in the matter.

John Pym was the catalyst who gave effect to the yet unstated views of parliamentarians. If Parliament was to achieve supremacy, the Crown and its ministers had to be reduced. In the past, criticism of the King had been muted. In law the King could do no wrong. If things went wrong it must be the fault of Ministers of the Crown. Persons who treacherously advised their monarch to adopt policies to the detriment of his subjects, the great Duke of Buckingham and his like, were subject to two forms of control; the threat of impeachment, a prosecution by the House of Commons before the House of Lords, and attainder, which could declare a victim dead in law (*civiliter mortuus*), for no better reason than Parliament regarding the victim better dead.

Pym was a veteran Parliamentarian: he had been a member of the dissenting left with Wentworth, Coryton, and the rest. He had learnt how to steer Parliament under the august leadership of Sir John Eliot himself.

There was another factor. The second Bishops' War had obliged Parliament to pay the Scottish Army of occupation in the north of England. Those professional soldiers, like Sir Richard Grenvile and his nephew George Monck and the men of their regiments, knew only too well the improbability of the King himself being able to pay them for their services. By voting monies for payment of soldiers direct, Parliament achieved a relationship with the military calculated to undermine the conception that the King alone was their commander-in-chief.

On 21 November 1640 Sir John Hotham, the governor of Hull, moved that monies voted by the city to pay both armies in the north should be despatched instantly. Another member, Alderman Pennington, pointed out that the City had already underwritten £20,000 but that more would be raised if it could be backed by security. D'Ewes records a list of those prepared to give their bond, which included persons like Sir Ralph Hopton and Sir John Culpepper, all of whom would prove themselves ardent Royalists. At the tail of the list he named 'Sir Edward Greenfeild' as surety for £1,000.

No such member of the Long Parliament existed. It seems that Bevill felt unable to show himself less capable than his colleagues to give bond for such a sum. Bonds for some £90,000 were volunteered in this way. Ironically, Bevill's gesture would prove another straw in the wind which would enable Parliament to raise and arm its own forces. How horrified poor Grace would have been to see her husband risking the little left to them.

The pent-up frustration of the progressives led to very understandable excesses. A London petition to Parliament for the abolition of the episcopacy was debated in February 1641. This move was a direct consequence of the Bishops' Wars. The authority of Kings being based on the sacrament of coronation, any attack on the bishops was an attack on the monarchy. Bevill, as a traditionalist, can be relied upon to have voted against such an innovation.

The division of members of the House of Commons into two parties, Royalists and Parliamentarians, was achieved by Pym in his attack on Strafford. Thomas Wentworth, Earl of Strafford, like William Coryton, was a turncoat. He had been an enthusiastic supporter of Eliot and a colleague of Bevill Grenvile's. Once the Duke of Buckingham had been murdered, Strafford had seized his opportunity to change sides and become an adherent of personal rule. He was intellectually some streets ahead of other ministers of the crown, and far more competent. He was in his native Yorkshire when word came from the King that he needed him in Westminster to advise him, and guaranteed his personal safety.

Strafford knew very well the danger of leaving the north of England or Ireland where he had both authority and armed supporters to guard him. His friends tried to dissuade him from venturing within the jurisdiction of the Houses of Parliament, but he felt he could not abandon his master in his hour of need. Within three days of his arrival in London he was arrested and imprisoned in the custody of Black Rod.

Eventually Strafford was brought to trial in Westminster Hall on an impeachment for treason. The prosecution had the difficult task of proving treason in a man whose every action had been in support of his King. Clotworthy was produced by Pym to assail Strafford's government in Ireland. Clotworthy was spokesman for the Irish Presbyterians with a history of repression against the Catholics. But his attack was so cleverly countered and every accusation blunted by the logic of the accused man's arguments that it was not long before the general public attending the trial, and a number of ladies in particular, showed their favour for him. As the trial dragged on the Lords, who were initially content to see the downfall of so powerful an upstart, became unsure among themselves. It looked very much as if he would be acquitted. Pym acted with decision, applying for an adjournment. Before the trial could resume, a motion for Strafford's attainder was brought before the House of Commons.

Bevill wrote to Sir Alexander Carew his fellow Knight of the Shire:

> 'Pray, Sir, when it comes to be put to the vote, let it never be said that any member of our country [Cornwall] should have a hand in this fatal business, and therefore pray give your vote against the bill.'

Carew replied:

> 'If I were sure to be the next man that should suffer upon the same scaffold with the same axe, I would give my consent to the passing of it'.

Bevill has been obliquely criticised for not himself voting against the bill, and the Journal shows he was given leave to go into the country for some convenient time immediately before the bill was debated. When the bill reached the Lords the King told them on 1 May that he was not satisfied in his conscience of Strafford's guilt, and could therefore in no circumstances agree to pass the bill against Strafford's life.

Had the Kind adopted any other posture, Strafford might have been saved. The Lords, having been assured that the King would not agree the bill in any event, saw no reason not to pass it. Believing it possible the King would not accept the bill, riots took place at Westminster with the mob baying for Strafford's head. The King sent for his bishops to advise him. They told him in effect that it was his duty to obey his Parliament. Strafford himself wrote to the King, offering his life in a chivalrous letter. He can hardly have supposed his offer would be accepted, but not caring to sign the death warrant himself, the King appointed a commission to do so. Strafford is said to have commented wryly: 'Put not your trust in princes'. His head was severed on Tower Hill amid the blood-thirsty yells of the mob. It was 12 May 1641.

Eight Cornish members voted against the bill of attainder, Richard Arundell, Sidney Godolphin, Nicholas Slanning and John Trevanion among them. The Venetian Ambassador noted that many members were leaving Parliament for the country that April.

While Bevill was in London news reached him that his son had left Oxford and returned to Stow. Dick appears to have 'dropped out' and Grace had written asking him not to be too hard on the boy.

> 'You will not have me take exceptions to your son for small matters', he wrote. [Dick has become 'her' son and not 'our son' by this stage.] 'But as I have forgiven what is past, so I should not be over sensible for the time to come. You should prevail in all. I shall use few words to him in any kind. I pray God to guide and bless him. He shall stand or fall by his own judgement, for mine is despised by him.
>
> The way I proposed was a path [that] would assuredly [have] led to wealth and honour. But he likes it not, and calls my advice the severest rigour. I took it not to be so when I gave it; but I thought, seeing I was prevented of leaving him a great estate, I should have done as well in putting him into a way to have gained one.
>
> If he otherwise conceive I cannot help it; I shall be sorry to see him live in want, but I hope some of his brothers will find the way to raise their fortunes by this course which he despises.
>
> So I leave all to God, resolving to trouble myself as little as I can hereafter.
>
> Pray let him spend his time as well as he may while he is in the country, and as soon as I can I will call him thence. The directions he hath from me for the country will do him no hurt to follow them, what course soever he take. Young Mr. Chichester doth sometimes ask kindly for him and wish for his company. Pray bid Dick to write a handsome compliment to him . . .'.

At Hartland Abbey are portraits of three boys. All are said to have been painted in 1636, according to their superscriptions. But the names attributed to each, and added at some date later than 1661, are clearly mistaken. One is entitled 'John, Earl of Bath aetatis sua 15'. The only one of Bevill's sons aged 15 in 1636 was Richard. I am persuaded that it is indeed a portrait of Richard and not of John. His father might well have had his three eldest sons painted in 1636, and they would have been Richard, John and Barnard. The pictures pretend to represent John, Barnard and Denis, but Denis was not born before 1637. The portrait of Richard, as I maintain, shows a boy who may well have been a difficult character to deal with.

He wrote to his father in the following terms:

> 'I was doubtful what to say that I blotted a quire of paper to write one letter, and so crossed it that it looked like an old mercer's book, and yet I am so far from knowing what to write as I was at the beginning. What can I possibly say, Sir, to retain your lost favour which you are possessed that it is an indifferent thing to me whether I enjoy it or not, and that all my unhappy errors proceeded from a heart to disoblige you.
>
> Unless you pleased, Sir, to change that opinion I cannot hope to give you the least contentment in the world. Could you see my heart you would find there engraved in a plain character all filial duty.

'I shall therefore beg a General Pardon for all my offences. My good intentions, which are best known to myself, embolden me thus once more to ask forgiveness. Pray pardon the frenzy of him who is so distracted that he cannot appear to be your most obedient and humbly affectionate son . . .'.

Bevill has had his absence from the House of Commons from immediately before the Attainder of Strafford remarked on by a number of writers. His grant of leave of absence must clearly have been by reason of Dick's illness. Dick seems to have died that April when in Cornwall. Both his parents were grief stricken.

Sir Nicholas Slanning left Westminster on 18 June 1641 to take up the post of Governor of Pendennis Castle commanding Falmouth harbour in Cornwall. In reply to an invitation from Slanning to join him there Bevill wrote:

'I am not yet fit after so late and heavy a loss (being the greatest that could have befallen me) to look upon so good company . . . I wish you mirth and comfort'.

Chapter Ten

THE OUTBREAK OF WAR

BEVILL was out of London from May until July 1641. In his absence the Commons, spurred on by Pym, had drafted a Remonstrance on the State of the Kingdom. It seems to have embodied the complaints against the King's conduct and government contained in a Protestation which included criticism for failing to punish Catholics, for ruling so long without a Parliament, for illegal taxation, for the raising of an army in Ireland (by the unfortunate Strafford), and for bringing 'the English army into misunderstanding of this Parliament'. The criticisms were confined to the preamble, but the protestation itself, pronounced suitable to be signed by every member, was unexceptionable. Each was expected to swear to defend the Protestant religion, the King's person, honour and estate, and also the powers and privileges of Parliament. To maintain the liberties of the subject and help punish those with contrary intentions.

All present took the necessary oath, and members coming up from the country added their names as they took their seats. Bevill Grenvile was the last to subscribe his name, and did so on 31 July.

The execution of Lord Strafford in May was to have far-reaching effects. His office as Lord Lieutenant of Ireland had been entrusted to Parliamentarians Borlase and Parsons. They were Protestants whose representative in the Commons, Sir John Clotworthy, had openly declared that:

> 'The conversion of papists in Ireland was only to be affected by the Bible in one hand and the sword in the other',

while Pym was reported to have said he intended to leave not one priest in Ireland. Strafford may have proved himself a hard task master, but the Irish knew they could expect reasonable treatment under his rule. A Parliament directed by Pym spelled the destruction of Irish religion.

After failing to save Strafford, the King set off for Scotland. Pym and his revolutionary-minded friends set about drafting a 'Remonstrance on the State of the Kingdom' and Bevill, having taken the obligatory oath at the end of July, managed to return home until the autumn.

Bevill was very busy raising money. He mortgaged Stow Barton and the manor of Kilkhampton for £3,000 in 1640; his Manor of Bideford had been mortgaged for another £3,000 the year before. In November 1641 he sold a 1,000-year lease on the Barton of North Leigh in Devon and two grist mills at Morwenstow in Cornwall for £1,000. In one way and another he had borrowed £20,000 and seldom, if ever, was able to pay the instalments due.

In October the Irish revolted with their customary barbarity, butchering their Protestant neighbours, men, women and children by the thousand. The Commons, which had refused the King supplies for his Bishops' Wars, now volunteered the sum of £200,000 to raise 3,500 foot and 600 horse and to pay for a fleet to transport them. The Earl of Leicester was directed to recruit men for service in Ireland and, not having the King's warrant under the Great Seal to do so, queried the legality of his orders. Parliament resolved on 9 November 1641 that Leicester should proceed as ordered by virtue of an Ordnance of Parliament. It was a momentous step, facilitated by the absence of the King of Scotland, and the emergency that had arisen.

On 22 November the Remonstrance in its final, much-amended form was debated in the Commons. It set out all the many complaints which radicals had listed against the manner in which the King had governed his country since the beginning of the reign. It was a comprehensive indictment of Stuart policy and was only passed by the narrowest of majorities, either nine or eleven votes.

There were still enough supporters of the King in the Commons for Pym and his friends to react violently towards any opposition to the course he had set. After the Remonstrance had been carried on division, a Royalist member, a Middle Templar called Palmer, asked that a protestation against the Remonstrance should be entered in the Journal over his name. Other Royalists cried 'All! All!', some waving their hats and others unsheathing their swords. As D'Ewes remarked: 'If God had not prevented it there was very great danger that mischief might have been done'. The clerk began preparing a list of those members who wished to support the counter-protestation, but the names have since been obliterated by ink smears and emphatic crossings out. Hotham moved that persons heading adverse factions to motions approved by the House as a whole were guilty of mutiny, and Palmer was committed to the Tower.

While these stirring scenes were taking place in London, Sir Bevill and his son and heir were heading eastwards from Stow. Jack was now 13 years old and Bevill considered it imperative to have the boy crammed with all possible speed for an education to befit him for his new rôle in life. His cramming to be undertaken under his father's watchful eye in London, and thence to Oxford, providing he could matriculate. Grace had now lost two sons, her beloved Richard and another boy Bevill, who died in 1636 aged ten. She was far from keen on Jack going to London with its endemic plague and smallpox, and made it clear that she disliked the plan. Father and son paused long enough at Holsworthy for Bevill to send Grace instructions which she may have been in no mood to listen to when her husband left home.

'Dear Love' she wrote, 'You are (I hope) confident of my readiness to observe all your directions to the utmost I can, both what you told me and since wrote of from Holsworthy. Brute hath set all your acorns and sycamore seeds, and Ching is about the barley ground according to your order. I hope to receive some money from [you] by Cottle and then will pay it according to your order, and put off such servants as are faulty and reform all disorders what I can. I still labour with the same desires of being profitable to you, though my misfortunes do every day more and more disable me.

It was impossible for me to part with you and continue well (truly Love!). The next day after we parted, I was most extreme sick with violent head-ache, fainting and several vomiting fits, so I doubted I should have failed my gossip at Stratton; but I ventured next day, finding myself somewhat better, and met my cousin Arundell there and Mrs Vigures in my cousin Bassett's room, who came not by reason of Sir Rob[ert] Bassett was suddenly taken so ill as they are think he is now bidding farewell to this world.

Dear love, I must not omit to thank you for your kind care and wishing me to be comforted, and 'tis my endeavour to submit to the will of God, desiring his mercy still, which I humbly acknowledge hath always been plentifully mixed with his corrections, and 'tis and shall ever be my prayer that I may make the right use of both.

I confess my late sorrow hath created so many new fears in me, as I hate to think how contemptable a creature it may make me in time if it continue so burthensome on me, which made me express my unwillingness so suddenly to adventure Jack, especially this Winter, doubting he is but crazy and not of so strong a constitution as perchance you imagine.

Wherefore for God's sake excuse me and consider of these particulars in season, that we may not seem by our earnest covetting his learning to pluck on new sorrows by hazarding death, without which he cannot learn at all. Let not I pray my tenderness cause a misconstruction, for God knows I desire heartily he may be a scholar, and can be well contented with his absence so he be safe, but the sad remembrance of my late loss and the doubt of the sickness being so dispersed abroad doth fill me with fears which I cannot conceal, though 'tis with much unwillingness I fall on anything contrary to your opinion.

I pray for your health and his, which is all I can do, and that I will not fail to perform beseeching you to shun danger and be careful in all points of your own health as well as his. Pardon my distracted lines . . .

My mother prays for your welfare and enjoins me to entreat you to confer with Hutchings and to use what means you can to gain her the possession.

I earnestly entreat you to get me and send it as speedily as you can, a bottle of perfectly good Blue Syrup of Violets, a pound of the Syrup I desire; it cost 6s. a pound the last: it came safe and was excellent good. I cannot want it for my own use, and oftentimes for the children also. Therefore pray hasten it to me. A dozen of white gloves I desire and two pairs of thicker gloves.'

By 19 November or thereabouts Bevill and Jack had reached Salisbury. Grace's next letter to her husband makes sad reading:

'I have received yours from Salisbury and am glad to hear you came so far well with poor Jack. Ye shall be sure of my prayers which is the best service I can do you. I cannot perceive whether you had received mine by Pom[eroy ?] or no; but I believe by this time you have met that and another since by the post.

Truly I have been out of frame ever since you went, not with a cough but in another kind much indisposed. However, I have striven with it and was at church last Sunday, but not the former.

I have been vexed with divers demands more of money than I could satisfy, but I instantly paid what you sent, and have entreated Mr. Rous his patience a while longer as you directed.

It grieves me to think how chargeable your family is, considering your occasions, it hath this many years troubled me to think to what a pass it must come at last, if it run on after this course. How many times what hath appeared hopeful, and yet proved contrary in the conclusion, hath befallen us, I am loathe to urge, because 'tis far from my desire to disturb your thoughts. But this sore is not to be cured with silence or patience either, and while you are loathe to discourse or think of that you can take little comfort to see how bad it is, and I as unwilling to strike on that string which sounds harsh in your ear (& the matter still grows worse) though I can never put it out of my thoughts, & that makes me oftentimes seem dreaming to you, when you expect I should sometimes observe more compliment with my friends or be more active in matters of curiosity in our house, which doubtless you would have been better pleased with, had I been capable to have performed it. And I believe though I had a natural dullness in me, it would never so much have appeared to my prejudice, but 'twas increased by a continuance of sundry disasters which I still met with, yet never 'til this year, but I had some strength to encounter them, but truly, now I am so clean overcome, as 'tis in vain to deny a truth.

It seems to me now 'tis high time to be sensible that God is displeased, having had many sad remembrances in our estate and children of late, yet God spared us in our children long, and when I strive to follow your advice in moderating my grief (which I praise God) I have thus far been able to do as not to repine at God's will, though I have a tender sense of grief which hangs on me still; and I think it as dangerous and improper to forget it, for I cannot but think it was a near touch and correction sent from God to check me, for my many neglects of my duty to GOD. It was the tenth and last plague GOD smote the Egyptians with the death of their first borne before he utterly destroyed them, they persisting in their disobedience notwithstanding all their former punishments. This apprehension makes me both tremble and humbly to beseech him to withdraw his punishments from us and to give us grace to know and amend whatever is amiss. Now I have poured out my sad thoughts, which in your absence doth most oppress me, 'tis my weakness hardly to be able to say thus much unto you, how brimful soever my heart be, though often times I heartily wish I could open my heart freely to you when 'tis over-charged. But the least thought it may not be pleasing to you will at all times restrain me, consider me rightly I beseech you and excuse I pray the liberty I take with my pen in kind.

And now at last I must thank you for wishing me to lay aside all fear, and depend on the Almighty who can only help us. For his mercy I daily pray, and your welfare and our poor boy's. So I conclude and am ever yours faithfully and only

Grace Grenvile.'

In a postscript she added:

'... Sir Robert Bassett is dead. I heard from my cousin Grace Weekes who writes that Mr. Luttrell says if you and he could meet, and liking between the young people, he will not stand for money you shall find. Parson Weekes wishes you could call with him, and that he might entice you to take the castle in your way down. She says they enquire in the most courteous manner that can be imagined. Dear Love: think how to farther this what you can...'.

Bessie Grenvile was twenty or twenty-one years old. The heir to Dunster Castle, with no requirement for the Grenviles to put up a dowry, must have been an attractive proposition: but nothing came of it. Grace's next letter was dated a week later, 1 December 1641, and addressed to Bevill at the Hatchett behind St Clement's church:

'Since I wrote last I have been very ill, and kept my bed most part of the time, but now praise God, I am much better; but dare not stir out of my chamber, and I doubt this new sickness will make me capable of a relapse into my old distempers especially this dead season of the year. I cannot so well inform you, by letter, in what kind I have been ill, but it hath weakened me as much as any child-bed ... I am glad you and Jack be well, I long to hear of your coming down, and [the] few things desired in my letters I need much...'.

Grace's last child had been born in June 1638 and died a year later. She was aged 43 and her symptons were not of pregnancy; it may be she had some defect of her pancreas.

Bevill must have just reached London, when on 1 December 1641 the House ordered Sir Edward Deering, or in his absence Sir Ralph Hopton, the member for Wells, to present and read the Remonstrance to the King at Hampton Court. Both members subsequently became Royalists, but not until after the Militia Bill. Sir Simon D'Ewes left the chamber during the debate on the Remonstrance, feeling unwell from a cold contracted the previous day and not liking some of the matters contained in it. In the outcome it was Hopton, accompanied by D'Ewes, who presented the Remonstrance to the King.

The King's return from Scotland was announced in a letter to Parliament read on 3 December. His was an unhappy home-coming. The Irish rebels were rumoured to be expecting help from Spain, and both the Venetian and Spanish ambassadors protested vigorously at their correspondence being tampered with. A motion was carried in the Commons that catholicism was not to be tolerated either in Ireland or elsewhere, the Queen's Chapel had been closed, her priests dismissed, and her confessor Robert Phillips arrested and thrown into the Tower. The Queen protested that even in Turkey such indignities would not be suffered.

On 7 December Sir Arthur Hazlerigg brought in a bill for placing the Militia or Trained Bands under a Lord General. Sir John Culpepper, a Royalist, pointed out that such a bill would take away the King's power to control the armed forces of the Kingdom and vest unlimited arbitrary power in another. It failed on division, but only by 33 votes, and Pym was in no way disheartened. Another bill was promoted that Christmas Eve for 'The better settling of a military power for the defence of the realm'. It was debated inconclusively, but a Committee was appointed to sit at the Guildhall to give further consideration to a Militia Bill on the last day of the year.

Alas for poor Grace! Bevill was to remain in London over Christmas with Jack for company. On 22 December Jack sent off a flowery letter of compliments to his grandmother Lady Smith, at Stow.

The force being raised by Lord Leicester for service in Ireland was gathering at Chester. George Monck had now outstripped his uncle in that Leicester appointed him colonel commanding 1,500 foot, and Sir Richard Grenvile, major, commanding 400 horse in his, Leicester's, regiment. The King had sanctioned the force retrospectively on 14 December, when he told the Lords he would agree on this particular occasion to the Bill for Impressment, but did so without prejudice to his prerogative. Sir Richard's letter from Chester, read to the Commons on 10 January 1642, said his men awaited embarkation for Ireland, but lacked arms, money, and the means of transporting them. Parliament ordered that money be sent to some reliable aldermen at Chester for the purpose, and the fleet eventually sailed on 21 February. This incident was the great watershed of the times: Parliament had raised an army and paid for it directly and without recourse to the King.

The King realised his position was critical. Pym was winning all along the line. Charles I had been forced into permitting the execution of his ablest supporter

Strafford, and his other wise counsellor, Archbishop Laud, had been imprisoned in the Tower by order of Parliament since 1 March 1641. His Lord Keeper Finch and his secretary Sir Francis Windebank had fled the country. From his point of view he had been driven into a corner and must needs act if he was ever to regain the initiative.

The King sent his recently appointed Attorney General, Sir Edward Herbert, to appear at the bar of the House of Lords with an indictment against Lord Kimbolton in the Lords, and Hampden, Haselrig, Holles, Pym and Strode in the Commons. They were charged with treason for having tried to subvert the laws and government of the Kingdom and to deprive the King of his royal power and on six similar counts. The Lords decided to await the Commons' reaction and do nothing until the following day. News then arrived that officers of the King's had seized and sealed up papers belonging to the accused members. The Commons ordered those who had done so to be brought before the House to answer for their contempt, and for the seals to be broken. The sergeant-at-arms then came to the House to demand the five members. Lord Falkland and a deputation were sent to the King to say the Commons held the members ready to answer any legal charge levelled at them.

The following day, 4 January, the King himself entered the Commons and, approaching the chair, said: 'By your leave, Mr. Speaker, I must borrow your chair a little'. The Speaker, Lenthall, knelt, and addressing the Commons the King told them that in cases of treason no person could claim privilege and that on the return of the five members they should be surrendered to him. The Commons, fearful for their personal safety, adjourned to the City where they sat in Grocers' Hall. On 10 January Sir John Clotworthy produced a Bill appointing a Captain Philip Skippon Sergeant Major General with power to raise men and use London's store of ammunition and cannon to provide for the safety of the King, Kingdom, and Parliament.

Upon the matter being reported to the King he left with his family, going first to Hampton Court and then to Windsor. The King had decided on war, and the Queen was smuggled out of the country to Holland for her safety. There was no looking back after the events of 4 January 1642. Moderate reformers such as Hopton:

'Excused the King coming hither with so great a number and so unusually armed, became we ourselves had divers of our servants attending in the lobby without the door of the House, armed in an unusual manner also with carabins and pistols, that the speech his Majesty made was full of grace and goodness, that he did not think we would appoint a grand committee to go into [the city of] London, nor would he have had us adjourned at all.

His divergence of view from Pym's led Hopton to follow Palmer into the Tower of London that March.

The Commons next penned a Petition to the King in which the members

'humbly beseech your sacred Majesty to raise up unto them a sure ground of safety and confidence by putting the Tower and other principal forts of the Kingdom and the whole militia thereof into the hands of such persons as your Parliament may confide in.'

Not unnaturally the King refused to do so, and on 28 February the Commons approved a motion to the effect that those who advised His Majesty to give such an answer were enemies of the State.

One of those principal forts of the Kingdom was Pendennis Castle, commanded by Sir Nicholas Slanning. When the King tried to arrest the five members, orders were sent to all ports to prevent them escaping abroad. Slanning passed this directive on to John Trefussis and Mr. Bassett for their compliance, and someone reported Slanning to the Speaker for having done so. Slanning was sent for by the Commons, but was too wise to comply. Another westcountryman, John Arundell junior of Trerice, left the House on 27 January, and he too did not return.

That spring Jack seems to have been sent to Oxford, and Bevill stayed on in London. They were puzzling times. The Earl of Pembroke who had been at the forefront of the Bishops' War and had invited Bevill to stay with him at Wilton after it finished, had spun around politically and was one of those who pressed the King to relinquish his command of the militia and forts. Parliament recommended Pembroke for the post of Lord Steward, and the King refused it.

At this crisis in the affairs of State Bevill fell ill. It was a sufficiently serious illness for the House of Commons on 1 March 1642 to grant him leave of absence to recuperate. Bevill wrote to Grace a week later:

'Dear Love: I perceive you received my letter but not the other things, which I did hope should have been with you as soon as the letter, but I hope they are before this and I wish they may fit and please you.

I will bring hats for the boys and am glad you say they learn well.

I thank God I have attained my health pretty well, though not fully my strength, but I resolve to come away this week. I am very glad to hear my sister is well and with you. I beseech God to keep her and her's so still.

I will bring your physic with me also. Write no more hither. Present my duty to my Lady Smith with my service to my sister, my cousin Frank and my nieces . . . make for me against my coming the purging ale that you were wont; be sure to put in all the ingredients and let it be well done: it will be wholesome this spring-time.

I hear not whether there be any provision of wine made for me as I appointed. We are undone if there be not and it must be had home speedily. Pray provide store of good salad herbs and increase the rampions . . .

Make it known to all my neighbours and tenants of the west side of our parish that I shall take it ill if they grind not at my mill, and let the tenants of Northlegh know that if they do it not, as they are bound, I will put them in suit.'

If Bevill really had intended returning to Stow the following week it seems strange that he should have given Grace such a number of chores more properly executed by himself. In the outcome he stayed on into April 1642. Having been granted leave of absence by the House it would be interesting to know how he was occupying his time in London. His next letter to Grace, dated April 1641, but clearly written a year later from the evidence it contains, gives no pointer:

'I am infinitely perplexed in mind with doubt of your health. I do fear you do not tell me the worst, and my grief is not small that I cannot yet come to you . . . There is but little appearance of the plague, but the smallpox is very common and mortal more than usual. Few or none do escape. Since Mr. Wise, his death, another good member of our house called Sir Hen[ry] Rainsford is also dead thereof and at least a dozen more of the House since our first meeting are dead of several diseases.

I am not without careful and passionate thoughts for those considerations which you touch both of our children and estate. I wish to God I could settle all things, but I will be tractable to any course, and at our meeting [will] confer with you hereof.'

The letter ends with directions regarding his stud and his brother Sir Richard's grey mare which had to be kept from the stallion and sent elsewhere for service.

It must have been shortly after the foregoing letter was sent that its writer followed it down to Cornwall. According to Sir Alfred Robbins:

'He saw sooner than most the bad designs that were forming, and apprehended very clearly the pernicious consequences which must follow from them. In this situation he conducted himself with equal steadiness and prudence. He adhered to what he took to be his duty to his King and country, but he would not plunge himself into the depths of party.'

Instead, 'he left London as soon as he could do it with safety, and retiring into his own country, employed himself in opening the eyes of other honest gentlemen to see that their welfare and happiness depended on the preservation of the Constitution in Church and State: for the support of which, therefore, he advised them, whenever it should become necessary to venture their lives and fortunes, as they could have no security for either if the Constitution were destroyed.'

The King meanwhile was making his way northwards where his supporters were said to be more numerous. He had reached Royston in February when Pembroke pressed the Militia Bill on him. He then approached Hull in Yorkshire and was refused admittance to that walled port and city by Sir John Hotham. The inconsistency of top people is evidenced by the fact that both Sir John and his son were beheaded by Parliament on Tower Hill for turning Royalist in 1645.

Both sides now prepared for war.

Chapter Eleven

BEVILL GOES TO WAR

THE PRECISE DATE when Bevill left London is doubtful. We know he had leave to go as early as 1 March 1642. It seems clear that he only remained there long enough to recover his health and be fit enough to face the week's journey to Stow.

On 16 June there was a roll call of the Commons and some 45 members were found to be missing without leave of the House. John Arundell, Edward Hyde, John Trevanion, Sir Henry Slingsby, Sir Ralph Hopton (who had been let out of the Tower after spending 11 days there in March), Endymion Porter, John Ashburnham, and Bevill were among them.

The House resolved that those absent members whose names had been read out should not sit in the House till they had made their excuse to the committee appointed to consider how the mulcts of money imposed upon the members absent, for whom no excuse was made and allowed, should be levied and paid towards the cost of civil war in Ireland.

On 22 July the Commons ordered Bevill and 14 other members to be summoned to appear before them, but Bevill had other matters to attend to in Cornwall.

By June 1642 Parliament was asking for money, plate, and horses: Sir Alexander Carew, Thomas Arundell, and Francis Godolphin, the members for the county of Cornwall, West Looe and St Ives, were sent down to assist the Deputy Lieutenants appointed by Parliament in raising the militia.

The militia consisted of trained bands commanded for each county by the Lord Lieutenant and Deputy Lieutenants. The system had been created in Tudor days for the defence of the realm against Spain, and armouries had then been set up with weapons and ammunition at different muster points in the county. By issuing what it termed its Militia Ordinance and appointing Deputy Lieutenants of its own, Parliament had declared war on the King.

An alternative method of raising men was to call upon the *posse comitatus*, which included all men of fighting age in the county. Men gathered in that way came under the command of the Sheriff.

A third variation was for the King to issue commissions of array, sending officers so commissioned into each county to muster its inhabitants. The King had had copies made from an ancient precedent of the reign of Henry IV, and such a document, issued under the Great Seal of England, was unquestionably more authoritative than any Ordinance published by Parliament. The 17th-century Cornishman was not only litigious but he also reverenced the law, and many who had opposed the King before now felt unable to support a Parliament so clearly in breach of it.

The King's commissions of array were despatched on 11 June to some counties: they do not seem to have had sufficient copies ready for all, the one sent to Lord Bath at Tawstock in North Devon was not signed until 19 July.

The King's commissioners in Cornwall were Bevill, his cousin John Arundell of Trerice, John Grylls the Sheriff, and Warwick, Lord Mohun.

On 12 July William Seymour, Marquess of Hertford, set off for the West Country. He carried the King's commission as Lieutenant-General of Hampshire, Wiltshire, Dorset, Somerset, Devon and Cornwall, including Bristol, Exeter, and Poole. He was accompanied by his brother Lord Seymour, Sir Ralph Hopton, and a few other gentlemen. He wrote to the Queen that day saying, 'I am with all speed to repair unto the West, to put His Commission of Array in execution, which I make no doubt to perform without any great difficulty'.

Seven days later the King signed a Commission of Array for Devon. It was addressed to Henry, Earl of Bath, then living at Tawstock near Barnstaple, his agent Sir Ralph Sydenham at Youlston nearby, and Sir John Chichester his step-son: also to Thomas Monck, George's brother at Potheridge and 22 other gentlemen of the county. The operative words were:

> 'We . . . have assigned, you or any three or more of you, to array and train all and singular men at arms and armed men and archers dwelling in the county . . .'.

On 21 July, Lord Mohun, writing to Francis Basset of Tehidy from Boconnoc, told him that

> 'To let you see what an impudent beggar I am, I have sent this bearer to you for the barrel of gun-powder you promised me; and likewise to give you notice that the Commissioners of Array do meet at Lostwithiel Wednesday next (27th July). Pray do me the honour to meet your friends Sir Nich[olas] Slanning, Sir Bevill Grenvile, and Mr. John Arundell of Trerice . . . where we shall confer about some business concerning settling of this county.'

And so they did. Additionally the sheriff, John Grylls, was present. No minutes exist of their meeting, but one can assume that contingency plans were drawn up and instructions despatched by messengers to the constables of the county. A day or so later another meeting at the same venue led to commissions in the militia being issued in the King's name: the commissioners were Francis Bassett, Sir Nicholas Slanning, Lord Mohun, Sir Peter Courtney, John Arundell of Trerice, George and John Trevanion, Walter Langdon, Samuel Cosoworth, and foremost among them all, Bevill Grenvile.

Meanwhile, Lord Hertford had reached Shepton Mallet, having been rebuffed in Marlborough, and Hopton published the Commission of Array for Somerset. Bevill and his fellow commissioners published their Commission of Array five days later, on 5 August, on which day the news of Hopton's action was reported to the Commons and he was 'disabled' from sitting and summoned to appear at the bar of the House as a 'delinquent'.

Somerset was strongly pro-Parliament. After a minor skirmish at Marshall's Elm large bodies of Roundhead levies began to appear and the Cavaliers left Somerset for Sherborne, Dorset. Some other people from that county, known as the 'Somerset Colonels', penetrated Cornwall on Parliament's behalf: as foreigners they would have been unlikely to achieve much on their own, but they had their local supporters, too: Sir Richard Buller, Sir Alexander Carew of Antony, Richard Erisey, and Francis Godolphin of Treveneague. These began raising levies in and around Launceston.

On 17 August the sheriff Grylls mustered his posse on Bodmin racecourse to test the ability of his constables to mobilise their men: only 180 turned up and most wore the Grenvile colours of white and blue; they were Bevill's friends, tenants, and neighbours. Some, if not all, had accompanied him to the northern marches for the First Bishops' War. Five days later the King raised his standard at Nottingham, and on 29 August Hopton was charged with High Treason in the Commons.

The publishing of the Commission of Array in Cornwall on 27 July was reported to the House of Lords, who sent word to the Commons on 16 August 'That Sir Ric. Greenvile and Jo. Arundell should be forthwith sent for as delinquents'. Sir Richard was soldiering in Ireland where he had acquired renown in Leicester's army, putting down the Irish rebellion. The Commons resolved on 22 July (coincidentally the same day they had summoned his brother Bevill to return to the chamber) to disband his and 14 other troops. Richard did not return to England, nor does he seem to have been disbanded because, the following year on 20 February 1643, the Commons received a letter from the Justices of Ireland relating to the good success which the King's forces had met with at 'Roskennel' and their desire that both Houses be moved to ask His Majesty to bestow on Sir Richard Grenvile, to reward his great service, the castle of 'Bali Britten' in King's County and all other properties of one Anthony Preston, his wife, and sister-in-law, worth about £300 per annum. This recommendation was referred to the Committee of Adventurers in Ireland.

At all events the Commons were not misled by the Lords getting the name wrong and Sir Bevill Greenvile and Jo[hn] Arundell were sent for.

On 19 September 1642 the answers of Bevill and John Arundell 'of Trerise' were read in the Commons. They claimed that they had been ordered by His Majesty's special command to continue in Cornwall to preserve the peace there. John Grylls the High Sheriff, who had also been sent for and who had answered in similar vein, was declared a delinquent and was sent for. The Commons resolved that Bevill was disabled from sitting again in the present Parliament and another committee was appointed to prepare a declaration concerning the absence of members upon His Majesty's special command and to set forth how their absence tended towards the Dissolution of Parliament. Bevill's and Arundell's replies were to be printed and attached to their declaration.

The committee consisted of Francis Rous of Landrake in Cornwall, the member for Truro and a half-brother of John Pym, Robert Goodwyn, a Presbyterian who was knighted by Henry Cromwell in Dublin in 1658, Robert Reynolds, a Presbyterian barrister of the Middle Temple, Alexander Rigby, another Presbyterian barrister, but of Gray's Inn, John White the M.P. for Southwark, and Miles Corbet the regicide, of Lincoln's Inn, who was executed in 1662. It was fortunate for both Bevill and John Arundell that the committee was never able to lay hands on them.

September 1642 proved an exciting month in the west country. The Marquess of Hertford, having been driven out of Dorset, retreated to Minehead in north-west Somerset, where he embarked in some colliers waiting to return empty to South Wales. Their flight was in no way impeded by the Roundheads, but they took care to skirt the larger towns such as Taunton. Hertford was a man of little resolution and made small contribution to the events of the Civil War. His embarkation for Wales was no great loss to the King's cause in the south-west.

Hopton was left onshore. He had a commission from Hertford appointing him Lieutenant-General of Horse in the West, and precious little else. He had with him Sir John Berkeley, Colonel Ashburnham, Sidney Godolphin, some other officers, 110 horse and about fifty dragoons. It was 24 September 1642.

Hopton led his tiny force by way of Dulverton, Exford and Chittlehampton, according to Roundhead reports; a remarkable route, if true. They are more likely to have ridden many miles to the west of Dulverton and across Exmoor, then dodging past South Molton, a Roundhead town, to Chittlehampton. The same Roundhead report from Barnstaple says that a servant of the Earl of Bath and of Sir Ralph Sydenham acted as their guide. Barnstaple, Bideford, and Torrington were all in arms for Parliament, and it was necessary to slip past them all, through the network of lanes which exist to this day, but a guide would have been a very necessary adjunct to a force boasting no-one from North Devon or North Cornwall.

After riding 75 miles, or thereabouts, they reached Stow on the 25th. Where they bivouacked en route is not known, but it must have been a very tired and dirty 160 which clattered through Kilkhampton that night.

The arrival of Hopton's force at Stow en route for Pendennis Castle at Falmouth was regarded as a breach of the Bodmin truce, agreed on 18 August, some five weeks earlier. The decision to retire from Minehead to Falmouth was very sound. Cornwall was regarded as likely to have a majority in favour of the King's cause. Forty-three gentlemen, seven thousand esquires, freeholders and others of Cornwall had petitioned the King in York in June:

> 'Never to suffer Your Subjects to be Governed by an Arbitrary Government, nor admit an alteration "in Religion" and pledged themselves to be "most ready to maintain and defend with their lives and fortunes, Your Majesty's Sacred Person, Honour, Estate, and lawful Prerogative against all persons whatsoever . . .'.

Sir Nicholas Slanning still commanded Pendennis, a very considerable fortification with the space to accommodate the troopers and with arms and ammunition to equip them. Having no foot soldiers, Hopton would require a safe base from which, after resting his horse, he could set about raising the county for the King.

Of Grace's eight surviving children, Jack was probably still at Oxford, his parents placing such store on his education, but one may imagine the stir and excitement of Hopton's arrival and the immense problem of showing hospitality to so many officers at such short notice. Bevill and Hopton were well known to each other having long been members of the Commons, and Bevill's influence in Cornwall, and his advice on how best to raise the county, were essential to Hopton's plans for the future.

A prolonged stay at Stow was out of the question. Sir Richard Buller at Saltash soon heard of Hopton's arrival in Cornwall and issued orders for the militia to gather at Bodmin on the 28th. On the 27th the Royalists, accompanied by Bevill, set off on the 15-mile journey through Stratton, Wadebridge, to St Columb Major, where almost a thousand foot had been mustered urgently.

The muster of so many infantry at such short notice may well be explicable by the proximity of Trerice. A messenger sent the morning before from Bevill to John Arundell would have enabled the latter to alert his local constables, who had the duty of rounding up men of military age.

The armouries within the district that Bevill was responsible for as Deputy Lieutenant had been stocked to arm pikemen and, with nearly a thousand such, Hopton felt capable of breaking off his march towards Falmouth to face up to the threat on his flank from the direction of Bodmin. His tiny force turned accordingly to the east and advanced as far as Castle an Dinas, an ancient earthwork nearby.

Buller's men must have been nearby, since Sir Alexander Carew and Humphrey Nicoll approached the Cavaliers and asked Hopton for what was virtually a renewal of the Bodmin Treaty. It must have been late in the day, and both sides were tired after long marches. A sort of truce was reached until the matter could be fully discussed the following day at Mitchell, three miles further on on the road to Falmouth. This enabled Hopton to send his pikemen home, and the Roundhead foot retired, too, towards the east.

Nicoll was a cousin of Bevill's and his son Anthony was known to him as a fellow Member of Parliament. Anthony was a nephew of John Pym, through whose influence he had gained a disputed election for that city. Humphrey was a much respected Roundhead, who died later that year, but not in battle. After Bevill 'defected' from the Commons he received a letter from Anthony criticizing his conduct. His letter is lost, but fragments of Bevill's reply are legible:

> 'My co[usin] Nicoll: Sir, what you moved me in, because I promised you, I have performed. Otherwise I should allow [it] appear that that I am as little bound to serve you as you are pleased to love me . . . [much illegible] . . . where I thought I had friendship, and where I bore so much, as I would not have refused to have spent my life and fortune for the House of London. But seeing I am taught another lesson, I must take notice that my friends are few.
> Yet I am, Sir, your well-wishing kinsman and servant.'

The Roundhead emissaries met Hopton the following day as arranged, but nothing could be agreed, save to differ. The Cavaliers were able to continue unmolested to Pendennis Castle to await events.

It cannot be doubted that Bevill must have counselled Hopton that Cornishmen reverenced the Law, and that nothing could be done in Cornwall without due respect to it. Two informations had been sent to Quarter Sessions, then sitting at Lostwithiel, one charging Buller and his Saltash levies at Launceston with unlawful assembly 'contra pacem' and the other charging persons unknown with the same offence. It seems unlikely that Bevill would have had time to pack the jury at Lostwithiel with so little notice, yet a Grand Jury found a true bill against Buller.

William Coryton and Ambrose Manaton, both of whom as magistrates had presided at Lostwithiel, rode to Launceston with copies of the indictment and the finding of the court, with a civil covering letter inviting the Roundheads to disarm and disperse. Coryton needs no introduction, but Manaton was both the Recorder and the Member for Launceston; he was an adherent of reform but a pacifist who wished to avoid bloodshed. He was eventually disabled from sitting in 1644, but only for non-attendance.

In accordance with custom, Quarter Sessions then adjourned to Truro, some nine or ten miles farther to the west. By this time one may be able to detect Bevill's influence at work. The foreman of the jury at Truro was a Mr. Noyes. His father, William Noyes, who died in 1634, had been the very learned Attorney General to Charles I who had unearthed the many ancient precedents which enabled the King to raise taxes without recourse to Parliament. Noyes had bought Bevill's birthplace, Great Brynn near Bodmin.

When at Truro the persons unknown were cited, Sir Ralph Hopton rose to his feet and claimed to be their representative. He produced his commission as Lieutenant-General of the King's Horse in the West, which Lord Hertford gave him at Minehead and, after discussion, the petty jury not only acquitted him of the offence with which he was charged, but its foreman Noyes thanked him for coming to the aid of the County.

The Royalists having won their legal battle, John Grylls, the High Sheriff of Cornwall, wished to raise a posse to drive the Roundheads out of Launceston. The newly elected mayor of Truro was doubtful of the popularity of such a move. It would interfere with tin mining, and Launceston was a long way away. Sir Richard Vyvyan of Trelowarren, the Member for Tregony, warned the people gathered in Truro that any failure to support their Sheriff might endanger their wives and children at the hands of the unlawful assembly the jury of Lostwithiel had proscribed. This argument won the day, and the constables were directed to summon a posse to gather at Moilesbarrow Down on 4 October 1642.

Some three thousand turned up. The county armouries were insufficient to arm so great a gathering, and many had no more than clubs as weapons. Hopton did what he could to form this body of peasants into military formations and then marched them to within a couple of miles of Launceston where they bivouacked over night.

The following morning the posse advanced on Launceston. The town was defensible against attacks from Devon across the Tamar or from the north, but there were few obstacles to an attack upon it from the west. When the posse reached Launceston, they found the Roundheads gone. Buller's force had retreated into Devon.

That pause at the end of a long day's march two miles or so short of Launceston was not at all to Bevill's liking. He wrote to Grace a few days later:

> 'I will detain Sym[on] Cottle no longer, nor can he bring you much more news than I sent you yesterday'.

Cottle or Cottell came from Morwenstow and as Captain Cottell he subsequently became treasurer to the Royalist army in Cornwall. Bevill continued:

> 'We found men enough at the place appointed [Moilesborough Down], well armed, and for my part I was impatient (as all my honest friends also were) that we did not march presently to fetch those traitors out of their nest at Launceston, or fire them in it. But some of our fainter brethren have prevailed so far with the Sheriff as there is a conference agreed on this day between six of a side to see if they can compose matters. But we will march on nevertheless to be [at] hand if they agree not.
>
> My neighbours did ill that they came not out and are punishable by the law in a high degree; and though I will do the best I can to save some of the honester sort, yet others shall smart.
>
> They were not in this to have commands from me; it is a legal course which the Sheriff is directed to by the Statute, and he is the commander in the business and not the [Roundhead] colonels, but he may take to his assistance whom he please.
>
> My neighbours did perchance look to hear from me, and if we proceed I shall expect they should yet come forth or they shall suffer, and they shall have further direction from me.'

Grace clearly had duty to pass the word around Kilkhampton, the last paragraph containing a face-saving clause for those who had defaulted. A contemporary letter commented:

> 'Sir Bevill Grenvile hath been a tyrant, especially to his tenants, threatening to thrust them out of house and home if they will not assist him and his confederates'.

The townsfolk of Launceston were so alarmed at the prospect of their town being besieged that they persuaded the Roundheads to leave. Hopton found the town gates open.

The Western posse had come far, Launceston had its share of inns and ale-houses, and the posse soon got out of hand. The houses of those suspected of favouring Parliament were looted, including the Recorder's house of Ambrose Manaton. Order was not finally restored until 8 October.

Hopton and some others were keen to advance with the posse across the Tamar into Devon. But the posse was under the command of the Sheriff, whose writ ran no further than the county boundary. Rumour from Devon spoke of a sizeable body of Roundheads only three or so miles away, at Lifton, under Sir George Chudleigh. The undisciplined nature of the posse, whose looting members were being rounded up in the town, must also have featured in their discussions. In the end it was decided not to invade Devon but, as remnants of Buller's force still occupied Saltash, a contingent was sent to turn them out. Colonel William Ruthven, a Scottish soldier of fortune, with some two hundred Scots en route

from Ireland to France for service under the French king, had put in there to
shelter from a storm at sea. On the advance of the Cornish the Scots hurriedly
evacuated Saltash for Plymouth.

The whole of Cornwall having been cleared of Roundheads and Scots, the posse
was disbanded and the men sent home. It was then that Hopton invited the Cornish
leaders to raise a regular army for the King's service. His success in clearing Cornwall for the King was no mean feat but, if Devon was to be brought back within
the King's jurisdiction, an army, rather than a posse, would have to be raised.

Bevill had the King's commission to raise a regiment of foot. That Hopton
should remark on it implies that the document was something more than the
command of the trained band raised around Kilkhampton. Others who volunteered to raise regiments were Sir Nicholas Slanning of Marystow in Devon (Sir
John Arundell relieved him of his post as Governor of Pendennis Castle to enable
him to take a more active part in the campaign), Colonel John Trevanion of
Carhayes, and William Godolphin. Additionally, Captain Edward Cosoworth
undertook to raise a troop of dragoons.

Trevanion was aged about thirty and had married Anne, the daughter of Sir
John Arundell of Trerice. 'He was a steady young man, of a good understanding,
great courage but of few words, yet what he said was always to the purpose'.
John Arundell (junior) is also credited with having raised a regiment, as were
Warwick, the second Lord Mohun, and Jonathan Trelawney.

Young Lord Mohun is an enigmatic character. He was not at the muster on
Moilesborough Down, nor did he take part in the advance on Launceston. Instead,
at considerable personal danger, he rode to Oxford to see the King. Knowing
nothing of what had happened in Cornwall he importuned the King for a commission for himself, Hopton, Ashburnham, and Berkeley (the latter two having
ridden to Stow with Hopton), giving any two of those persons the command of
the King's forces in the south-west in the absence of Lord Hertford in Wales. This
was one of many instances where the King was prevailed upon by importunate
courtiers to award divided commands with all the difficulties that such appointments invariably give rise to. Hopton gave him credit that, upon his return to
Cornwall with the sought after document, Mohun 'showed himself very active and
forward to advance the business'.

Bodmin was decided upon as the centre for recruiting this new force. Its
weapons were taken from the armouries at muster spots for trained bands, and
their pay was either subscribed by the colonels personally, or by other Royalist
sympathisers in the county. Thus Trelawney, Trevanion and Bevill paid for their
men out of their own pockets, and persons like Jonathan Rashleigh of Menabilly
lent their silver plate to the value in his case of £104.

Once back in Bodmin to recruit his regiment, Bevill saw no reason to drink
at his own expense. The Mayor's accounts for that November 1642 has an
entry for the payment for three gallons of sack for Sir Bevill Grenvile. His letter
to Grace, already mentioned, must have been started at Launceston and finished
at Bodmin on 18 October. Having related what seemed to him the 'non-event' at
Launceston, he completed his letter with the gossip of the day:

'The gallant Prince Rupert goes on gloriously in his Uncle's service. He hath given another blow to the enemy greater than the former, and hath well nigh cut off all their cavalry with his. So as the great Cuckold [by whom he meant the Earl of Essex, whose wife had strayed] is forced to shut himself up with his foot within the walls of Worcester, not being able to keep the field.

Witherward the King is moving with his army to give the last blow, being able to bar him from all relief, and his army is mightily increased.

Cottle hath a note. Publish it to your friends. I have sent it already to my cousin Cary [at Clovelly].

I hope we shall shortly see good days again. My noble friend the brave Wilmott had a shrewd wound, and the Prince himself slightly hurt, but they killed two thousand of the enemy with little loss.'

Bevill knew very well that Grace would disseminate any propaganda he sent her as gospel in North Cornwall. As a wife she would have probably preferred a few endearments, but the letter ended 'Yours, Bevill Grenvile'.

In retrospect it is difficult to imagine how Bevill raised the money to keep, say, three hundred men under arms. He had already sold the lands he had inherited from his parents save those around Stow in North Cornwall, the manor of Bideford in North Devon and the island, Lundy, in mid-Bristol channel. His cousin, young Thomas Stucley at Affeton in Devon, was obliged to mortgage his lands to the Chichesters for a thousand pounds to raise a regiment of horse. A regiment of foot, admittedly armed from the county's armories, must still have presented an enormous outgoing for his reduced estate. Many of his regiment were likely to have been tenants, whose rents he may have foregone, but they needed food and boots to march on, and that required funds.

While Bevill recruited at Bodmin, the problem of Mount Edgcumbe arose. For historical reasons there were then (and still are) two enclaves subject to Devon rule west of the Tamar. One of them consisted wholly or in part of Edgcumbe lands around their house of Mount Edgcumbe. The area was occupied by troops out of Plymouth, and the posse could not be called upon to attack them. It followed, therefore, that the first military engagement of the Cornish campaign by means of regular troops was to drive the Roundheads stationed there back to Plymouth.

It so happened that young Mohun's regiment and Captain Cosoworth's dragoons were most conveniently placed to undertake that task. Piers Edgcumbe, according to his monument, was 'a master of languages and sciences: a lover of the King and Church, which he endeavoured to support at the time of the Civil Wars to the utmost of his power and fortune'. Colonel Walter Slyngesby, of Hopton's Minehead ride to Stow, was sent to Mount Edgcumbe to sound out the squire. Edgcumbe opted for the King.

Mount Edgcumbe was uncomfortably close to Antony, the seat of Sir Alexander Carew. Some minor skirmishing ensued, with Carew turning out Slyngesby, and Slyngesby eventually turning out Carew. The northern enclave, near the former Grenvile house of Penheale, presented no problem, and the end result was that Tamar was once again the ancient frontier of Cornwall.

Chapter Twelve

BATTLE OF BRADDOCK DOWN AND A CESSATION

WHILE the Cornish army was being recruited and armed, the Royalist gentry of Devon were keen to combine their efforts with those of Cornwall. Devon was basically Parliamentarian; Plymouth, Exeter, and even Bevill's own town of Bideford, were unanimously opposed to the King. The gentry were fairly evenly divided in the county as a whole, but a preponderance of Royalists occurred in South Devon.

In the South Hams lived John Fortescue of Fallapit (near Kingsbridge), Sir Edward Seymour of Berry Pomeroy Castle near Totnes, his son Edward one of the two knights of the shire for Devon, Mr. Henry Champernowne of Modbury, and many others eager to demonstrate their loyalty to the King.

The then Sheriff of Devon was Richard Culme of Canonsleigh near Tiverton (who was to be savagely fined by Parliament in due course). He was about to be relieved of his post by Sir Edmund Fortescue, another Royalist appointee. Culme and his friends sent Sir Henry Cary of Cockington (Torquay) and Mr. Robert Trelawney, a successful businessman of Ham House by Plymouth, to seek out the Royalist leaders at Bodmin.

Their proposition was that they would call a posse at Tavistock, which by nature of the richness and greater population of South Devon would be greater than Cornwall could achieve, and if the Cornish army moved into Devon within 14 days, the combined force would be able to conquer Devon.

The new Cornish army crossed the Tamar and marched into Devon on the day appointed. To everyone's surprise, far from Tavistock being the rendezvous of countless Royalists, it was still garrisoned by Roundheads. Fortunately for all concerned the garrison retreated to Plymouth without bloodshed, and after the Cornish occupied the town it must have been a rather crestfallen collection of Devon Royalists who arrived to explain that their real power lay further to the south-east, in the South Hams of Devon, and to invite the Cornish to move in that direction.

Hopton was to discover that the promises of Devon Royalists were more easily made than performed. The army, with no problems of supply or lengthening lines of communication, moved south-east and occupied towns and villages between Plympton in the west and Totnes in the east. The Cornish had their wages and could steal what they could not afford. Well scattered among the hamlets of South Hams the Cornish were well billetted. The problem was to concentrate them quickly in time of trouble.

Ruthven, who was now credited with the title 'General' Ruthven, had quite given up his idea of enlisting with his men in the King of France's army. The burghers of Plymouth were delighted to find this professional and competent soldier available to help them. Driven out of Plympton, he retreated to Plymouth to plan his next move.

This incursion into Devon spurred Bevill into writing a number of letters to Grace and to the many cousins who sought his help; the name Pollard recurs frequently in Bevill's affairs, and Hugh Pollard, then a man of about 33 had achieved a certain notoriety. Henry, Lord Wilmott, William Ashburnham and he had been arrested in June, charged with High Treason. Their offence was a somewhat half-baked military coup on behalf of the King. Hugh Pollard was bailed from the Gatehouse on 30 June but appears to have jumped his bail, since the Earls of Bedford and Essex were ordered to forfeit their recognizances for his non-appearance on 7 July.

Pollard no doubt fled to his native Devon, where his father's house then stood at King's Nympton; Wilmott had been fighting and was wounded at Edgehill; Colonel William Ashburnham was now with the Cornish army. It was natural for Pollard to gravitate towards South Devon.

Bevill wrote to Mr. Henry Champernowne:

'I cannot forget that promise of yours, which did incline much to honour and favour me, namely that when our noble friend H[ugh] Pol[lard] did visit this place, you would make my happiness complete by meeting him.

I am now given to understand that he will be here in or about the beginning of the next week, and I shall think my happiness not small if you then please to honour me with your company also.

I have nothing more to say while I know your pains and penance must be great, and no ability of mine can requite it. But it will add a link more unto that chain by which I am already tied to be your faithful friend and servant ...'.

It seems unlikely that the hoped for meeting ever took place.

Sir Edmund Fortescue of Fallapit, being newly sworn in as High Sheriff of Devon, and other Royalist Devonians, then with the Cornish at their Plympton headquarters, thought it would assist the cause if a posse were summoned to muster at Modbury, Champernowne's village in the South Hams. Hopton, Slanning, and a few others rode over to Modbury on the day appointed, hoping to find well-armed foot-soldiers capable of laying siege to Plymouth. But, as Hopton relates,

'though there appear'd a great concourse of people, yet it was rather like a great fair than a Posse, there being none but the Gentlemen that had any kind of arms or equipage for war; insomuch as Sir Ralph Hopton . . . could not procure above twenty men arm'd, nor so much as a Patrol of twenty horse to ride out. All the Gentlemen of the County being so transported with the jollity of the thing that no man was capable of the labour and care of discipline.'

Bevill was not there. His regiment had been sent to occupy Totnes, but when Hopton saw the unarmed throng at Modbury he sent couriers galloping to Totnes for half Bevill's regiment to be sent to guard such sheep from the slaughter.

Other orders were intended to station picquets of horse between Modbury and Plymouth to give advance warning of any advance from that direction.

General Ruthven, that competent professional soldier, left Plymouth that night with seven or eight hundred horse and dragoons and managed to get within half a mile of Modbury before anyone noticed their arrival. It was an outstanding victory for Ruthven. The posse of unarmed peasants was dispersed, and among the prisoners sent to London for imprisonment in 'The Clinke' at Southwark were

> John Fortescue of Fallapit, Esq.,
> Sir Edmund Fortescue, Knight, the Sheriff.
> Sir Edward Seymour, Knight & Baronet.
> Edward Seymour, Esq., Knight of the Shire.
> Arthur Bassett, Esq.,
> Henry Champernowne
> Edmund Tremayne

and 12 others. Hopton and Slanning narrowly escaped being taken prisoner themselves. It was fortunate, too, that Hugh Pollard was not with Henry Champernowne at the time.

Upon the arrival of half Bevill's regiment and the return of the picquets who had proved so incompetent, an attempt was made to rescue the Devon worthies, but their captors reached Dartmouth with their prisoners before anything could be achieved. With Ruthven in Dartmouth, and Plymouth strongly held for Parliament, the Cornish army split. One half based itself on Totnes, up-river from Dartmouth, the other half on Plympton to cut Plymouth off by land from Dartmouth. I assume the Grenvile regiment to have been reunited at Totnes.

Those Royalist Devonians who had not been captured at Modbury next suggested an attack on their county town of Exeter. They said its garrison was weak and that a certain Captain Nott would be there with a ship to ferry the army across the river Exe. (One cannot help wondering whether this was Pirate Nutt of Torbay now turned into a respectable citizen.)

Hopton and his joint commanders, Ashburnham, Mohun and Sir John Berkeley had three alternatives: they could retreat to Cornwall recognizing their reverse at Modbury as final for that year's campaign; or remain quartered in the South Hams and hope for recruits; or finally, to accept Devonian promises again and venture all in an attack on the walled city of Exeter.

The Cornish army had now become a sizeable force. William Ashburnham served as Major-General of the foot, Sir John Berkeley commissary-general in charge of supplies. Bevill's regiment had grown to consist of 500 men, and the force was reported to total 10 times that figure. The Cornish were never anxious to leave their native county and Berkeley had been obliged to award a bounty to each man before crossing into Devon. This maintenance of so many men under arms required a considerable back-up team in Cornwall raising the necessary money. Devon was not coming up to promises or expectations.

The Queen, in Holland, had arranged for the Cornish to trade their tin for munitions. The Commissioners of Array were empowered to levy money from recusants, Parliamentary commissioners, and those unfit to bear arms.

Sequestration of rebel estates was another source of income. The funding of the army with Plymouth and Dartmouth in enemy hands must have been a hazardous undertaking.

One new recruit to the Cornish army was Jack Grenvile, Bevill's eldest surviving son. He was 13½; precisely when he left Gloucester Hall at Oxford is uncertain, but we know he took part in the Exeter campaign.

It was in November 1642 that the Cornish moved out of Totnes and Plympton and advanced on Exeter. The city walls on their Roman foundations, with a river at one side and a great Norman castle at the other, represented a formidable target. The Roundheads claimed to have 8,000 men under arms to man the defences.

One part of the Cornish force occupied the villages of Powderham, Alphington and Ide and crossing the Exe up-river dug in facing the walls with three iron demi-culverins. Bevill's and William Godolphin's regiments crossed over to Topsham by means of a ship seized by Pirate Nutt (if it was he) only to be left without any line of retreat — Nutt losing his ship 'by neglect'.

On 30 December Hopton and Ashburnham sent a summons to Christopher Clarke, Mayor of Exeter, to surrender his city. Clarke knew very well that the Earl of Stamford with sizeable reinforcements was on his way, and should he have had any doubts about the matter, they were soon dispelled when the redoubtable Ruthven arrived with a strong force of horse and dragoons, slipped through the Royalist lines, and joined the defenders.

Ruthven very sensibly decided to attack the smaller Royalist force to the east. Hopton was there with Bevill and William Godolphin and perhaps a thousand men. The Cornish put up a stiff fight. It was reported that Bevill and Hopton 'like men of resolve stood it out to the uttermost', but they were driven out of their lines. The promises of substantial assistance from Devon Royalists had once again proved illusory. The Cornish were restive, being short of powder and match and far from home. Mutiny was brewing. Exeter had proved no less invincible than Plymouth. Hopton decided to return to Cornwall.

The Roundheads were well aware of Hopton's difficulties. A courier was intercepted with a message to the Mayor of Barnstaple relating Hopton's difficulties and asking for help in attacking the Royalists on their homeward trek and particularly to seize their cannon.

The Royalists retreated in good order to Crediton, Bevill having to march round Exeter anti-clockwise. After a night there and at Bow, a straggling village of cob and thatch, they reached Okehampton, the guns being sent forward to Bridestow. It was at Okehampton that Ruthven launched his attack on the retreating column. The Cornish, now they were heading home, had recovered their spirit, and defended themselves so well that Ruthven was driven off. The following day the Cornish crossed the Tamar and were home again at Launceston.

From Launceston on 6 January Bevill wrote to Grace at Stow:

Launceston Jan 6 1642 [3]

'Dear Love
I shall be willing that Jack may repose himself a while at home seeing our actions abroad are not more worthy of his bestowing his time in. There comes with him a rare

man one Mr. Coxe, a Divine though for some employment which he hath it is not amiss to have him sometimes in a grey coat. His learning, his parts, his conversation are excellent, I hope he will retire himself for a while at Stow, and thereby imprint some forms in the boy which, if he have the wit, to make use of, may season him while he lives.

Pray afford him the best usage and respect you can both in diet and lodging and attendance. Lodge him in the Red Chamber and because your Chamberlain is sick, let some trusted body see his bed well furnished, with neat linen and all things appertaining sweet and clean with good fires both beneath and above, all which I leave to your discretion.

And myself for ever to remain
Your own B. Gren.

I am of a mind to billet some companies in the parishes about you as namely five companies five parishes, by one in a parish for a defence against plunderers. Wherefore, Mr. Rous to prepare the inhabitants of Kilkhampton, Morewenstow, Stratton, Poughill, and Lancells to diet a hundred men a parish in several houses. They should be allowed for each man two shillings by the week which is enough from a poor soldier, and to be brief if they will not do it willing, they shall do it whether they will or no.

And in this I expect a speedy answer.

Since the writing of this Mr. Coxe cannot come.'

Dr. William Cox, a Prebendary of Exeter, sometimes relinquished his cloth for a grey coat because Hopton employed him as a Royalist courier or spy. Hopton had no scout-master, but was hospitable to clergymen and his messages were often carried by trustworthy men of their cloth.

By 13 January Henry, Earl of Stamford, lord general of the Parliamentary forces in the West, was on his way to Cornwall. Ruthven had beaten the Devon posse at Modbury, sent the Cornish army besieging Exeter back whence it came, and must have formed the opinion that the Cornish were in such poor shape as to be no longer able to offer more than some token resistance. Fired by his successes he saw no reason to await Stamford and launched an attack on Cornwall, hoping no doubt, to be the hero of the hour.

Within a few days of Bevill arriving at Launceston three warships and a battery of cannon on the Devon side of the Tamar gave Saltash a battering. The bombardment lasted a week. While that was going on a strong force of Roundheads crossed the Tamar at Newbridge by Gunnislake, seven miles further north. The bridge had been demolished, and earthworks erected, but the Roundhead horse and dragoons forced their way across, fording the river with covering fire from their foot. Two Royalists were killed and 40 prisoners taken.

It looked as if Launceston would be outflanked and Hopton wisely ordered a general retreat towards Bodmin, surrendering Saltash and evacuating Millbrook in the south. The Cornish posse was ordered to muster, at the usual rendezvous on Moilesborough Down.

Ruthven crossed to Saltash and, joining up with the Newbridge contingent, marched to Liskeard.

By now the Cornish had got themselves into reasonable order and advanced to Boconnoc, Lord Mohun's park, where they encamped that night. Picquets of horse rode out and reconnoitred to the eastward. Their reports made it clear where Ruthven was, and a council of war at Boconnoc agreed that it was essential to attack Ruthven before he was joined by Stamford. It may be they knew from such reports that Ruthven had no great artillery train, four brass cannon (two twelve pounders) and one iron saker. Hopton had two small iron guns called 'drakes' provided by Mohun. The rest of his cannon was still at Bodmin.

Braddock Down, sloping up from Boconnoc to Braddock Church, is thickly wooded today but then consisted of two heaths, a wasteland of low shrubs, connected by a lane, itself flanked by hedges. Ruthven's army was drawn up on a ridge skirting the northern sector of the area, and the Royalists took station on a similar hump of rising ground to the west. By common consent, Hopton now was commander of the force as a whole.

By far the best account of the battle which then took place is that of Bevill himself, writing from Liskeard immediately after it occurred. If Bevill's pikemen were all fully accoutred each man would have worn a broad brimmed pot (helmet), a gorget about his neck, a breast- and back-plate, and a pair of large one-piece tassets, about eighteen pounds of steel, capable of providing protection against pistols and even muskets. Although Bevill claims the victory was without loss of life among the Royalists, Hopton says few of the Roundheads were killed. No figures are given of casualties on either side, yet the rival armies had fired at each other for two hours before Hopton charged.

Endorsed 'This messenger is paid, yet give him a shilling more'.

'My dear love,
   It hath pleased God to give us a happy victory this present Thursday being the 19th of January for which pray join with me in giving God [thanks]. We advanced yesterday from Bodmin to find the enemy, which we heard was abroad; or, if we miss him in the field, we were resolved to unhouse him in Liskeard or leave our bodies in the highway. We were not above three miles from Bodmin when we had view of two troops of their horse to whom we sent some of ours which chased them out of the field, while our foot marched after our horse. But night coming on we could march no further than Boconnoc Park where (upon My Lord Mohun's kind motion) we quartered all our army that night by good fires under the hedge.
   The next morning (being this day) we marched forth at about noon, came into full view of the enemy's whole army, upon a fair heath between Boconnoc and Braddock Church. They were in horse much stronger than we, but in foot we were superior as I think.
   They were possessed of a pretty rising ground which was in the way towards Liskeard, and we planted ourselves on such another against them within musket shot, and we saluted each other with bullets about two hours or more, each side being willing to keep their ground of advantage, and to have the other to come over to his prejudice. But after so long delay, they standing still firm and being obstinate to hold their advantage, Sir Ra[lph] Hopton resolved to march over to them and to leave all to the mercy of God and valour of our side.
   I had the van; and so, [after] solemn prayers in the head of every division, I led my part away, who followed me with so good courage, both down the one hill and up the other, that it struck a terror in them. While the seconds came up gallantly after me, and the wings of horse charged on both sides.
   But their courage so failed them as they stood not our first charge of foot but fled in great disorder and we chased them divers miles. Many were not slain because of their quick disordering, but we have taken about six hundred prisoners, amongst which Sir Shilston Calmady is one, and more are still [being] brought in by the soldiers;

much arms they have lost — eight colours we have won, and four pieces of ordinance from them.

And without rest we marched to Liskeard and took it without delay, all their men flying from it before we came.

And so I hope we are now again in the way to settle the country in peace.

All our Cornish grandees were present at the battle with the Scotch general Ruthin, the Somerset colonels and the horse captains Pin and Tompson, and but for their horses' speed had been all in our hands.

Let my sister and my cousins of Clovelly, with your other friends, understand of God's mercy to us. And we lost not a man. So I rest.　　　　　Yours ever

Bevill Grenvile.'

The great charge led by Bevill and so ably backed up by the rest must be credited in part to the chink of silver in the pockets of his Cornish soldiers. Two days before the battle, on 17 January, a fleet of 40 sail bound for London had been forced by the weather to take shelter in Falmouth harbour. Sir Nicholas Slanning seized their cargoes and put them under guard in Pendennis Castle, and so many weapons were taken and such money was found in the ships that each man in the Cornish army was paid his arrears and given a fortnight's pay in advance.

This windfall persuaded Hopton to try once again to capture Plymouth. Bevill, as his last letter shows, was content with having cleared Cornwall of the enemy and hoped for a lasting peace. The Cornish siege of Exeter had shown that the tin miners among them were better with spade and shovel, digging entrenchments and sapping walls, than with pike and musket.

With the impetus of victory and having rested the night at Liskeard, the Cornish army divided. Lord Stamford with reinforcements had arrived at Launceston to be met by the fleeing remnants of Ruthven's army. Had Ruthven been content to await his arrival the outcome might well have been different at Braddock Down. As it was, Stamford prudently withdrew to Tavistock in Devon, but he was not to be left there in peace. Berkeley and Ashburnham, with the regiments of Bevill, Slanning, and Trevannion with half the horse and dragoons, set off for Tavistock; the remainder for Saltash.

Both Saltash and Tavistock were occupied without resistance, Ruthven having crossed over to Devon from Saltash by boat with only 260 of his men. A further 100 are said to have been drowned, and 140 taken prisoner. Saltash fell on the 22nd.

Stamford needed time to reorganize his army. He proposed a conference between himself, Sir George Chudleigh, and Francis Buller with Lord Mohun, Hopton and William Godolphin representing the Cornish. The proposal was that those who wished to do so should be allowed to rejoin the King's main army, on the condition that Devon and Cornwall should both be declared a neutral zone.

'The new garrisons in them to be slighted, the old garrisons restored into King's hands, and kept with the wonted guards as in time of peace, that no armed troops should be received into either county of either part[y], no contributions exacted to the war, no pressing, or levying of volunteers, but that whosoever stood affected to either party might singly go out with his retinue and goods to either party, as he should think fit . . .'.

After some disagreement over the venue for this meeting it was agreed to meet at Robert Trelawney's Ham House near Plymouth. The conference lasted an hour and a half and failed to agree over the return of the old garrisons to the King.

This impasse having been reached, Hopton decided to invest Plymouth. The Cornish trained bands refused to cross into Devon and his forces were much depleted. The volunteer regiments moving into quarters around that city. Sir John Berkeley and William Ashburnham with Bevill's regiment and others occupied Plympton and the surrounding countryside.

Sir George Chudleigh lived at Place (now called Lower Barton) at Ashton, on the eastern extremity of Dartmoor. He and his son James were very active on the side of Parliament, James being major-general of the Roundhead foot. James raised a body of men at Totnes to relieve Plymouth, and began operating behind the Royalist lines. By early February the threat to the rear was sufficient for a detachment from Plympton to be sent to disperse such Roundheads as were mustering in the north. Bevill wrote on the 9th:

> 'Dear love; I will write a hasty line by my cousin Porter. We marched with some foot and horse from Plympton to prevent the enemy from gathering power at Tavistock, where he forbore to come for fear of us.
>
> We then marched to Okehampton to find him, we being sure they were there with five thousand men, but they ran away before we came.
>
> Then were sent some horse and dragoons to Chagford to pursue them in the night, but for want of good foot, and the approach to the town being very hard, our men were forced to retire again after they were in. And some loss we have sustained that is invaluable, to wit Sydney Godolphin is slain in the attempt, who was as gallant a gentleman as the world had. I have time for no more.'

Sydney Godolphin was a poet and courtier who had accompanied the army throughout its campaign. He was William Godolphin's second son, born in 1610. Although small of body and of a sensitive and retiring nature, his mind, according to his friend, Hobbes, was characterised by 'clearness of judgement . . . largeness of fancy, [and] strength of reason'. He was newly married and left a daughter. I assume he served in his father's regiment, but without any particular command. 'He had received a mortal shot by musket, a little above the knee, of which he died on the instant, leaving the misfortune of his death upon a place which could never otherwise have had a mention in the world!' He is said to have fallen by the 'Three Crowns Inn' facing the churchyard, which still rates two stars in guidebooks today.

Everyone loved Godolphin, and it was a saddened body of men who returned to Plympton to maintain their blockade of Plymouth. By sea no such blockade was possible – water supplies had been restricted by damming up Sir Frances Drake's culvert which carried fresh water to the city from the moors.

On Tuesday 20 February Parliament sequestrated all Hopton's lands in Somerset; others, too, were under threat. Bevill's brother-in-law John Harris (whose brother Christopher had married Gartrud Grenvile) had garrisoned his great house of Radford across the Catwater from Plymouth for the King. He was then aged about 46 and was the member for Liskeard. His house commanded the entrance to the harbour of Plymouth, if the fort on what is now called Mount Batten could be held.

News reached Bevill that Radford was likely to be attacked and Harris asked for help. His draft reply, much crossed out and re-written, shows how dangerous it was to send letters anywhere near the Roundhead lines.

> 'Sir', he wrote. 'The fault shall not be in me if ['the K's forces' deleted and 'Arbitra-tors' inserted] meet not at the prefixed time, for I will send them notice with the best speed I can. Only I have some fear that my friends can scarce be ready upon so short a warning.
>
> If I cannot attend in person, yet my obligation that you are my brother-in-law, I shall not need to tell you [much illegible] I have ever conceived very honourably of you and shall still merit as well of you as I can by my actions . . .'.

Harris was eventually disabled from sitting in the Commons and fined £600 for his malignancy. Of his house nothing remains.

On 20 February Bevill wrote home to Grace. The inactivity at Plympton was about to end. He was aware that James Chudleigh was likely to threaten Modbury, which lay between Totnes and Plymouth, a little town which both sides regarded as of great tactical importance. The unfortunate Henry Champernowne lived there. He had been lodged 'In the Clinke' on 27 December last, and was unlikely to have been exchanged yet. His house was consequently at risk.

The letter, even though entrusted to Grace's messenger, had to be carried some 50 miles across country, yet it contained information which was of considerable interest to the Roundheads if it was intercepted. That the messenger got through safely to Stow does not excuse the total lack of security in Royalist communications. The Roundheads were no less casual about theirs.

Bevill's letters, as always, were filled with propaganda to enable his wife to dispel any alarm or despondency that might have arisen in Cornwall. The teenage Jack, having been sent back to Stow after the Exeter debacle, continued at Stow. His studies at Oxford were disrupted by the Civil War, and Bevill made such arrangements as he could to complete his heir's education. Grace was, as usual, having to cope with North Cornish affairs. Fortunately, her mother, the widowed Lady Smith, was with her:

> 'My dear love,
>
> Your great care and good affection, as they are very remarkable, so they deserve my best thanks, and I could wish that the subject which you bestow them upon could better requite you.
>
> I shall return your messenger with but little certainty concerning our present condition. Our army lies still in several quarters. Sir Ra[lph] Hopton with my Lo[rd] Mohun is upon the north side of Plymouth with two regiments; Colonel Ashburnham, Sir Jo[hn] Berk[eley] and I are on the east side with two regiments; and Sir Nic[holas] Slan[ning] and Jack Trevan[ion] and their two regiments were sent the last week to Modbury to possess that quarter before the enemy came, being the richest part of this country, whence most of our provisions and victuals do come; and if it were taken from us we might be starved in our quarters.
>
> Modbury lies six miles to the eastward of us, and now the enemy with all the power that they can gather of those that we dispersed at Okehampton, at Chagford, and other [places] advanced within two miles of [our forces] at Modbury. There are many

thousand as the report goes, and we are like to have speedy work. We have sent more aid to them both of horse and foot. God speed us well.

Plymouth is still supplied with men and all sorts of provision by sea, which we cannot hinder, and therefore for my part I see no hope of taking it.

So, now, the most danger that hangs over the King's side is in these parts, for he hath great success in those parts where he is. Cirencester which Prince Rupert took, hath drawn in all Gloucestershire. The cities of Gloucester and Bristol do offer to rend themselves without force, and they are places of great importance. The Earl of Newcastle hath given the Parliament's power a great defeat in Yorkshire. The Queen is coming with good aids to the King. The Parliament did attempt to force several quarters where the King's army lay, and were beaten off with great loss to themselves in all places.

We have advertisement that some aid is coming from His Majesty to us, but it is so slow as we shall need it before we see it.

But God's will be done. I am satisfied I cannot expire in a better cause.

I have given some directions to Jack for his study. Pray cause him to put them in execution, and to make some exercise in verse or prose every day. Entreat my Co . . . Bar: Geal. to take a little pain [with] him.

I have released the prisoners that Bar: Geal: wrote for.

Let Cap[tain] Stanb: know it is all one to me whether he go by Bideford or Padstow so he make haste.

And now to conclude. I beseech you take care of your health. I have nothing so much in my prayers. Your physician Jennings is turned a traitor with the rest, whereby he hath lost my love, and I am doubtful to trust you with him.

Present my humble duty and thanks to your mother and I beseech God to bless our young people.

I rest your own ever

Bevill Grenvile

My new cap is a little too straight.

I know not what form of certificate it is that Jo Geal: desires, but if he will send it to me drawn, I will get it signed.'

James Chudleigh was now in a position to launch something larger than the forces previously engaged in skirmishes behind the lines. The Devon Roundhead posse was mustered at Totnes and on Monday 20 February they marched the 13 miles to Kingsbridge, and an advance guard pressed on up the road towards Modbury to secure the bridge over the river Avon. That same night another force marched out of Plymouth on the Modbury road and visited Fleet, a fine house belonging to Sir Thomas Hele, Baronet. Hele was a cousin of the Rolle family, and indeed of Sir Alexander Carew. His house had been seized as an outpost by the Royalists, and Roundhead reports claimed they had seized 20 horses and some prisoners there, on the march towards Modbury.

Modbury was now being advanced upon by some 8,000 clubmen of the Totnes posse from the east, and a strong force out of Plymouth from the west, the latter making up by their better equipment what they may have lacked in numbers. Most of the posse had agricultural implements and clubs.

Sir John Berkeley defended Modbury with two regiments, those of Slanning and Trevannion, at most a thousand men. The nearest help lay at Plympton, eight miles away to the north-west (as the crow flies). Bevill's regiment was at Plympton, and does not appear to have been sent for to reinforce Berkeley. It looks as if Hopton, apprised of the great superiority of the enemy so

far as numbers were concerned, had already resolved on a fighting retreat to the
Cornish borders.

The battle of Modbury which followed was a foregone conclusion; Berkeley
retreated house by house through the town and finally made a stand at the
Champernowne's manor house to the west of the town. It was militarily hopeless,
and after 12 hours' fighting, Berkeley pulled his men out and retired in good
order on Plympton to the north.

How many men were killed on either side? Grenvile says less than ten, Roundhead reports admit the loss of seven and some prisoners. The Royalists say they were
obliged to retreat for lack of powder, so a lot of banging must have gone on. The
Roundheads claimed 100 dead and 150 prisoners. I favour the lesser figure quoted.

Hopton appointed Roborough Common as a rendezvous for all Royalist forces
in Devon and, having mustered there the following day, they marched into
Tavistock, still in Devon, to await events. The Cornish army was becoming professional, but had insufficient sinews of war to equate with the huge bodies of
Devon peasants who turned up with their sickles to evict the foreign Cornish
from their beloved land. As two Parliamentarian baronets reported to Westminster: 'The Devon trained bands are sufficient to defend their country against
a small invasion, but not to follow the enemy into Cornwall'. It was Braddock
Down in reverse.

Bevill wrote to Grace from Tavistock:

> 'There have been some changes since I wrote last. We have raised our seige of
> Plymouth which for my part I never expected could have been successful, yet in sub-
> missions to better judgements I gave way. And we are now at Tavistock, united again in
> one body.
> The party of ours which was at Modbury endured a cruel assault for twelve hours
> against many thousand men, and killed many of them with the loss of four, and some
> hurt. But ours at last were forced to retire to Plympton for want of ammunition, having
> spent all their stock.
> We are still threatened, but I hope God's favour will not forsake us. Your neighbour
> of Souldon I hear is one of the dead at Modbury, and will not now plunder your country,
> if it be true.
> If my soldier Hugh Ching continues sick, pray let there be care had of him, and let him
> not want what you can help him. Bid Tom Anstey have special care of the business I have
> now writ to him. Give my duty to your mother, and I beseech God to keep and bless
> you all, and if it be His will, to send us a happier meeting; so prayeth yours faithfully,'
> and he added: 'I have sent home some pear grafts. Let them be carefully grafted, some by
> Brute and some by Jo: Skinner.
> I beseech you make Jack to pursue the directions I have given him. I did sent home
> pear grafts from Truro about Michaelmas, let them be carefully grafted also, and note
> which is one and which the other'.

Jack's education was rightly regarded as more important than soldiering at the
age of thirteen. According to Roger Granville: 'Your neighbour of Souldon' who
fell at Modbury was Humphry Prideaux of Soldon (the husband of Honor
Fortescue of Fallapitt. Humphry was the second son of Richard Prideaux of
Thuborough by Katharen Arundell of Trerice). His Bevill blood entitled him to be
regarded as one of the family by Sir Bevill.

This branch of the Prideaux family had lived at Thuborough since about 1500. The Grenviles had maintained close contact with them ever since Sir Barnard married the Bevill heiress. Writing as long before as in 1618 he told his son Bevill of one Bevill Prideaux:

'D[ick] Tremayne comes even now from Bideford where Bevill Prideaux arrived with a bark of corn from Ireland or Wales, and hath made great boast to my cousin M. Weekes and others that he will have Bevill's land from us being next heir unto it by an especial entail. I cannot but smile to see how the fools feed him fat!'

The unfortunate Bevill Prideaux had died by 1620 (the year of the Visitation) and Richard Prideaux the eldest surviving son inherited their property at Thuborough.

It must have been before the Civil War when Bevill wrote to his cousin John Harris at Radford. (John did not inherit Radford until his brother Christopher died childless in November 1623.)

'My no[ble] Co[usin], I am entreated by a poor gent[leman] of a very good family, which hath been of much worth in provident times, and is not without it in the present, and the man himself for ought I have heard hath in him no other thing to be disliked but his poverty.

But my pity to him is more stirred up by the view of his poor estate than by the consideration of his alliance. It is a brother of my co[usin] Prid[eaux] of Thuborough [that] hath importuned me to be a suitor to you in his behalf, that you would be pleased to move the noble young Mr. Hele of Wenbury to have a little pity on him, in respect of a business which he can better express than I: but I take it briefly to be thus; This gentleman in the times of his better fortune contracted with Sir Warwick Hele for a lease of some good value, and (as he informs me) paid a greater part of the fine. But being unable to pay the rest, was forced to lose his hoped for living, and to stand at Sir War[wick's] mercy for the money. Who nobly gave him some back again, and retained (as he had reason) the rest, and might have done all if it had pleased him.

And methinks it had not been amiss if it were for no other reason but to teach Co[usin] Prid[eaux] and all others so much with as not to undertake bargains as they cannot perform . . . For mine own part, though there [is] nothing either in law or equity to relieve him, and that he hath no other avail but to the nobleness of Mr. Hele's disposition, yet I leave you to perform his suit, to that noble gent[leman] whose worth and fame I love and honour though I have not yet the honour to know his person. And for myself I have no other suit but that you both will excuse my boldness; who could deny to be thus far pitiful to an Ancient gent[leman] of whom I know no ill . . .'.

John Harris lived only eight or nine miles away from the Heles at Fleet, and whether he managed to prevail on them for the return of Humphry Prideaux's money is a matter for conjecture.

Humphry was at Soldon, a farm on the estate of his eldest brother Richard, and lived there with his wife and son. He served as a Captain in a regiment raised by a Mr. Rolle, the son of Sir Samuel Rolle of Heanton.

Sir Samuel Rolle (c. 1588–1647) was one of the largest landowners and one of the richest men in Devon. His great house at Heanton Sackville near Petrockstow was destroyed by fire earlier this century, but his descendants continue in a house built on the site.

Sir Samuel subscribed £1,000 towards putting down the rebellion in Ireland, and worked vigorously in the Roundhead cause until ill health retired him. As

early as 5 August the previous year the King appointed Arthur Bassett Colonel
with authority to appoint Captains of the trained bands commanded by Rolle.
The commission would have had no more effect than a Parliamentary appointment to command Grenvile's regiment in Cornwall. The Rolle regiment must
have had many Rolle tenants among its ranks, and with one of its Captains,
Humphry Prideaux, living only seven miles from Stow, Grace may well have
feared he might plunder her country.

Bevill wrote home again on the 26th:

> 'Dearest; I shall write to you without delay having a little alarm at this instant, and so
> we had last night, which [has] kept me up late. Our loss at Modbury was little, the
> enemy's great. We had not ten men slain, the enemy about 300, some say 500 . . .
>
> Tell my cousin George Cary I give him great thanks for his favour to Jack, which I
> entreat him to continue. The boy doth amend his hand a little. Let him continue to do
> so and he shall be the better for it.'

George Cary of Clovelly had a daughter married to John Arundell (junior) of
Trerice and was otherwise connected to the Grenviles. The grey-coated Doctor
Cox having failed to turn up at Stow, Jack may have been sent to Clovelly to
continue his education.

> 'There is yet no aid coming to us', he continued. 'But I hope there will be — though
> I fear too late'.

No men or money having reached the Cornish from the King for so long, and
the seige of Plymouth raised for want of both, the two sides agreed an armistice
or truce for seven days on 28 February, the Cornish vacating Tavistock and
crossing the Tamar back into Cornwall. Bevill and his regiment quartered in
Launceston while the grandees on both sides, nine from each county, met at
Stonehouse outside Plymouth, and swore to uphold the Protestant religion, the
prerogative of the King, and the privileges of Parliament. To make the truce
binding each took a personal oath and the sacrament.

The war being over, or so it must have seemed, young Prideaux, Humphry's
son, called on Bevill to confirm the rumour of his father's death and to solicit
his help. Mr. Rolle was about to replace Captain Henry Prideaux with another,
and his son was very keen to follow his father in the regiment. One thus gets a
curious glimpse of the strength of family ties in Civil War; the Colonel of a
Royalist regiment begging a captaincy in a Roundhead regiment for a young
cousin. There may have been self-interest involved in the matter: for if hostilities
should break out again, young Prideaux might feel constrained to leave Grace
and her household in peace.

> 'To Mr. Rolle: Most hon[oured] Sir. I hope I have obtained your pardon for that I
> could not lately wait on you in person when I was near you. Truly it was much against
> my will to be kept from you, and I will not be long before I come purposely to kiss
> your hands.
>
> Sir, I am emboldened at this time to trouble you with a word or two in a business that
> I hope will not offend you. There is one of the old Captains of your regiment lately
> dead (my cousin Pri[deaux] of Thub[orough]). He hath left a son who is a gent[leman]
> of singular virtue and worth, and whom I am persuaded is ordained by God to repair

those breaches which the old man hath made in his fortune. He is willing to serve you in the quality of Captain, as his father did, and I hope you will respect a gent[leman] of so great merit, and not confer it upon a stranger — rather upon a son — while there is so much desire in him. His habitation is also most convenient for the company, being in the midst of it, and thereby most fit on all occasions to attend his duty.'

In case the letter should fail to reach Mr. Rolle or carry insufficient weight by itself, Bevill wrote to a Mr. Rawlings, presumably Rolle's agent:

'My good friend; I have written unto my noble friend your m[aster] in the behalf of my young Cousin Prid[eaux] of Thub[orough] that it would please him to confer on him the command which his father had within Mr. Rolle's regiment . . . I will also entreat you if Sir Edmund Fowell be with you to acquaint him with this business, and desire his good word in it in behalf of my Cousin Prideaux who married his niece . . . You see how bold I am with you, but it is because I love you, and am confident of yours and will ever rest your faithful friend.'

The peace treaty had been in operation little more than a week when Grace, not unnaturally, wished to know when she might expect to see her husband. In reply to her enquiry he wrote:

'Dearest, If you account yourself fallen from any happiness by the want of me, I have a thousand time[s] more reason to be miserable when I am divided from you. Pray be of comfort however things go, and I beseech God to enable me to deserve your love.

For news, there is a cessation agreed on for 20 days, from whence for my part I look but for knavery.

We hear that the Queen is landed in the North, for whose guard the King hath sent those forces which should have come to us, whereby we are prevented a while longer: so one thing or other hinders us still, but I hope God will not forsake us.

The force which was at Tavistock is all disbanded. Enquire whether my regiment may be billeted in good houses of the Hundred of Stratt[on] during this cessation, and then I will be nearer home. Pray keep me some Pearmains.'

The Queen had indeed landed in England with the proceeds of pawning the crown jewels in Holland. Neither Sir Bevill, nor his regiment, were keen to continue at Launceston. His men used the church as a barracks; its splendidly carved granite must have been as cold as death in early March. Bevill had already sounded out the householders of Stratton, having returned thence on 6 March, when by reason of the 'great company' the Mayor had to find wood and candles. Two days later the Mayor ordered a bottle of sack to be given to Bevill, costing 2s. 4d., a considerable price. The letter of 9 March, throwing the responsibility on Grace to find billets for Grenvile's men near Stow, shows Bevill to have much preferred mess life to domesticity.

Although Bevill had mortgaged Bideford to Margaret Lady Cholmely for £3,000 in 1639, he was still Lord of the Manor. It must have galled him that his town of Bideford was staunchly pro-Parliament. His house on the quay was no longer a safe retreat for him to visit. The cessation, as both sides called the period from 28 February to 22 April, was so uneasy a peace that both sides accused the other of breach of faith.

According to 'Certain Information', a pamphlet in Thomasen's Tracts dated 10–17 April 1643:

'The toune of Beddiford in the North part of the County of Devon should have been betrayed and delivered up to Sir Ralph Hopton in this manner; Sir Bevil Greenvill sent some of his soldiers into the toune like countrimen, one after one, who confederated themselves with some of the malevolent Townsmen, to surprise the Watch of the Towne and to cut their throats in a certaine night, and then an alarm should have been given by them as a call to the rest of Sir B. G.'s regiment which should have attended neere to the Toune to have come to their aide and finished the exploit: but it pleased God in his mercifull providence to discover the Treachery thus; One of the Conspirators being a Tounsman happened to be drunke the afternoon before the dismall night, and in his drunkenesse openly babbled out what feates he and the rest of his Complices meant to perform the night following; which being taken hold of and thoroughly examined, the Conspiracie was discovered and all the Conspirators were instantly apprehended together with all Sir B. G.'s souldiers that were then in the Toune . . .'.

We know Bevill regarded the cessation as an opportunity for knavery by the other side. Parliament had shown itself more than displeased by the cessation. Neutrality was, for Parliament, defeat. To prevent extensions of the cease-fire the Commons forbade the Mayor to permit Hopton to enter Exeter for further discussions. The Cornish commissioners, on being refused access, left Devon on 17 April. The Roundheads were complaining that the Cornish were in contact with the French, who were advancing money for the Royalist cause. I think it unlikely that Bevill, a mere colonel in the Cornish army, would have attempted to take Bideford by stealth, or would have countenanced what he would have considered a breach of faith. On balance I think the so-called plot to breach the cessation and seize Bideford was an ale-house fantasy.

Chapter Thirteen

THE BATTLES OF STRATTON AND LANSDOWN HILL

PARLIAMENT had no intention of allowing Devon and Cornwall to opt out of the Civil War; of becoming, in effect, a neutral peninsula. While complaining of Royalist trafficking with the French and their repairing the defences of Saltash, Lord Stamford was busy raising three new regiments of foot at Exeter with a view to invading Cornwall the moment the truce expired, at midnight Saturday 22 April 1643. The inhabitants of Barnstaple and Bideford were reported to have sent 5,000 foot and nine troops of horse to Holsworthy, and news to that effect must have reached Grace at Stow. Cornwall's natural defensive line, the river Tamar, peters out into small streams in the extreme north of the county, and Grace must have felt her children and herself unduly exposed. Her letter suggesting she should join Bevill at Launceston has been lost, but his reply reads:

> 'Dear love: Use your own discretion in removing where and when you think fit. I will not for a world stay you against your mind, and I am now doubtful whether I shall advise you to come hither, because the enemy is come so near us as Holsworthy. But there is a cessation concluded again till Saturday night; they cannot stir in the meantime unless they be devils. Yet do what you please; it shall please your B: Gren: '

Grace very sensibly moved out of Stow and went to stay with the Arundells at Trerice; it was to prove a wise move on her part. If, as I suppose, Jack was at Clovelly, he too no doubt left Devon for the safety of Newquay, 20 miles away to the south-west.

The Cornish themselves were busy. A meeting of the gentry at Bodmin on 10 April agreed to raise £750 a week to pay for their army, and Lord Mohun and others lent their plate to the value of £3,000. Munitions were reaching Falmouth from Bordeaux, and a general muster of the Cornish army at Launceston was ordered to take place on Sunday, 23 April.

Stamford had re-organised his army, which now consisted of 3,500 foot and eight troops of horse, but he himself was immobilised with a severe attack of gout. Bevill and his men were able to take advantage of the cessation to snatch a few days' leave, but he and his regiment were back in Launceston by the 14th.

The last night of the truce was celebrated by the Mayor of Launceston giving a dinner party; his guests were Hopton and Bevill, Francis Bassett of Tehidy and his brother Sir Thomas, William Coryton, Colonel Ashburnham, Ambrose Manaton of Trecarrel and Paul Speccot of Penheale. Ashburnham had turned over his post as major-general of the army to Sir Thomas Bassett and was about to leave and join the King. The party may have been to bid him farewell; it was certainly the prelude to a storm, and one hopes the sack was good.

Such intelligence as had reached Hopton spoke of enemy forces mustering at Lifton, four miles away in Devon. To safeguard himself against a surprise attack, he and Bassett posted dragoons at the Tamar crossings that morning. Major General James Chudleigh marched out of Lifton at first light with 1,500 musketeers, 200 pikes, and five troops of horse. The only Royalists in Launceston were Grenvile's 1,200 men, billeted as usual in the church, when news of Chudleigh crossing Polson bridge reached the town.

Hopton send half Bevill's men to man Beacon or Windmill Hill commanding the road from Devon, and lined the banks and hedges with musketeers. No sooner were they posted than Colonel Godolphin's regiment arrived and joined them. The opposing forces were now about equal, but Chudleigh launched an attack on the hill at 10 o'clock. Grenvile's men were well placed and caused some loss to the enemy before being driven back.

At 11.00 Lord Mohun's regiment arrived together with Sir John Berkeley's horse and dragoons. Hopton now had sufficient men to try and cut off Chudleigh by seizing Polson bridge in his rear, but Chudleigh too received reinforcements. They found the bridge held by 700 of Meyrick's London Grey Coats and a hundred Devonians of Sir John Northcote's regiment.

The battle continued all day, and both sides suffered casualties. Captain Bassett, commanding Mohun's regiment, was killed, amongst others, and the tide only turned on the arrival of Slanning and Trevannion's regiments at 7.00 p.m. Hopton Berkeley and Bassett then led three separate columns in a charge on the enemy's line, Chudleigh's men fell back and he was obliged to retreat over the bridge back into Devon. It was a well managed rearguard action by Chudleigh, which Hopton was unable to turn into a rout. What might have been a decisive victory was spoiled by the Cornish who 'according to their usual custom after a fight grew disorderly and mutinous'. Such pursuit as was attempted was deterred by the explosion of a powder store in a little barn which 'scalded' many of the victorious Cornish.

The Cornish had fought long and hard, and some had marched considerable distances before being committed to battle. A day was needed to rest and regroup, but on Tuesday 25 April they set off for Okehampton, getting no farther than Lifton that evening.

On Wednesday the Cornish advanced to Bridestowe, six miles from Okehampton, intending to quarter there before advancing farther. At some point of their march they were joined by a party of Devon Royalists commanded by the new Royalist High Sheriff of Devon, Sir Henry Carey of Cockington (Slanning's brother-in-law). The column now totalled 3,000 foot, 600 horse and dragoons, and four brass guns, of which two were 12-pounders taken at Braddock Down.

At Bridestowe there was a brush with Chudleigh's scouts and a 'friend' arriving from Okehampton reported that Chudleigh's men were in very low spirits, and that Chudleigh himself was only awaiting help to evacuate his cannon and powder before retreating to Exeter.

Hopton's men were still fresh, the news from Okehampton was not inaccurate, and it was decided to march on through the night and assault Okehampton at first light. Between Bridestowe and Okehampton lies Sourton Down, the highest, bleakest part of the road where it crosses a spur of Dartmoor. Once over Sourton Down the road drops away down to Okehampton, an indefensible town sunk in a valley below the moor.

The army with its picquets already posted was called to arms, and a long column, with its cannon in the centre and its foot divided equally before and behind the guns, with horse and dragoons in the van and rear, set off with little thought of meeting any resistance on the road to Okehampton. They had overlooked the courage and resource of young James Chudleigh.

News of the Royalist advance only reached Chudleigh at nine o'clock that night. Many of his men had deserted after Launceston, and his cannon were not available. His force had been reduced to about 1,000 foot and 108 horse. Ordering his foot to the western limits of Okehampton, he led his horse onto Sourton Down. It was a pitch dark night with a storm brewing. On Sourton, Chudleigh posted his dragoons in small groups under resolute officers at different points on either side of the road.

Hopton, Mohun, Berkeley and Bassett were 'carelessly entertaining themselves' at the head of the dragoons in the van as they started crossing Sourton Down. Scouts rode ahead and on either flank, according to Hopton, but no one detected the ambush that lay ahead. His army was 'never as they conceived in better order, nor in better equipage, nor ever (which had like to have spoiled all) in lesser apprehension of the enemy'.

At eleven o'clock the trap was sprung. Chudleigh's dragoons charged the Royalist column from either side, firing their weapons and cutting through both horse and foot in Hopton's van. The Roundhead officers shouted, 'Charge on, charge on! They run, they run!' And run they did. Sir Henry Carey had his horse shot under him and the leading dragoons, presumably newly raised in Devon and therefore politely allowed to lead the Cornish into their county, broke and fled. Falling back onto the horse behind them they, too, were panicked. Roundhead horse rode through them and the foot, and penetrated as far as the cannon.

Had it not been for Bevill and Mohun who stood firmly in defence of their cannon train, Hopton's defeat would have been total. As it was, he lost about 60 killed, 20 taken prisoner, 100 horses, and a quantity of muskets and powder. But even worse, the Roundheads killed Hopton's secretary and seized his portmanteau in which were lists of Royalist supporters in Devon and the King's orders to Hopton to march into Somerset. This windfall was to cause the gouty Lord Stamford to 'leap out of his chair for joy' when the spoils reached him at Exeter. He declared that the sequestrations to be levied on such evidence would be worth £40,000 to the Roundhead cause.

Mohun and Grenvile's regiments having saved the guns, Slanning moved forward from the rear and those who had not fled were deployed along a ditch in line with musketeers on their left and the remnants of the cavalry on their right. The cannon were placed and protected from assault by rows of 'Swede's feathers', long iron-tipped staves set into the ground at angles designed to rip out the bellies of any horse which charged them.

By now Chudleigh's foot had arrived from Okehampton and his little force advanced on the Royalist line, their slow matches glowing in the dark. Two cannon were fired at the advancing Roundheads as soon as they came within range and the storm, which had been building up throughout the night, burst. Thunder, lightning and torrential rain discouraged the men of either side. Chudleigh charged with his horse in a feint for the guns, but the 'Swede's feathers' deterred him. He then retreated in good order to Okehampton, leaving slow-match gleaming like glow worms hanging from furze bushes behind him. Not realising the road to Okehampton was now open to them, the Royalists trailed miserably back to Launceston to regroup.

Carey, who had been unhorsed, returned home to Cockington, disguised as a woman. Another Royalist, Chichester Wrey, was taken prisoner but, being only 15, no one imagined he would be a Captain in Mohun's regiment, and being loosely guarded, made his way off in the night. It was a noteworthy victory for Parliament and Hopton was back where he started.

Regrouping at Launceston took several days; routed stragglers trickled in, and in the hope of collecting more in Devon, Tavistock was occupied once again, but news of Stamford's advance westwards made it imperative to draw back behind the Tamar line.

Stamford's gout had moderated. Appreciating the difficulty of a frontal attack on the Cornish protected by their river he had evolved a masterly plan to circumvent it by a right hook into North Cornwall. The Cornish were obliged to defend a line about 50 miles long, extending from Plymouth Sound in the south to the Bristol Channel in the north. Royalist regiments were spread at intervals along that line. Bevill and his regiment were posted around Stratton in the north; his house of Stow lay in that narrow strip of land running northwards to Hartland Point in Devon and the Tamar in that region was no more than a stream, offering little or no protection. Sir Francis Hawley, with two hundred of the more reliable troopers available, guarded the bridge at Bridgerule against any advance into Cornwall from Holsworthy. But Holsworthy was only nine miles away from Stow, and Grace was to be congratulated for her foresight in travelling down to Trerice.

Stamford had 1,400 horse and dragoons, 5,400 foot, and a train of 13 brass cannons and one mortar. He was plentifully supplied with money, rations, and powder. His intelligence, suggesting that the Cornish were short of everything, was accurate.

According to a newsletter dated from Plymouth on 15 May 1643, the Cornish army now consisted of seven regiments of foot: those of Slanning, Thomas Bassett, John Trevanion of Caerhayes, Mohun, William Godolphin, Charles Trevanion of Caerhayes (whose lieutenant-colonel was John Arundell junior of Trerice), and Bevile Grenvile. He gives the names of Bevill's officers: lieutenant-colonel Sir Peter Courtenay, Sgt.-Major M. Deroy, and Captains Piper, Estcot (Escott?), Ford, Porter, Smith, Watts and Penvowne. Jack Grenvile is not mentioned, nor Anthony Payne, the Cornish giant, but the latter may not have held a commission. The fact that the Roundheads were conversant with the nominal rolls of their opponents, however inaccurately, argues an intelligence network far superior to that available to Hopton.

On 11 May the Earl of Stamford set out from Exeter with the intention of conquering Cornwall. A rendezvous for the trained-bands had been ordered at Okehampton. Knowing his army to be both better armed and twice the size of Hopton's volunteers, he had only two worries; one was that the High Sheriff Grylls would muster a posse and even up the disparity of numbers, the other that the Royalists might escape the pincer movement he had designed to entrap them. These considerations persuaded him to detach his horse from his foot. Sir George Chudleigh (father of Major General James Chudleigh) was detached with 1,200 horse to cross the Tamar farther south, presumably at New Bridge, and to surround Bodmin where the posse would be discouraged from mustering. The few horse he retained he sent to Stratton to seek a suitable encampment for his foot. The infantry and artillery train set off to the westward through Holsworthy and soon reached the border and crossed into Cornwall, heading for Stratton. Stamford was now west of the Tamar and Cornwall must have appeared his for the taking.

The advance guard of Stamford's horse chose Stratton Hill as the best base from which to mop up the Cornish. It had a level top, remnants of an iron-age fort, and steep sides. Save for Chamond Grenvile at Poughill nearby, the inhabitants of Stratton were thought to be inclined more towards Parliament than towards the King. Grenvile had billeted his regiment thereabouts and no one likes to have troops of any complexion billeted on them. Bevill was probably at Efford, south of Stratton and the river Neeth, a house which belonged to his cousins the Arundells of Trerice.

Stamford's main body was able to camp on the hill without opposition in mid-May, but their arrival was known to Hopton within hours. Hopton resolved to concentrate his field army and to strike at Stratton when Stamford was without his main body of cavalry. He marched in easy stages to allow those regiments in the south to join him. The first day's march out of Launceston took him no farther than four miles, to North Petherwin, where on an open common the army 'lay together all that night, and as well the best of the officers as the soldiers were all well contented with a dry biscuit apiece for want of other provisions'.

The following day, being Sunday, prayers were read by the chaplains of each regiment, and on they went again. Their advance was delayed by skirmishes with Stamford's dragoons, Hopton fearing that their appearance presaged a major battle with Stamford's foot. The Cornish moved forward cautiously to Week St Mary, only six miles north of their previous bivouac. Roundhead horse harried them there as well, and the Cornish were not only hungry but deprived of their sleep. But they had attained a point only five miles away from Stratton Hill.

Bevill, with his regiment of 1,200 men, must have been greatly relieved when the main body of the Cornish army appeared at Efford that Monday evening. Grace and the children were safe with the Arundells at Trerice, and the days of wanton destruction were yet to come. There is no suggestion that Stow was sacked by Stamford's men, although lying as they did between Bevill and his home.

Of the battle of Stratton which followed there are, or have been, three contemporaneous accounts; one written by Bevill to Endymion Porter for the King's information which has been lost, one contained in Hopton's *Bellum Civile*, and a third of Clarendon's clearly based on Hopton's account. Hopton having been in command of the field, his account can best be relied on. It had not been printed by Charles Healey when Roger Granville gave his account, based on Gardiner and Fuller, and his suggestion that the *Tree Inn* at Stratton was the Royalist headquarters before the battle seems unlikely. Efford House was a more likely venue, and the line of the river the logical line to have been held against any further incursion by Stamford into Cornwall.

> 'The next day by sunset they were advanced so far as Efford House being within the parish of Stratton about a mile from the town, and immediately with their forlorn hope beat in a party of the enemy's, and recovered the pass over the river at Efford Mill which lay between them and the enemy's camp. There the commanders of the Cornish army called a council of war, where it was quickly resolved, notwithstanding the great visible disadvantage, that they must either force the enemy's camp, while the most part of their horse and dragoons were from them, or unavoidably perish.
>
> And so in the beginning of that night a great part of the army was drawn over that pass and placed in the enclosures towards the enemy's camp, and stood all night at their arms ready to receive the enemy, which was expected to fall upon them.
>
> But nothing was acted till the next morning about the break of day, and then it was discerned that the enemy had lined hedges within half musket shot of them, and then immediately musket shot began to be exchanged between both parties.
>
> And within a while after the rest of the Cornish army were drawn over likewise, and the foot being about 2,400 divided into four parts, and the cannon being eight pieces equally distributed to every part. The first part being commanded by the Lord Mohun and Sir Ralph Hopton [900 men from Liskeard] undertook to assault the enemy's camp upon the south side, next Sir John Berkeley and Sir Bevill Grenvile [with 1,200 men] upon the avenue next to them upon the left hand, Sir Nicholas Slanning and Colonel Trevannion [1,000 from Saltash and 700 from Launceston] the next avenue to that upon the left hand of all [that they were to assault from the north side has been erased in Hopton's manuscript] and Sir Thomas Bassett and Colonel Godolphin upon the left hand of all. Mr. John Digby with the horse and dragoons being then about 500, stood upon a sandy common where there was a way leading up to the enemy's camp, with order to charge anything that should come down that way in a body, but else to stand firm in reserve.'

The figures in brackets are taken from Coates, and suggests that the total men available to Hopton rather exceeded 2,400.

> '[The enemy] had with them but a few horse, but they had 5,400 foot by poll as Mr. Chudleigh their Major General afterwards acknowledged. They had likewise thirteen pieces of brass ordinance and [a] mortar piece with a very plentiful magazine of provisions and ammunition, and all very strongly encamped and barricaded upon the flat top of a very high hill that had very steep ascents to them every way.
>
> In this order on both sides the fight began Tuesday the 16th day of May 1643 about five o'clock in the morning. The Cornish foot pressing those four ways up the hill towards the enemy, and the enemy as obstinately endeavouring to keep them down.

The fight continued doubtful with many countenances of various events till about three of the clock in the afternoon, by which time the ammunition belonging to the Cornish army was almost spent.'

Clarendon adds this to the account: 'Towards three of the clock in the afternoon, when word was brought to the chief officers of the Cornish that their ammunition was spent to less than 4 barrels of powder; which (concealing the defect from the soldiers) they resolved could be only supplied with courage; and therefore, by messengers to one another, they agreed to advance with their full bodies, without making any more shot, till they reached the top of the hill, and so might be upon even ground with the enemy . . . and the enemy, in wonder of the men who outfaced their shot with their swords, to quit their post.

It fortuned that on that avenue where Sir Bevill Grenvile advanced in the head of his pikes in the way, and Sir John Berkeley led on the musketeers on each side of him, Major General Chudleigh with a stand of pikes charged Sir Bevill Grenvile so smartly that there was some disorder, Sir Bevill Grenvile in person overthrown, but being presently relieved by Sir John Berkeley and some of his own officers, he reinforced the charge, and there took Major General Chudleigh prisoner.'

Hopton continues:

'In fine, the endeavours of all the four parts of the foot succeeded so well, as growing nearer together as they ascended, and the enemy giving way, and leaving the possession of some of their dead and some of their cannon to them, between three and four o'clock the commanders happened to meet altogether in one ground near the top of the hill, which the enemy had acquitted in a rout.'

Clarendon says:

'But the enemy no sooner understood the loss of their major-general but their hearts failed them; and being so resolutely pressed, and their ground lost, upon the security and advantage whereof they wholly depended, some of them threw down their arms and others fled, dispersing themselves, and every man shifted for himself.'

Hopton comments:

'In that fight God blessed the King's party so well that they lost not . . . men in all, though they were the assailants, but killed about 300 of the enemy in that place and took seventeen hundred prisoners, whereof their major-general was one, and about thirty other officers. They took likewise all their cannon, . . . and all their ammunition being seventy barrels of powder, and all other sorts of ammunition proportionable, and a very great magazine of biscuit and other provisions.'

Lord Stamford remained with his horse who were never ordered to charge the Cornish as they fought their way up the hill. There were only six or seven score of them, but resolutely led they might have turned the tide of battle; their only function seems to have been to escort Stamford as he fled ignominiously to Exeter. All concerned were full of praise for Chudleigh who 'behaved himself with as much courage as a man could do'. James Chudleigh was so impressed by the behaviour of the Cornish that he changed sides and advised his father to do likewise.

Sir George Chudleigh had carried out his rôle admirably. Having occupied Bodmin he successfully prevented the posse from gathering, and was now awaiting Lord Stamford and his victorious army.

Hopton marched south to cut him off, but failed to do so.

Bevill was left with his regiment at Stratton, when he may well have lodged at the *Tree Inn*. His duties included guarding the prisoners and the Roundhead cannon train and powder. He would have been less than human if he failed to ride north to Stow to see if all was well there.

His next surviving letter to Grace was dated eight days after the battle. It being the last letter of Bevill's in existence I give it in full:

'To my best friend the Lady Grace Grenvile these ——

Okehampton May 24 1643

Dear Love

I have received several letters from you since I wrote last, and in all do see your excellent affection & mine own obligation. God reward you if I cannot. You are doubtful lest my bruises stick by me. I thank you, but I hope it is prettily over, though I am something sore, & did spit blood two days and bled at nose much. I had no slatt, neither do I now need it I think, but I did wish I had some at that time.

You may safely return to Stow, and I am persuaded you would have had no hurt if you had stayed.

Our Army is at Okehampton: and what further will become of us I know not, we are sure of your good prayers as you are of mine who will ever remain

Yours constantly

Bevill Grenvile.

Present my duty to your mother, and my best service to my noble cousins at Trerice.'

Slatt or powdered slate was thought to have medicinal qualities. If Grace and her mother still continued at Trerice, her son Jack must by now have joined his father at Okehampton. The comment that Grace might have stayed safely at Stow suggests that Bevill did indeed visit his old home after Stratton and that the Roundheads did not.

The same day he wrote to Grace, the King wrote to Bevill:

'To our Right Trusty and Well-beloved Sir Bevill Granvill at our Army in Cornwall: Charles R.

Right Trusty and Well-beloved Wee greet you well. Wee have seen your Letter to Endymion Porter Our Servant. But your whole conduct of Our Affairs in the West doth speak your Zeal to Our Service and the Public Good in so full a Measure as Wee rest abundantly satisfy'd with the Testimony thereof. Your labours and your Expenses Wee are graciously Sensible of, and our Royal Care hath been to ease you in all that Wee could. What hath fallen short of our Princely Purposes and your Expections Wee know you will attribute to the great malignity of the Rebellion Wee had and have here to wrestle withall.

And Wee know well how effectually a diversion of that mischievous strength you have made from Us at your own hazzards. Wee assure you Wee have all tender sense of the hardness you have endured and the state wherein you stand. We shall not fail to procure you what speedy relief may be. In the mean space Wee send you Our most hearty thanks for some encouragement and assurances on the word of a Gracious Prince that (God enabling us) Wee shall so reflect upon your faithful Services as you and yours shall have cause to acknowledge our Bounty and Favours. And so Wee bid you heartily farewell. Given at our Court at Oxford the 24th May 1642/3.'

At the Restoration, Charles II slipped the patent for the Earldom of Bath into Jack Grenvile's pocket before leaving Holland for England. Some say it had been promised to his father Bevill, but the King's letter makes no mention of it, and Hopton, the victorious general at Stratton, was only made a baron.

Another hero of the Stratton battle was Bevill's henchman Anthony Payne. At the Restoration, Charles II made him Halberdier of the Guns at Plymouth Citadel, and Sir Godfrey Kneller was commissioned by the King to paint his portrait. It hung in the great hall of the palatial house built by Bath at Stow. After the house had been demolished, Gilbert, the Cornish historian, found it in a farmhouse on the estate. The farmer's wife described it as a 'carpet with the effigy of a large man on it'. It was rolled up, full of holes, and thick with dirt. She or her husband had been given it by the landlord's steward and gladly sold it to Gilbert for £8. After Gilbert's death it was sold at Devonport for £42 to a connoisseur of paintings, who took it to London, where it fetched £800. It now hangs in the Royal Institution of Cornwall at Truro.

Born at Stratton, he measured seven feet when at the age of 21 he became part of Bevill's household at Stow. He grew a further two inches subsequently. He was not only tall but immensely broad and strong and there are many stories told about him. One relates how, after the battle of Stratton, Payne had the grisly task of helping bury the dead. Trenches to contain 10 men at a time had been dug, and Payne was carrying one corpse under his arm when the supposedly dead soldier started to kick and plead for his life.

'Surely you won't bury me, Mr. Payne, before I am dead?' said he. 'I tell thee man', replied Payne. 'Our trench was dug for ten and there's nine in it already; thou must take thy place.'

'But I be'ant dead I say', said the soldier. 'I haven't done living yet — be massyful, Mr. Payne — don't ye hurry a poor fellow into the earth before his time.'

'I won't hurry thee, thou canst die at thy leisure', was the reply, but he carried the man back to his wife and cottage in Stratton.

Another story relates how one Christmas a boy had been sent with a donkey to bring in logs for the fires at Stow, but was a long time returning. Payne went in search of him and returned carrying the loaded animal on his back which he set down by the hearthside shouting:

'Ass and fardel, ass and fardel, for my lady's yule.'

He had accompanied Bevill into Stratton on another occasion when there was a commotion in the yard of the inn. Bevill sent him to find out what was going on and he returned with a man under each arm whom he had arrested for brawling.

'Here are the kittens', said Payne, and continued to hold them while Bevill gave each a thrashing with his riding whip. Magistrates had rather greater scope in the 17th century than they have today.

Bevill in charge of the prisoners achieved a notable convert. James Chudleigh had found himself cold-shouldered by the Court after giving evidence against the London plotters, Hugh Pollard and his friends, and joined the Roundhead army out of pique. His courage in the battle of Stratton and during his attempt on Launceston had won him the respect of his enemies, who treated him with the utmost civility. He soon noticed that Parliamentary propaganda, painting Royalists as godless debauchees, was ill-founded. He wrote to his father:

'I never saw any army freer from vice, nor more religiously inclined than I perceive the whole genius of this Army to be'.

Chudleigh's defection was blamed for Parliament's defeat at Stratton. He was accused of treachery. His father could not be persuaded to change sides, but resigned his commission and retired home.

Meanwhile Hopton had returned to Launceston where he met the mysterious Doctor Coxe, dressed no doubt in his grey coat rather than his canonicals. It was he who brought the news that Lord Hertford and Prince Maurice were marching westwards at long last and hoped to meet Hopton and his Cornish army in Somerset.

Bevill was sent for with his regiment to join the army at Okehampton. We know that Jack and the Cornish giant Payne went, too. The enormous expense of keeping so many men under arms may well have been the gravamen of Bevill's letter to Endymion Porter. But the King had no money to spare.

The Cornish army at Okehampton had a very considerable cannon train, taken from Stamford and Ruthven, a good stock of powder, and above all a resounding victory against heavy odds behind them.

Lord Stamford's army having melted away, the foot not taken prisoner making off towards Bideford and Barnstaple, and the horse accompanying their general back to Exeter, there was no field army in the South West to oppose Hopton. Nor could there be any reason for not acting on the orders brought by Doctor Coxe to join up with Lord Hertford's forces moving south-west from Oxford.

One large centre of population, the city of Exeter, not only provided a Parliamentary stronghold, but might prove an inconvenience if by-passed. Sallies from behind the walls and forts of Exeter could harass Hopton's lines of communication with Cornwall in his rear.

It was hoped that Exeter might be persuaded to submit now that Roundhead prospects seemed so dim. Parliament was lagging in supplying the sinews of war, and Lord Essex, their commander-in-chief, was in no position to march west himself. According to the parliamentary news-sheet 'A Perfect Diurnal':

'The Parliament party in Somerset, with the view to prevent the junction of Sir Ralph Hopton with the Marquess of Hertford summoned the whole County to rise and keep their rendez-vous at Taunton Deane. Colonels Popham and Strode were at Shepton [Mallet] with 4,000 men with the same object.'

Hopton moved out of Launceston and started concentrating at Okehampton. Upon his approach the local field commander fled, leaving four iron cannon behind him. Word was sent to Bevill to join him with his regiment from Stratton.

While this was going on, Doctor Coxe with a trumpeter was sent to summon Exeter to surrender. Sir George Chudleigh had reached Exeter safely with his horse, and the reverend doctor carried with him a letter to Sir George from James Chudleigh, suggesting he should follow his son's example.

According to 'A Perfect Diurnal', the Chudleigh letters

'were intercepted about [the person of] a Jesuit Doctor, Doctor Coxe, whom Sir Ralph Hopton sent to Exeter under colour of another treaty, but it is found out that the intent of sending him was no other but to put in practice another damnable design to betray Exeter by blowing up the East Gate with the help of a vault under it.'

According to Hopton,

'the Doctor being come into Exeter was presently secured and strictly examined, and upon suspicion of swallowing some papers was enforced to take a vomit by command of the Earl of Stamford, which together with his strict imprisonment and other hard usage produced a very dangerous sickness, under which he laboured a very long time after.'

It seems as unlikely that Doctor Coxe, with only a trumpeter in attendance, could have had about his person sufficient explosives for such an act of demolition as that he had turned Jesuit, being a Prebendary of Exeter Cathedral. He seems to have succeeded in passing James Chudleigh's letter to Sir George before being arrested, and his subsequent ill-treatment may be placed at the door of a defeated and humiliated Stamford. As already recounted, Sir George took no further part on the Roundhead side.

When Bevill and his regiment arrived at Okehampton on 24 May he was in doubt where the army would next be directed to. News of Doctor Coxe's failure must have come in that evening because the decision to march by way of Crediton was made and the Cornish occupied Crediton the following evening. It was a march of some 17 miles, arguing a complete absence of opposition on the way.

A few days were spent at Crediton seeking intelligence of enemy forces, and it was learnt that Colonel Weare of Halberton was preparing to defend Tiverton for Parliament.

Tiverton lies 12 miles to the north-east of Crediton and has a bridge over the river Exe commanded by a castle. Resolutely contested, Tiverton might have presented no mean obstacle to Hopton's advance. To guard his right flank he sent two companies of foot and a troop of dragoons to Sir John Acland's house at Column-John, which lay between Exeter and the Tiverton road. The Cornish reached Tiverton on Sunday 28 May, but Weare had fled and the barricades were unmanned. The town was occupied without incident.

Two or three days were spent at Tiverton 'to settle the affections of the country' and the army set off again through Bradninch and Cullompton, where bridges at both span the river Culm. They marched only six miles, but the going is hilly and the roads were rough. Some Roundhead cavalry were seen in the distance which, too, may have sounded a note of caution. The enemy horse were reputedly from Honiton, and the Cornish marched accordingly in that direction. It was an 11-mile march over high land by Hembury, and the 'forlorn hope' (an advance guard of horse) had a skirmish on their approach to that town, but the enemy fled Honiton, too, and the place was occupied without difficulty.

The next day they continued eastwards towards Axminster, a further 10 miles or so, and were now only a short distance from the border with Dorset. It speaks much of the bonds forged between officers and men that the Cornish, who had formerly shown such reluctance to leave their native county, had traversed the whole of Devon in good order and perfect discipline. They had become a united band of high morale.

A Captain of Hertford's staff met the army as they approached Axminster with the news that Lord Hertford and Prince Maurice had reached Yeovil in Somerset, only 20 miles away. After a night in Axminster the army swung northwards to Chard, Hopton and his staff spurring onwards to Crewkerne to wait on the Marquess and Prince Maurice that same evening.

For Hopton it must have been an emotional moment, crossing into his native Somerset and meeting the son of his old friend Elizabeth of Bohemia. Lord Hertford had been busy and successful since he fled onboard the collier from Minehead: all Wales was held for the King (as the Northern Counties were held by Northampton). Now that the south-west had been subdued, all those supporting the King must have had high hopes of eventual victory. Colonel Strode still acted as sequestrator of Hopton's Somerset estates, but the rank and file had failed to muster in Taunton Dean. A King's army of nearly 7,000 men on the march towards them had cooled their enthusiasm for Parliament.

Sir William Waller was a roundhead general of considerable renown. His successes elsewhere had led to his being given the soubriquet 'William the Conqueror'. Essex sent him orders to leave Bristol and do what he could to stem the Royalist tide from Cornwall. He had been a friend of both Bevill's and Hopton's for many years. As long before as 1633 Bevill had sent him a three-year old 'nagg' with a letter saying:

'I beseech you name not money between you and me, it is a thing so much beneath my thoughts. If it please you to vouchsafe the acceptance of him, I am more than satisfied.'

When Waller, smarting under what he considered to be an unjust judgment against him in the Star Chamber, joined the Presbyterians, Bevill wrote to him again:

'The fullness of my grief for the irreparable loss which both I and our country doth sustain by being deprived of you, I cannot express . . .'.

and then continued to ask for a loan of £2,000 on the security of his Manor of Bideford. In a postscript he thanked Waller for having been kind to his son Richard at Oxford and mentions the death of Sir Barnard.

Since that date Waller had resolutely followed the Parliamentary line. Although his orders were to march with 2,000 horse and dragoons 'with all haste to Devonshire' to counter Hopton's advance, the speed of events had overtaken them. On 2 June 1643 the two Royalist armies met at Chard, in Somerset.

Hertford led 1,500 horse and 1,000 newly-raised foot. He had an artillery train of 10 or 11 cannon. Hopton commanded 3,000 foot, 500 horse, and 300 dragoons, all seasoned soldiers with four or five cannon.

The Oxford cavalry were a high-spirited, undisciplined force accustomed to live off the land by looting. They were credited with the view that all rich men were Parliamentarians. Hopton's army was regularly paid, severely punished for ill behaviour, and each regiment had its chaplain to enforce the Sabbath. The two disparate forces must have eyed each other with little enthusiasm; it may not have helped that the Cornish, having reached Chard first, had presumably achieved the best billets.

Hertford intended to subdue West Somerset and then take Bristol. With this object in mind the combined force marched from Chard towards Taunton the following morning, moving across the rich lowlands of Taunton Dean. Taunton, the county town of Somerset, Bridgwater and Dunster Castle in the north all accepted Royalist occupation without hesitation, Taunton agreeing to raise £8,000 towards the maintenance of the army, a sum sufficient to pay it for several weeks.

After Taunton the army marched to Glastonbury and Wells with no more than smirmishes between the horse of both sides. The Oxford cavalry, venturing into the Mendips, had a sharp encounter with Waller's horse, but the infantry remained in the lush lowlands about Wells for 10 or 11 days. It was from Wells that Hopton wrote to Waller suggesting a meeting. He must have hoped to convert Waller as Grenvile had converted Chudleigh.

Waller's reply to this overture dashed any hope there might have been of marching unopposed on Bristol.

'Certainly my affections to you are so unchangeable that hostility itself cannot violate my friendship in your person, but I must be true to the cause wherein I serve. The old limitation "usque ad aras" holds still, and where my conscience is interested, all other obligations are swallowed up. I should most gladly wait on you according to your desire, but that I look upon you as you are engaged in that party beyond a possi- bility of a retreat, and consequently incapable of being wrought upon with any persuasion. And I know the conference could never be so close between us but that it would take wind and receive a construction to my dishonour.

That great God, which is the searcher of my heart, knows with what a sad sense I go upon this service, and with what a perfect hatred I detest this war without an enemy . . .

We are both upon the stage and must act those parts that are assigned to us in this tragedy. Let us do it in a way of honour, and without personal animosities, whatsoever the issue be. I shall never willingly relinquish the dear title of Your most affectionate friend . . .'.

Waller had about as many men as Hertford, but a higher proportion of horse. Sir Arthur Hazelrigg, with his famous regiment of cuirassiers known as 'The Lobsters' by reason of their rusted armour, was under his command. But he had insufficient money with which to pay them. He and Hazelrigg wrote jointly to the Speaker of the Commons, Lenthall:

'We have long and often supplicated you for money. Find us but a way to live without it, or else we humbly beg a present supply. If not, this horse will certainly disband, which thought makes our hearts to bleed.'

The heights of Mendip were better suited to a defence by cavalry than the longer route from Wells through Shepton Mallet, where Colonel Strode's 4,000 men failed to appear, to Frome. From Frome the Royalists took the Bath road heading for Bristol.

Waller placed a strong force on Monkton Farleigh Hill beyond Bradford-on-Avon as an ambuscade. When Hopton advanced northwards out of Bradford it was the regiments of Grenvile, Godolphin and Trevannion who broke up Waller's ambush and forced him to retire on Bath.

Bath, with its cathedral and Roman springs, lies to the north of the river Avon. By his advance through Bradford-on-Avon, Hopton had outflanked the city's river defences. Until Cromwell and Monck, both sides adhered to the feudal view that armies were best commanded by great noblemen. Hence the Earl of Essex on one side and the Marquess of Hertford on the other. Hertford, an indolent easy-going sort of man, was quite content to leave the day-to-day management of his army to professionals like Hopton, as Essex perforce had to leave things to Waller. Both had served in Germany and knew how to manœuvre an army in the field Bevill was not on the staff. He was not a professional soldier; but he had proved himself a first-rate colonel of his regiment. His views seem to have been asked before the siege of Plymouth was attempted and he may have been called in on the counsels of war which were held from time to time, but any contribution he may have made was no doubt as muted as his contributions to the debates he attended in Parliament. He does not seem to have been a man of words, but of action.

Hopton, being free to pass to the eastwards of Bath and advance on Bristol, must have preferred to choose his own ground on which to knock out Waller. He could not very well continue against Bristol with Waller in his rear. The obvious and only practicable way to threaten Bath was to seize Lansdown, the great limestone escarpment which looms to the north of that city.

Lansdown had only one road which zig-zagged up precipitously from the city itself, traversed the level ground on top, and after dipping several hundred feet rose again to Tog and Freezing Hills towards Marshfield. But Waller had put up a stiff fight at Farleigh Hill and the cavalry sought better quarters than a camp in the open at 700 feet. They quartered at Batheaston in the valley, and the staff and foot toiled up the steep ascent to Cold Ashton and Marshfield. It seems almost certain that Bevill and his regiment occupied Cold Ashton, while the staff found billets at Marshfield. Had a more forward policy been adopted a great many lives would have been saved.

When the sun rose on 4 July it became clear that Waller, a man with a consummate skill at anticipating his opponents' movements and a quick appreciation of the lie of the land, had encamped his forces at the northern extremity of Lansdown, and was even then completing the breastworks embracing his cannon commanding the sole approach to his position. Waller could be congratulated on his choice of a virtually impregnable position defending Bath.

By common consent, we are told, Hopton was given command of the field. I suspect that if Hopton had not been overshadowed by the Marquess, Prince, and Lord Carnarvon, the position would have been reversed, with the Cornish atop the hill ready to storm down upon Bath.

At first light the two armies approached each other, the dragoons of each side expending a great deal of powder with little effect. The only way out of the impasse was to feign a retreat. The Royalists withdrew. Waller, from his commanding position on Lansdown, released a strong party of horse who were more than a match for the Cavaliers.

'The regiment of cuirassiers [The Lobsters] so amazing the horse they charged that they totally routed them, and standing firm and unshaken themselves, gave so great terror to the King's horse who had never before turned from an enemy, that no example of their officers who did their parts with invincible courage, could make them charge with the same confidence and the same manner they had done. .

However, in the end, after Sir Nicholas Slan[n]ing with 300 musketeers had fallen upon and beaten their reserves of dragoons Prince Maurice, and the Earl of Carnarvon, rallying their horse and winging them with the Cornish musketeers, charged the enemy's horse again and totally routed them.'

The Cornish foot, left unsupported by the horse, stood firm. The lobsters having failed, Waller committed his reserve of cavalry.

'They had (like provident soldiers) placed their best horse in the rear, who being compelled, turns about and fights desperately — but our horse, being still assisted by the foot, at last beat them down Tog Hill, where in the bottom they were cruelly galled by our foot that they drew up thick on Tog Hill.

Now did our foot believe no men their equals, and were so apt to undertake anything, that the hill upon which the rebels stood, well fortified, [a] little without musket shot (from whence they raked us with their cannon) could not deter them, for they desired to fall on, and cried: "Let us fetch those cannon!"'

The northern slopes of Lansdown are incomparably steeper and higher than Stratton (or as it is now called, Stamford) Hill but in one sense they were less dangerous to climb, since the cannon on the top could not be brought to bear on anyone climbing the steep sides after leaving Freezing Hill until they reappeared near the lip or crest of Lansdown.

Hopton sent his musketeers to right and left to climb the wooded sides of Lansdown hoping to outflank Waller's line. But the main body was obliged to advance frontally along the line of the road.

'They had much to do, by reason of the disadvantage of the ground, the enemy's foot and batteries being under cover of their breast-works, and their horse ready to charge upon the very brow of the hill where the King's forces were five times charged and beaten back in disorder.

The [Royalist] horse were to pass up the high-way, but were at first repulsed. Sir Bevill Grenvile then stood [at] the head of his regiment upon Tog Hill; Then Sir Bevil Greenevil advanced, with a party of horse on his right hand (that ground being best for them) and his musketeeers on the left; himself leading up his pikes in the middle, and in the face of their cannon and small shot from their breast-works, gained the brow of the hill having sustained two full charges of the enemy's horse; but in their third charge, his horse falling and giving ground, he received, after other wounds, a blow on the head with a pole-axe, with which he fell.

And many of his officers about him. Yet the musketeers fired so fast upon the horse that they quit their ground, and the two wings who were sent to clear the woods having done their work and gained those parts of the hill, at the same time they beat off their foot, and became possessed of their breast-works, and so made way for their whole body of horse, foot, and cannon to ascend the hill; which they quickly did, and planted themselves on the ground which they had won; the enemy retiring about demi-culverin shot behind a stone wall upon the same level and standing in a reasonable good order.'

Bevill's henchman Antony Payne hoisted young Jack Grenvile into his father's saddle. His letter to Grace after the battle is said to have been found in the old chest in Stowe Barton farm and read:

'Honoured Madam. Ill news flieth apace. The heavy tidings no doubt have already travelled to Stow that we have lost our blessed Master by the enemy's advantage. You must not, dear Lady, grieve too much for your noble spouse. You know, as we all believe, that his soul was in heaven before his bones were cold.

He fell, as he did often tell us he wished to die, in the great Stewart cause, for his country and his King. He delivered to me his last commands and with such tender words for you and for his children as are not to be set down with my poor pen, but must come to your ears upon my heart's best breath.

Master John, when I mounted him upon his father's horse, rode him into the war like a young prince as he is; and our men followed him with their swords drawn and with tears in their eyes. They did say they would kill a rebel for every hair of Sir Bevill's beard. But I bade them remember their good master's word when he wiped his sword after Stamford's fight: how he said, when their cry was "Stab and slay", "Halt men, God will avenge". — I am coming down with the mournfullest load than ever a poor servant did bear to bring the great heart that is cold to Kilkhampton vault. O! my lady how shall I ever brook your weeping face? But I will be trothful to the living and the dead. These — honoured Madam, from thy saddest truest servant Antony Payne.'

The dying Bevill was carried back over Freezing and Tog Hills to Cold Ashton, a village aptly named from which the scene of Hopton's pyrrhic victory can be viewed to the south-west. He was carried into the Parsonage beyond the Manor House which suggests the Parsonage was his billet before the battle. The house still stands, much added to in Victorian days. Its present owner tells me that the chair which used to be shown to visitors as the chair in which he died, is now unknown.

Sir John Hinton, M.D. in his memorial to Charles II records: 'In his extremity I was the last man that had him by the hand before he died'. Bevill died the day after the battle on 6 July 1643. On his person was found the letter written on white sarsenet (fine silk) from the King. It was endorsed in his own hand 'Keep this safe!' Also found among his belongings was his 'Camp Plate' in its shagreen case. The silver plates, porringers and other pieces present a fascinating problem to any historian. Why do some of the pieces bear the Bath coronet? Why is the hallmarking 30 years too late? And how did it get into the hands of the Chichester family if adopted, hall-marked, and coronetted by his son Lord Bath? These three questions are unlikely to be resolved.

His body was carried from Cold Ashton to Launceston, and thence to Kilkhampton, where it was interred with his ancestors in the family vault on 26 July 1643.

ENVOI

WHAT HAPPENED to those actors remaining on the stage? After Lansdown, Jack Grenvile remained his his father's regiment and took part in the siege of Bristol when the two remaining 'wheels of Charles's wain' were killed later in the month. Nicholas Slanning and John Trevannion. The decimation of the Cornish at Lansdown and Bristol, and particularly the loss of their leaders, demolished the great impetus they had given to the King's case. An occasional victory was yet to illuminate the Royalist scene – but eventually – in 1644, the wealth and power of Parliament prevailed, and the remnants of the King's army, defeated in the final battle at Torrington, laid down their arms in Cornwall.

Parliamentary commissioners sequestrated the estates of all malignants including those of the Grenviles, but this proved a blessing in disguise. Since Bevill had mortgaged everything he had, and the mortgagees were unpaid the monies due to them, they were prevented from foreclosing on such lands as had not been sold outright. When, after the Restoration in 1660, Jack Grenvile had become John Granville, Earl of Bath, he was able to upset some sales of trust property made by his father, and redeem other lands with the great wealth available to him from his grant of the Stannaries.

Stow, on which his father had lavished so much love and money, was torn down, and a great palladian mansion, Stowe, erected nearby.

Of Bevill's daughters, Grace married Colonel Robert Fortescue and lived at Wear Giffard, up-river from Bideford, and Elizabeth Sir Peter Prideaux of Netherton in East Devon. Their mother Grace was fortunate in not having let Bevill tinker with her lands. She was able to retire to Madford, her father's old home outside Exeter, and both those daughters were with her when she died in 1647.

It was on 19 April 1647 that Grace Grenvile dictated her nuncupative will. Part of it reads:

> 'These two jewels or pictures, I give one to you [speaking to her daughter Prideaux] and the other to my daughter Fortescue.'

The jewelled locket, containing a portrait of Sir Bevill by David des Granges, passed by descent from the Prideaux family to the Chichesters of Hall. The present head of that ancient family, Major Charles Chichester, remembers his grandmother, who always wore it at Bideford Horseshow, lamenting its loss. In about 1890 her husband received a letter from Queen Victoria saying that she would be very pleased if Mr. Chichester would sell his locket to a great friend, Mr. Rothschild. Obeying the royal command Mr. Chichester accepted £1,000 for it. It is now exhibited in the Hoddesdon Collection of the British Museum.

The Camp Plate, if it or part of it ever belonged to Sir Bevill (experts disagree on its provenance), seems to have been appropriated at some stage by John, Lord Bath. How it passed to his sister's descendants the Chichesters can only be surmised. Did she, when attending her brother's funeral, help herself to the shagreen case and its contents? This too passed out of the hands of the Chichester family when the unmarried squire of Hall found himself obliged to give it to one of his unmarried sisters as the price for her taking herself off to a nearby manor called Huddiscott and leaving him in peace. She left it to a niece, who gave it to the Lord Fortescue of the day under the mistaken belief that he was a descendant of Sir Bevill's. It continues in the possession of the present Earl.

APPENDIX I

SIR JAMES BAGG of Saltram, who in his various capacities as Vice-Admiral and Commissioner was charged with the collection of monies in the West Country, was eventually brought to book in 1639. A jury found he had embezzled various sizeable sums of money over a period of years, or had failed to account for their receipt. To recover the outstanding sums, an enquiry was made into his land holdings in Cornwall. This revealed his purchase of Killigarth and other lands in the parish of Talland in August 1632. The sale was not publicized, and it is clear that Bevill never told his wife (see her letter of 30 May 1639, p. 85). Meanwhile the net was closing on Bagg. He conveyed Killigarth to one Thomas Marsham for £5,000 in February 1633 as tenant for a thousand years with the duty of paying Bagg a red rose at Pentecost if asked for. This assignment was set aside and the lands were seized in payment of Bagg's debt to the Crown. During the Commonwealth, the estate passed to the Lord Protector, Cromwell. John Grenvile (afterwards Granville, Earl of Bath) had the temerity to claim Killigarth for himself in 1655. His claim was firstly that his father died at Killigarth in April 1644 (when everyone must have known that Bevill had been killed fighting Parliament in July 1643); secondly, that the land had been put in trust for Bevill's heirs male in 1625 (which may be true, the deed being lost); and thirdly that he was the heir at law, his elder brother having died. His claim was struck out on his failing to appear at court in 1659.

PRINCIPAL SOURCES

Original Documents in Manuscript:
Grenvile Letters the property of Major Munthe (Munthe MS)
    „   „   „   „   „ Lord Bath (Longleat MS)
    „   „   „   „   „ The Huntington Library, Los Angeles, U.S.A. (Huntington MS)
    „   „   „   „   „ Devon Records Office, Exeter (Devon R.O.)
    „   „   „   „   „ The Victoria and Albert Museum (Forster MS)
State Papers, Domestic Series, Public Records Office (SP)
Talland/W.Looe Legal Records and Grafton MS (Northants Record Office)

Copy Grenvile letters printed in the following:
    History of the Granville Family (infra)
    Sir John Eliot (infra) (Forster or Port Eliot MS)

Printed Matter:
1547–1642	Journals of the House of Commons.
	CSP. Domestic Series. British Museum
1642–6	Thomasen's Tracts. B.M.
1878	Transactions of the Devon Association
1879	Return of the Parliaments of England 1213–1702. H. of L.
1881	Visitations of Devon. Edited Colby
	Visitations of Cornwall, Vivian
	Dictionary of National Biography, Vol. 8
	The Complete Peerage

Other Authorities:
Ashley, M., *General Monck*, 1977
Brunton, D. and Pennington, *Members of the Long Parliament*, 1954
Bushnell, G. H., *Sir Richard Grenville*, 1936
Callender, G., *Sea Kings of Britain*, 1925
Clarendon, Lord, *History of the Rebellion . . .*, D. Macray, Ed., 1888
Coates, M., *Cornwall in the Great Civil War*, 1963
Cotton, R., *Barnstaple during the Civil War*, 1889
D'Ewes, Sir S., *Journal*, W. Notestein, Ed., 1923
—— W. H. Coats, Ed., 1942
Du Maurier, D., *The Winding Stair, Francis Bacon*, 1976.
Edgar, F. T. R., *Sir Ralph Hopton*, 1968
Forster, J., *Sir John Eliot*, 1864

Fraser, A., *King Charles II*, 1979
Fraser, J. A., *Spain & the West Country*, 1935
Gardiner, S. R., *History of the Gt. Civil War* (U.S. Edn 1965)
Gilbert, *Parochial History of Cornwall*, 1838
Goaman, M., *Old Bideford & District*, 1968
Granville, George (Lord Lansdown), *The Genuine Works of*, 1736
Granville, Roger, *History of the Granville Family*, 1895
Hobhouse, Christopher, *Oxford*, 1939
Hopton, R., *Bellum Civile*, Ed. Somerset Rec. Soc., 1902
Hoskins, W. G., *Devon*, 1954
Huxley, G., *Endymion Porter*, 1959
Irwin, M., *That Great Lucifer (Ralegh)*, 1960
Johnson & Cole, Eds., *Commons Debate of 1628*
Keeler, M. F., *The Long Parliament: 1640-1*, 1954
Kippis, *Biographia Britannica*, 1773-1780
Langham, *Lundy*, 1960
Lawrance, W. T., *Parliamentary Representation of Cornwall*, 1925
Lewis, G. R., *The Stannaries*, 1908
Lysons, D. & S., *Magna Britannia* (3), 1814
Miller, A., *Sir Richd. Grenville of the Civil War*, 1979
Morgan, E., *Sir Bevill Grenville of Stowe*, 1969
Newman & Pevsner, *Dorset*, 1972
Pryce, W., *Mineralogia Cornubensis*, 1778
Robbins, Sir A. F., *Sir Beville Grenville*, 1884
Rogers, Colonel, *Battles and Generals of the Civil War*, 1968
Ross, J., *The Winter Queen*, 1979
Round, J. H., *Family Origins*, 1970
Rowse, A. L., *Sir Richard Grenville*, 1937
Rushworth, *Historical Collections*, 1703
Salzman, L. F., *English Life in the Middle Ages*, 1926
Skinner, T., *Life of General Monk*, 1724
Stucley, Sir L., *The Humble Petition of . . .* , 1618
Teide, *Historia de Espana*, 1979
Tregellas, *Cornish Worthies*, 1884
Verney, P., *The Standard Bearer*, 1963
Wedgwood, C. V., *The King's Peace: 1637-1641*, 1955

INDEX OF PERSONS

INDEX OF PLACES

LIST OF SUBSCRIBERS

Countess Badeni
The Revd. Anthony Ball
Leni Baltazzi
J. Barber
C. W. Beckerleg
A. F. Bennett
Margot Louise Russell
  Bennett (née Beville)
The Hon. Mrs. Julian Berry
Philip George Billing
Lt.-Col. R. D. D. Birdwood,
  M.C., D.L.
John Bowater
John James Bowater
Viscountess Boyne
Miss Eileen F. Brady
Damien Brook
Brotherton Library,
  University of Leeds
Simon D. Brown
Ronald de Bunsen
Miss Lydia Burge
K. J. Burrow
John Buxton
Dr. Roger A. H. Casling
Charles Chichester
Mrs. Norman Colville
Sir James Colyer-Fergusson,
  Bart.
R. D. Cooper
Kathleen W. Coryton
Guy Cruwys
J. A. S. Davey
Jean Denham
Devon & Exeter Institution
  Library
Mary Catherine Bowater
  Dixon
Betty W. Farrell
Mrs. H. R. Ferdinando
Mrs. J. T. Fetherston-Dilke
T. G. Field-Fisher, Q.C.
The Earl Fortescue
Lady Margaret Fortescue
James Fox-Andrews
Eric Frankcom
Charles and Cheryl Granville

Miss Sarah Ayshford Turner
  Frederick
David W. Gale
Mrs. Margaret M. Gilpin
Dr. Terry Glanvill, T.D.,
  C.St.J.
Rupert and Pia Granville
  Glover
Muriel Goaman
Christopher Richard Granville
Dennis Granville
R. Granville
Mrs. R. St. L. Granville
Captain P. J. P. Green, M.C.
Mr. C. Dennis Gregory
Jane Grenville–Beville
Grenville College, Bideford
P. R. Grotian
David L. Hall
Viola Hall
Innes Hamilton, D.S.C.
Richard Lionel Harding
Mrs. Valerie Harvey
Mrs. Ruth Hayden
Mrs. Gerald Hohler
Mrs. W. M. Hood
R. A. Hutchinson
Lt.-Col. G. S. Ingledon-
  Webber, T.D., D.L.
J. L. Jervoise
Robert F. Jewell
Theodore Giffard Landon
His Honour Judge Lavington
Lord St. Levan
W. Ronald Loosemore
Donald McCorquodale
Geraldine Mackeson-Sandbach
Lt.-Col. J. K. La T. Mardon
Edward A. Martin
Julian and Julianna
  Monsarrat
Anthony Moore
Phil Mottram
Charles Murland
Wing Commander Ayshford
  Peter Norman
Lt. Col. John Granville

Miss Phyllis Ayshford Norman
Tommy and Christine Oliver
A. F. Oppé
Mr. and Mrs. Martin Parr
Horace Parshall
Lady Paskin
Richard Carew Pole
R. M. Prideaux
C. A. Ralegh Radford
Stuard A. Raymond
John Anthony Reeves
Vice-Admiral Sir Geoffrey
  Robson
Professor Ivan Roots, M.A.,
  F.S.A., F.R.Hist.S.
Dr. A. L. Rowse
Mrs. Louise Rutherford-
  Savelli
Mrs. Elizabeth Scott
The Hon. Mrs. McNair Scott
Mrs. Ann Sheridan
Audrey Maynard Sim
Mr. and Mrs. David G. Spear
Anne Stevens
Sir Dennis Stucley, Bt.
Commander Bruce R. S.
  Symons, R.N.
Miss Betty Talbot
Talland Bay Hotel
Dr. L. F. Thomas
John G. Thynne
H. N. W. Toms
Professor G. E. Trease
J. M. Treleven
J. Tremlett
Dr. G. F. Trobridge
J. E. Tsushima
Maurice Whinney
His Honour Judge W. C.
  Wingate, Q.C.
Mr. and Mrs. R. D. Woods
Miss G. Yeo
Brigadier Peter Young, D.S.O.,
  M.C., M.D., F.S.A.
Priscilla, Countess Zamoyska
Z. I. S. Zamoyski

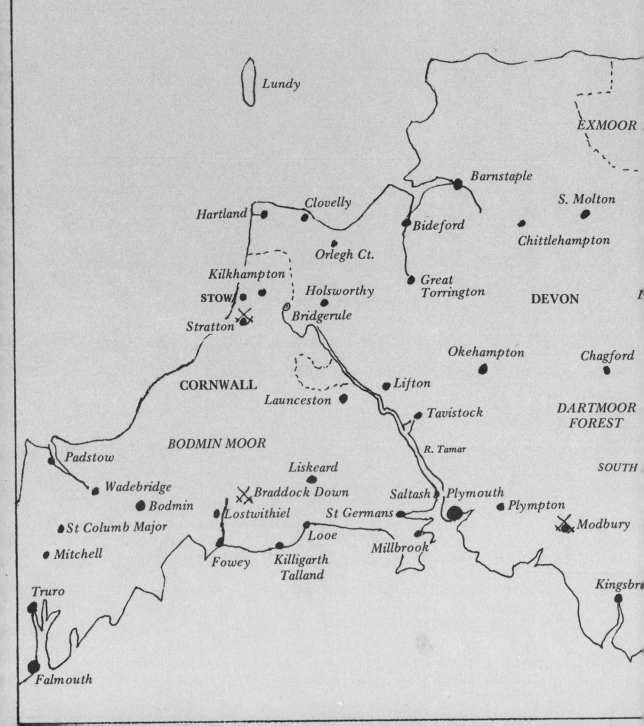

BRIST

Lundy

EXMOOR

Barnstaple

S. Molton

Clovelly

Hartland

Bideford

Chittlehampton

Orlegh Ct.

Great
Torrington

Kilkhampton

DEVON

STOW

Holsworthy

Stratton

Bridgerule

Okehampton

Chagford

CORNWALL

Lifton

DARTMOOR
FOREST

Launceston

Tavistock

BODMIN MOOR

R. Tamar

SOUTH

Padstow

Liskeard

Wadebridge

Braddock Down

Saltash

Plymouth

Bodmin

St Germans

Plympton

St Columb Major

Lostwithiel

Modbury

Looe

Mitchell

Fowey

Killigarth
Talland

Millbrook

Truro

Kingsbr

Falmouth